Teen Talk

How do today's teenagers talk? What are the distinguishing features of their style of language, and what do they tell us about the English language more generally? Drawing on a huge corpus of examples collected over a fifteen-year period, Sali A. Tagliamonte undertakes a detailed study of adolescents' language and argues that it acts as a "bellwether" for the future of the English language.

Teenagers are often accused of "lowering the standards" of the English language by the way they talk and text. From spoken words – "like," "so," "just," and "stuff" – to abbreviated expressions used online, this fascinating book puts young people's language under the microscope, examining and demystifying the origins of new words, and tracking how they vary according to gender, geographical location, and social circumstances.

Highly topical and full of new insights, the book is essential reading for anyone interested in how teenagers talk.

SALI A. TAGLIAMONTE is Professor of Linguistics at the University of Toronto, and a member of the Royal Society of Canada. She has published five books on varieties of English, dialects, variation, and how to observe, analyze, and understand language.

Teen Talk

The Language of Adolescents

Sali A. Tagliamonte

CAMBRIDGE
UNIVERSITY PRESS

University Printing House, Cambridge CB2 8BS, United Kingdom

Cambridge University Press is part of the University of Cambridge.

It furthers the University's mission by disseminating knowledge in the pursuit of education, learning and research at the highest international levels of excellence.

www.cambridge.org
Information on this title: www.cambridge.org/9781107037168

© Sali A. Tagliamonte 2016

First published 2016

A catalogue record for this publication is available from the British Library

Library of Congress Cataloguing in Publication data
Names: Tagliamonte, Sali, author.
Title: Teen talk : the language of adolescents / Sali A. Tagliamonte.
Description: Cambridge : Cambridge University Press, 2016. |
Includes bibliographical references and index.
Identifiers: LCCN 2015036021| ISBN 978-1-107-03716-8 (Hardback) |
ISBN 978-1-107-67617-6 (Paperback)
Subjects: LCSH: Teenagers–Language. | Body language. | Communication. | BISAC:
LANGUAGE ARTS & DISCIPLINES / Linguistics / General.
Classification: LCC P120.Y68 T33 2016 | DDC 428.00835–dc23 LC record
available at http://lccn.loc.gov/2015036021

ISBN 978-1-107-03716-8 Hardback
ISBN 978-1-107-67617-6 Paperback

For Duncan
Father of our children:
Adrian, Freya, Dazzian, Shaman, Tara
I love you,
Sali

Contents

Figures

Tables

Preface

My husband, Duncan, and I have five children, currently between the ages of 12 and 31. We have a busy household! Kids are always coming and going. Family suppers on Sunday evening can comprise what we call our "mini family" – us and one or two of our children – or we might have up to 16 attendees at the table, including the kids, their partners, and friends. Life with children – no matter what their age – is fraught with complexity and challenge. Among the best pieces of advice I ever received about children was the following: embrace the little opportunities in your day to spend time with your children, even if it's simply driving them and their friends all over the place or standing outside the front door for a brief chat as they wait for the bus. The next part of the advice is the difficult part: parents are advised not to talk, but listen. Up until the time I was a mother I had spent my career studying the language of older people, senior citizens/old age pensioners. Often these people inhabited small communities in remote locales. Their linguistic features were strange and wonderful. I thought I was studying the most interesting dialects in the world. But when my children reached pre-adolescence the kitchen table became an unexpected laboratory. As I listened to them talk I realized something even more interesting was going on. A whole new type of creativity and innovation in language erupted into my life in the most varied of words and phrases. I had entered a new frontier – one infrequently studied using natural unmonitored data – the language of teenagers.

This book comprises linguistic analyses of some of the most frequent, innovative, but also intensely ill-reputed, features of teen language circa late twentieth and early twenty-first centuries. The studies are based on extensive corpora I have collected over 20 years of my academic career. The book is generously peppered with examples from these informal conversations with teenagers so that readers will virtually enter into the world of this sector of the population. In fact, taken together the examples throughout the book provide a mini-corpus that readers can use to observe and explore the many facets of teen language. Sprinkled throughout the book are quips and comments from individuals that my research team and I have interviewed over the years. Their words corroborate and sometimes contrast with the results of linguistic analysis in colorful ways. You will also find mention of the many students that worked with me in this research. I have profited immensely from their input and collaboration because, in this case, they are often precisely the teenagers and twenty-somethings that are the population of study. I am particularly indebted to my (current) Ph.D. student Marisa Brook, who read through the completed manuscript with her eagle editing eyes and the inherent savvy of the very generation that promulgated many of the innovations you will read about. At one point, her comment in the margin was: *"I suddenly feel like I'm being stared at . . .: P."*

Each chapter ends with a linguistic puzzle based on data from the corpora and focuses on the feature under discussion. Readers will gain firsthand experience of teen language using the examples in the book and companion materials on the CUP website. Any one of the phenomena I discuss could be studied wherever readers are located. Although most of my data come from a large city in North America (Toronto, Canada), the individuals come from a wide range of ethnicities and social backgrounds. Moreover, the features that I focus on are typical of teen language wherever English was spoken or written natively during the same time frame. But if English is not the local vernacular, simply look out for the same features or their ilk in the varieties at hand!

One of the overarching goals of this work is to show readers how fascinating teen language is and where it fits in with the rest of the population – in fact teenage language is critical to the advancement of language evolution and society itself. When I hear people disparage youth and their language, I am always defensive. Teenagers are the innovators and the movers and shakers of language change and they are the hope for the future. Let's hear what they have to say.

1   What's all the fuss about teen language?

> There's always going to be a generation gap because you're never going to change teenagers. Even in the fifties they were like being rebellious and going against them by wearing poodle skirts and burning their bras in the sixties. So teenagers aren't ever – are never gonna change.
>
> (Mindy Chow, 17)[1]

This book is about the way teenagers talk. It is not about the way adults think teenagers should talk. It is about the way they *do* talk. What you will read about in this book is based on what I have learned from listening and questioning and from doing what sociolinguists do – analyzing everyday talk. In this chapter I bring together the prevailing ideas about teen language.

The rise of teen power

As a backdrop for the investigation of teen language, it is important to contextualize the historical and cultural context. Consider the events and developments that have typified the twentieth century. There have been two world wars. The United States has risen as a world power. Public broadcasting has developed, including talking movies in the 1920s and, after 1950, television. There have been colossal, widespread technological developments, including the World Wide Web in the 1990s. English has become a global language (Crystal, 2003).

These developments have innumerable implications for language change, and for the English language in particular. Class structure, a vital concomitant of language variation and change (e.g. Chambers, 2003a) has flattened and literacy has risen (Chambers, 2003b: 100–101), rural dialects have declined and urbanization has increased. There have been unprecedented changes in communication and media, and popular youth culture has developed. Many of these changes converge in grandstanding the very youngest sectors of the speech community. The notion of the teenage years as a discrete stage in life did not even exist before the twentieth century, let alone tweens (the 8–12-year-olds) who are now becoming a major advertising market. Moreover, the focus on youth is strengthening with pervasive geographic, social, and occupational mobility, as well as the increasing tendency towards new types of communication (i.e. text messaging, email, instant messaging, etc.), which are fundamentally changing the types of contacts young people have on a daily basis. As we shall see, all these sociocultural changes may have added to the influence of teenagers as the drivers of language change.

Language, is changing, but not for a good reason. It's because a bunch of self-centered, self-focused new generation people are saying, "I don't need to learn how to speak correctly!" You understand what I'm saying? (Loreen Kowalski, 50)

The problem of teen language

An influential view of teen language is that it is "fast becoming dreadful in the hands of young people."[2] A common conclusion is that teen language is filled with "slang." What is slang? Slang is informal language, but in addition to its casual nature, it also has a particular set of characteristics. Slang is associated with a relatively local and confined age group of speakers considered less responsible than the adult members of society. Who would that be – teenagers of course! Slang is also the label typically given to words associated with social groups outside of the mainstream or with local peer group identity. This is the reason why teenagers, in particular, with their emphasis on peer group relation-ships, are often blamed for the origin and cultivation of slang. Slang items are characteristically synonyms for everyday words. To put it another way, the individual who uses the slang word knows darn well there's a mundane alternate word but chooses not to use it. The slang term is an intentional, deliberate replacement of a neutral conventional term, a flaunting of an antith-esis of the mundane. You can probably remember a time when you purposely used slang to shock someone. Teenagers love to flaunt the newest trendiest words when they are talking to their elders. For example, when I told my kids I was writing this book, one said "Mum, that's sick!" and another said simply, "Dope," perhaps because they wanted to shock me. But I knew they meant it positively. Listen out for the latest new word in your neighborhood. Finally, slang items are usually perceived as having a short life span. Some, in fact, do, especially those associated with local peer groups; however, many others have staying power. Think of the word *cool* for example, to mean something positive, compared to *wicked*, which is fast becoming stale compared to *groovy*, a word that I don't think anyone (at least that I know) uses anymore. I do not know how long *sick* or *dope* might last as a synonym for *good* either, but they are two of the trendier terms at the moment. According to Mencken (1971: 365), "slang originates in an effort, always by ingenious individuals, to make the language more vivid and expressive." Keep this in mind.

Language is a dynamic function. It must grow or die, right? (Loreen Kowalski, 50)

Why are teenagers distinctive?

The teenage years are well known to be the most turbulent phase in human life, a veritable "social hothouse" (Eckert, 2000: 16). Physically, physiologically, socially, intellectually, teenagers are in a constant state of flux. The social forces that dominate adolescent life, including increased independence, wider contacts, the imperative to separate from parents, and solidarity with peers have a corresponding impact on language (e.g. Eckert, 1988: 205–206; Kerswill, 1996: 198). How does teen language reflect this? Teenagers specifically set out to use words that their parents do not. Sometimes this is a conscious selection of one word over another (in one generation the use of *groovy* instead of *good*, in another the use of *sick* instead of *great*). Sometimes, however, it is much more subtle, and teenagers themselves do not know just how marked their difference from the older generations really is.

[046] do u argue w ur parents [8] YES JOKE!!! (Andre Luc, 18)

In-group vs. out-group

Teenagers are cliquish to the nth degree. Group identity and membership is where it's at. Much of the literature about teenagers comes from the study of their social networks, groups, and gangs (e.g. Bucholtz, 1999, 2011; Eckert, 1989, 2000, 2003; Kiesling, 2001). Language is one of the primary means of marking group norms. Teenagers use language to include other teens and to exclude out-group members, such as parents and teachers and even other teenagers. Acceptance by one's peers is crucial and isolation is not simply undesirable, but literally terrifying. This is why use of language becomes a powerful tool. It signals to others what group you belong to (Fortman, 2003).

Teenagers and language change

Most sociolinguists agree that adolescence is the "focal point for linguistic innovation and change" (e.g. Chambers, 2003a; Eckert, 1997, 2000; Kerswill, 1996; Roberts, 2002). This means that children and adolescents, in particular, are the key individuals to look to when it comes to trying to find out what is changing in language and where language is headed.

Let's explore this broad statement in more detail. First, it is necessary to understand how language changes from birth to adulthood. Labov (2001) proposed that language changes according to a model of Incrementation.

First, I need to explain Incrementation. The model of linguistic change represented in Figure 1.1 is taken from Labov (2001: 448, figure 14.1). An individual acquires language from their primary caregiver, usually the

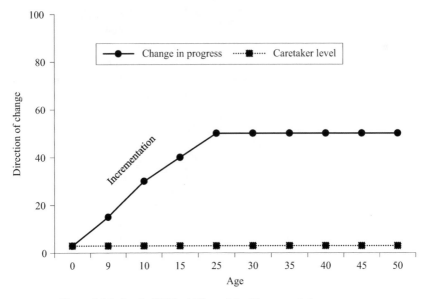

Figure 1.1 Labov's (2001: 448) model of Incrementation

mother. A form undergoing change will be acquired at the same frequency as used by the model. This level is represented by the dotted line labeled "Caretaker level." As an individual goes to school and becomes part of the community, the frequency of innovating forms increases, or increments, until late adolescence represented by the diagonal line labeled "Incrementation." In late adolescence, the grammar stabilizes. Individuals stop incrementing (i.e. increasing their use of incoming forms). The hypothesis is that their grammar remains constant for the rest of their lives, represented by the level line across the adulthood years.

Let's make this practical by imagining this process with the alternation between *have got* and *have* (e.g. Kroch, 1989; Tagliamonte et al., 2010). For example, my mother used *have got*, as in "*I've got a cat*" most of the time, with a few *have* tokens here and there. So, I acquired this ratio of *have got* to *have* as well. However, when I entered school and extended my social networks my use of *have* increased, e.g. I started saying "*I have a cat, I have a car, I have a headache.*" This continued until I was in late adolescence or early adulthood. By the time I settled into adult life, my frequency of *have* stabilized at a frequency much higher than my mother's. At a certain point, the use of *have got* probably started to seem old-fashioned. When I became a parent, my children acquired my frequency of *have*. Their grandmother was much older and she used a lot of *have got*, but by then this sounded old-fashioned. When my grandchildren acquire language they will acquire their parents' frequency of *have*, not mine (which still has the occasional *have got*). And the cycle will continue.

All three of these mechanisms – (i) acquisition of variation from the language of caretakers, (ii) incrementation of incoming variants in adolescence, and (iii) stabilization – are critical to understanding how language changes. Adolescence is a key phase. It is the time of rapid development. The teenage years are a period of instability for many reasons, especially for language change. If there are changes going on in language, this is when they take off. By early adulthood the grammar is set. Individuals are expected to keep the same frequencies and patterns for the remainder of their lives.

What's a variant?

I will use the term "variant" to refer to different forms of words and phrases that alternate with each other in language use. For example, a quotative verb in English comprises several different variants, *say, tell, go, think,* etc. Another variant is *like* which is an innovation in contemporary English, as in *I'm like, "oh no!"*

Let's go into some detail about how the model of acquisition, incrementation, and stabilization in Figure 1.1. maps from individual life spans onto the life span of change in the community over generations.[3] Figure 1.2 is reproduced from Labov (2001: 453, figure 14.5) and Tagliamonte and D'Arcy

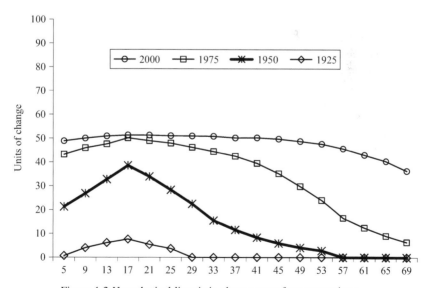

Figure 1.2 Hypothetical linguistic change over four generations

(2009: 68, figure 5). First, I will describe what the figure shows. Then, I'll demonstrate how it works step-by-step.

Figure 1.2 represents a hypothetical language change over four generations, fixed at 25 years each: 1925, 1950, 1975, and 2000. It is important to highlight that Labov's model makes a distinct contrast between female and male speakers. Figure 1.2 shows the profile for females who increment changes in adolescence as shown by peaks at certain stages of the change. Males are thought to have no incrementation component and so are predicted to have smooth trajectories and few, if any, peaks (Labov, 2001: 457). As we will see, this opposition is not so clear cut in practice.

By the last period, the circle line, the innovating form has leveled out at approximately 50 percent of the system of which it is a part and appears to have stabilized across the age span (with a slight downturn among the individuals that are 60+). The figure is based on the "apparent time construct" (Bailey et al., 1991). In an apparent time study, generational differences are compared at a single point and are used to make inferences about how a change may have taken place in the (recent) past. The speech of individuals of different ages is taken "to reflect the language as it existed at the time when that generation learned the language" (Bailey et al., 1991: 242). Apparent time offers language scientists a surrogate for chronological (or real) time, enabling the history of a linguistic change to be studied with data from the existing population.

Let's track a hypothetical change moving through time. It begins in 1925 (the diamond line at the bottom of the figure). The change is incipient, so low in frequency probably no one notices it. Community members over the age of 25 are not affected by it, and neither are the 5-year-olds (at the far left) because their 29-year-old mothers do not have it. The 5-year-olds are at level zero and so are all the adults from age 29 onwards. But older children have started acquiring the change from peers and they are increasing the frequency of use of the new form in adolescence. Observe that 9-year-olds use the new form a little, 13-year-olds use it more, and 17-year-olds are producing the most advanced realization of the change. A peak in apparent time is just visible here. This peak is an important indication that a linguistic change is beginning to take off.

Now, let's move to 1950, 25 years into the future (the starred line). At this point, the 17-year-olds in the 1925 line have aged 25 years and are 42. Based on the model of linguistic change, they stabilized after age 17, and so their use of the new form remains at the same level as they had in 1925. In contrast, the former 13-year-olds, 9-year-olds, and 5-year-olds have all increased their use of the new form in adolescence. They too have stabilized, but due to the fact that they increased the frequency of the new form through their adolescence, they have reached a higher frequency of the incoming form. The 13-year-olds had four more years in which to increment before stabilizing at 17, so they have advanced only a little since 1925. The 5-year-olds had 12 years of incrementation, so they have advanced more – past their slightly older peers. Language change is moving along.

This same process continues every year, so the 17-year-old peak is very high. Again, those 17-year-olds will now stabilize, so that in 1975 they exhibit the same frequencies as they did in adolescence. However, as before, their younger peers continue to increment past their rates before they, themselves, stabilize. In 1975, a peak is barely visible. Between 1975 and 2000 the rate of change slows down as language change evolves. This results in a lessening of the increment between childhood and adolescence. By the year 2000 the change has slowed to the point where no peak is visible. The patterning of linguistic change in apparent time is therefore a critical diagnostic of its nature. The slope of incrementation in adolescence will depend on how far the change has progressed in the community.

From Cedergren's study in Panama in 1973 and 1984 (Cedergren, 1973, 1984) to research in North America (Bailey et al., 1991; Tagliamonte, 2006b), this model has been shown to match well with community changes in apparent time (e.g. Cedergren, 1988; Sankoff and Blondeau, 2007; Sankoff and Evans Wagner, 2006; Tagliamonte and D'Arcy, 2009). When a linguistic change is at mid-pace, you will find a peak in apparent time among adolescents, likely at around 17 years of age.

A correlation between patterns of linguistic features and speaker age can also identify other types of change in the speech community. Sometimes there is change in progress in the underlying grammatical system (language change). In this type of change the whole community is involved and the language itself is changing (as in Figure 1.2). Sometimes speakers change the way they speak but this is a product of their age. This is called "age grading." In this case, the language itself is not changing. Instead speakers change the way they speak at different phases in their life. Sometimes both types of change happen at the same time. The only way to tell which phenomenon is in evidence is to tap into language patterns and interpret them.

This is my departure point into teen language. The processes of Acquisition, Incrementation, and Stabilization and their timing in the life span are intimately tied to how language change works. Keep this model in mind as I explore the analyses of linguistic features among teenagers in the coming chapters.

[Interviewer] Yeah, I mean then the influence of how your kids say "like" all the time? [077] It's a terrible habit I have. I hate to think how many times I've said it on this tape. It's a dreadful habit that I try to break myself ... (June Watson, 49)

2   Teens talking

> I think the natural inclination of anybody is to get lazy and sloppy and not think. So there's more and more slang and people dropping their G's and things like that that frankly grates on me. I hate it! Then again, I find myself doing it sometimes.
>
> (Sara Kempt, 49)

In this chapter I introduce the data from which the book will draw its information. I will also describe the data collection methods and procedures, the fieldwork experiences, and corpus compilation procedures. Who are the teenagers and young adults who make up the animated conversations I cite? Readers will get to know them through the many examples of their conversations in this chapter and sprinkled throughout the book.

When people talk about teen language, they often have based their views on anecdotal observation and/or extrapolation from small samples. In this book, I rely on an immense collection of conversations that were collected under unique circumstances – teenagers talking to first-year university students who were familiar to them.

The data come from a research program that I have been conducting for many years. The earliest data I will discuss come from 1995; the latest from 2010. The corpora span many different projects, most of them conducted within the auspices of the undergraduate curriculum of universities where I have taught over this period (the University of Ottawa, the University of York, UK, and the University of Toronto). In order to study teen language, it is important to be able to situate it more broadly. How can you say that a word or an expression is a "teen" thing if you do not know what everyone else in the community is doing? How do you know it's a "new" thing if you haven't checked the historical record? A researcher must have a solid comparative perspective from people of other ages and other times and places. Without the comparative perspective from across the age span, something that seems exclusive to teenagers may actually be a development that began a long time ago among people much older than contemporary teens. For example, everyone thinks that *like* is a teenage thing, or at least a young person's thing. However, when I started studying *like* I discovered that researchers have been complaining about *like* for a very long time. Consider this quote from Jespersen:

Like is very much used in colloquial and vulgar language to modify the whole of one's statement, a word or phrase modestly indicating that one's choice of words was not, perhaps, quite felicitous. It is generally used by inferiors addressing superiors. (Jespersen, 1933: 417–418)

Given the time Jespersen was writing, *c.*1933, it is likely that many parents reading this book had grandparents who used *like*. Moreover, the American Heritage Dictionary[1] cites the non-standard use of *like* as an "expletive to provide emphasis or pause." Observations such as these provide us with great insights into the use of forms beyond simply claiming that a certain sector of the population uses them. It also highlights how important it is to study the whole population when attempting to analyze teen language.

Collecting authentic data from teenagers

How does a middle-aged academic gain access to the world of teen language? A critical goal is to record individuals when they are not concerned about how they sound or what they say. Casual conversations are required. However, when teenagers talk to adults, they do not use the typical interactional characteristics that they would normally use with each other. There are unavoidable sociocultural reasons for this. Teenagers often are at odds with adult members of society, especially those in positions of authority, teachers and parents. In example (1) one of my students interviewed her younger sister.

1.   a. [Interviewer] Do you talk different, like when you're around people?
      b. [019] I guess teachers.
      c. [Interviewer] Really?
      d. [019] Really. I'm talking to a teacher, I'm not like consciously but like, not
         'cause I want to. But just, I don't know, I feel weird talking to teachers.
         I don't know why. I've always felt that way. (Rahim Vasanji, 19)

Moreover, there is an irrepressible clash of generations and opinions across people of different ages. Consider (2), where Clara talks about her father's reactions to the difference between herself and her sister

2.   Daddy doesn't think that I get high enough marks to like his standards.
      Because you came along and got all these nineties! But like, I don't know
      like I understand that it's hard for me because like I'm different from you. And
      like I'm just not – my learning strategies and stuff, the way I learn is just
      totally different from you. And like I don't know it's just we do our own thing.
      But like Daddy just wants me to be like exactly like you! (Clara Felipe, 16)

These social and psychological barriers make it almost impossible for adults to hear what teenagers are talking about among themselves, and by extension their "real" language. To obviate these problems, my projects were designed so that young people themselves were participant observers in the data collection and I (as the scientist behind the scenes) was nowhere near the interview situation. This method resolves many of the issues and problems surrounding fieldwork among teenagers and opens unprecedented doors into the word of teen language. Of course my eavesdropping on my own tweens and teenagers notwithstanding!

Sociolinguists typically enter the speech community they are interested in in such a way as to optimize observation of the "vernacular," the style of language people use in everyday talk (e.g. Labov et al., 1968; Milroy, 1987; Trudgill, 1974). This is crucial in the study of teen language, which to an outsider's ear is non-standard. In order to tap this type of language, the fieldworker must either be an in-group member, or have some affiliation with the community so that he or she can be perceived as a legitimate presence in the local milieu. In this case, I have employed a specific and, I think, unique strategy. My students – all in their late teens or early 20s – were the fieldworkers: by their age and many other social factors, they were inherent insiders.

In this way, all the teenage materials described in this book come from face-to-face conversations among peers. This is a very important fact. It means that the data were not collected by people who would have influenced the nature of the language, i.e. middle-aged people, "old" people, adults, etc. Due to this fact, the materials contain rich grassroots language comprising a wealth of rarely recorded discourse typical of spoken English language in the first decade of the twenty-first century. There are innumerable "slang" words and expressions. There are unusual sounds. There are unexpected twists in the arrangement of sentences and in the way sentences begin and end. There are little-known and rarely described conversational rituals. There are many things that are strange and exotic; there are some things that are unheard of and yet others that are hauntingly familiar. In many cases, features alien to adult language are present – the voices in the written and audio record echo with both the sanguine sophistication of thoughtful individuals and the crazy expressions of youth. All the examples in this book are orthographically transcribed verbatim from the written or audio records.[2]

All the teen language materials are young people talking to other young people. This makes these corpora among the few data sets collected by in-group members of youth culture.[3] Each of the interviewers was trained in sociolinguistic interviewing techniques and charged with engaging in friendly banter with a young person for about an hour. In each case a small, unobtrusive tape-recorder was employed, with a lavalier (tie-clip) microphone, clipped within 20 cm of the mouth. The interactions focus on informal topics such as school activities, hobbies, sports, friends, and lots of commiseration about problems with parents, boyfriends and girlfriends, etc.

It is important to acknowledge that all the corpora discussed in the book were collected under ethical guidelines and underwent an ethics review process. All participants, interviewees and interviewers, correspondents and friends signed consent forms permitting the academic uses of the materials reported in subsequent chapters. In the next sections I provide details of each of the corpora in turn.

The Storytelling Corpora: 1995–2004

One of the best ways to gather language data is storytelling. Everyone has a story to tell and teenagers are no exception. From 1995 to 2004 I taught a course called the Linguistics of Storytelling. In each class my students asked their friends and brothers and sisters to tell them stories from their lives, producing an eclectic collection of experiences, tales, and confessions.

Stories are an ideal way to find out about how people use language. A story is a structured speech act with distinct parts. Events are understood to have occurred prior to the moment of speaking, i.e. they are in the past. Labov and Waletzky (1967: 12) and Labov (1972b: 359–360) define narrative as a recapitulation of past experience, whereby narrative clauses are ordered iconically, i.e. in the temporal sequence in which the events actually occurred. Further, narratives have a universal structure. They typically begin with an "Orientation," which describes the setting: *It was a dark and stormy night.* The action takes place in a series of clauses referred to as the "Complicating Action." This is where the main line of the story is. These sentences answer the question: *And then what happened?* Interspersed among Orientation and Complicating Action clauses are sentences that provide evaluating statements that highlight the impact of the stories, what is important and why: *It was so scary!* This is called the "Evaluation." Stories can also have an "Abstract," a series of clauses that summarizes the story at the beginning, kind of like an advert: *This is the story about how I learned to swim.* Narratives can also have an ending sequence that sums up the story and bring the discourse back to the present time, *And that was the end of that.* The story in (3) illustrates a typical narrative structure. Several features of interest are marked with italics and will be explained below.

3. Sleepover Story
    a.   Just before school started my friends   ORIENTATION
         and I had a sleep over
    b.   And one of my friends, she just came back from Europe and had jet lag.
    c.   fell to a deep sleep   COMPLICATING ACTION
    d.   And we took advantage of it.
    e.   And we used a marker

f.	And drew a mustache and like scars all over her face *and everything.*
g.	Yeah, *so* when she woke up,
h.	She went into the bathroom,
i.	*So* we managed to keep a straight face and everything.	EVALUATION
j.	She just went into the bathroom	COMPLICATION ACTION
k.	And saw her- (laughs)
l.	And yeah she*'s like,* "What the hell did you guys do to me!"
m.	It was funny. (STC, female, 18)	EVALUATION

Many features of teen language can be studied effectively with corpora that contain plenty of stories. As we shall see in Chapter 4, personal narratives are the prime locus for quotative verbs, which introduce dialogue, as in (3l). The early storytelling corpora from 1995 and 1996 in my archive enabled me to catch a new innovation, the use of *like* as a quotative verb, before most people knew it was rising. Stories are also an ideal site for the examination of discourse markers such as *so*, as in (3g, 3i), which I'll explore in Chapter 6.

However, to comprehensively study features of language among teenagers, you need a lot more data than a few stories. You need long conversations with many types of discourse, descriptions, stories, and interactions, enough to document how teens talk with each other when they are not thinking about how they talk.

The Toronto Teen Corpus: 2002–2006

The Toronto Teen Corpus (TTC) is a large compilation of materials that were collected by student researchers within a special undergraduate program called the Research Opportunities Program (ROP) in the Faculty of Arts and Science at the University of Toronto. Every year between 2002 and 2006 a small team of students joined me in a project that focused on teen language in Toronto. During the course, the students enlisted the help of members of their own social and familial networks to assist them in data collection. The project focused on tweens and teens between the ages of 9 and 20, the sisters, cousins, neighbors, friends, etc. of the students. The interviewers for the TTC were thus well known to their interviewees. They hung out with their interviewees and talked about things that were relevant to them – friends, computer games, pets, etc. Everything that was said was captured in high quality digital sound. The recordings were orthographically transcribed and made ready for analysis.

The data that arose from this six-year study contain nearly 1 million words of spoken conversation.[4] To my knowledge there are very few corpora of teen language that are this large. Table 2.1 shows the distribution of individuals in the TTC by age and sex.

Table 2.1 *Toronto Teen Corpus (ROP 2, 3, 4, and 6)*

Sex	9–12	13–16	17–19	20–22
Male	10	15	19	2
Female	8	13	20	3
Total	18	28	39	5

Table 2.1 documents the sample design: 90 speakers between the ages of 9 and 22. The age groupings correspond to the different education levels in Canada: primary school (grades 1–5); middle school (grades 6–8); and secondary school (grades 9–12).

The TTC can be put into perspective by comparing it with other influential studies of teen language based on the collection of spoken conversations. Perhaps the most influential linguistic studies on teenagers is Eckert's (1989) research on adolescent social networks in a Detroit high school. The largest corpora I am aware of are based in England. The first one is the Bergen Corpus of London Teenage Language (COLT)[5] (Stenström et al., 2002). It comprises 500,000 words from 31 boys and girls in living in London, England, who were between the ages of 13 and 17 in 1993. A few years later, in 1997 a corpus of 13–14-year-olds (8 girls; 8 boys) was collected in Glasgow, Scotland (Stuart-Smith, 1999). In 2003 a follow-up study recorded 36 Glasgow adolescents aged between 10 and 15 in groups of two boys or two girls. The youngest speakers (10–13) were recorded again in 2004 (Stuart-Smith, 2002–2005). These corpora comprise just over 150,000 words. Another study from London has collected interviews with 72 teenagers aged between 16 and 19 in 2004 from two boroughs of the city (Havering and Hackney) (Kerswill and Cheshire, 2004–2007). Other studies of teen language have been primarily small scale using anthropological and ethnographic methods. Because my goal in this book is to tap into language variation and change, I have focused on the plethora of materials in my own corpora that can be compared and contrasted across a broader spectrum of the population. However, the book is designed so that any number of studies could be replicated with a small, carefully designed sample of teenagers. Table 2.2 sketches one possible template with 16 individuals across the key age milestones of the incrementation model of linguistic change (Figures 1.1–1.2).

Our general impression is that the teenagers put an effort into expressing their identity as young Londoners, in ways that are playful, creative and innovative. [Speaking about the contents of COLT corpus] (Stenström et al., 2002: 17)

Within the social and cultural information contained in the TTC are dozens of linguistic features worthy of investigation. Many are common to teen language

Table 2.2 *Teen language corpus template*

Sex	9–12	13–16	17–19	20–22
	Pre-adolescents	*Teenagers*	*Teenagers (at putative age of stabilization)*	*Young adults*
Male	2	2	2	2
Female	2	2	2	2
Total	4	4	4	4

across the major varieties of English and have also been studied in other teenage corpora, including quoting *like,* intensifiers, tags, general extenders, etc. (Cheshire, 2007; Cheshire et al., 2007–2010; Stenström, 1999, 2000, 2002). Examples (4a–c) offer some typical examples from the TTC:

4.
  a. The scariest thing that happened was when me and mom went on the Matterhorn, and I got *so* sick and the ride was going *so* fast around in circles and I was *so* nauseous. And I *was like* "Mommy!" And then Mommy'*s like* "I'm here! I'm here!" But *like*, she's getting nauseous too right. *So* it's not really *like* anything you can do. It's not like you *can be like* "Stop the ride!" But *like*, it was *so* scary. (Clara Felipe, 16)

  b. Yeah, *like* my dad watches the Simpsons, right. And they used to be really bad. Because when I was younger, he used to watch it at night 'cause it was on. He'd laugh. But my mom would always come in *like*, "Don't watch that horrible show," *right. Or whatever.* And *so* I *was like*, "Hm, what's this show?" So I'd watch it, *right.* (Antonio Silvaggio, 16)

  c. Actually one of the craziest things, well not craziest things I ever did, but one of the coolest things I did in Montreal was um- we had this um- it was sort of a survival thing and we had to go through this maze of um mud and by the end the mud-. It was *like* a big mud bath and it reached our chins. *Like* I was- we were told to bring- we were told to bring shoes and pants and shirts that we- we could throw out afterwards. *So* we'd have to find like a whole bunch of clues. We had to do all these obstacle courses *and stuff.* And everything was in mud. And we're like "Oh you know, we're not that dirty. *Geez* I don't have to throw out these pants at the end of the day." But by the end we had to go through, I think it was something *like* four, maybe two kilometers. Is that? Two kilometers is *pretty* long *eh*? Something like a two kilometers um mud bath where it was like through a forest too so we couldn't even- we couldn't see anything and we're getting *all like* scratched with branches and- It was *really* fun. (Lisa Neville, 18)

Teenagers use an overwhelming number of *like's*, and they use a lot of "fillers" in general, such as *well, right, eh, all*, etc. Are these simply examples of "bad" language, a degradation of language, a lapse in good grammar?

This way of speaking is unlike any variety of English that has ever existed before. Even data from individuals in their late teens and early twenties that I collected in another Canadian city in the mid-1990s do not look like this. It certainly isn't the way I talk. It is even farther away from the way my grandparents talked. Why? What is going on with teen language?

By the middle of the 2000s there was something new and intriguing on the horizon – the Internet. Teenagers were embracing it en masse, not only for what it offered in terms of viewing and discovering things but also the ability to communicate with friends well beyond the telephone. In my house my oldest daughter, then a pre-adolescent, started to use the family computer a lot more than ever before. I could hear her tapping away very quickly and I remember wondering how she had learned to type so fast! At first, I thought she was doing homework. Then, I realized that what she was really doing was "talking" to her friends. The computer was dinging all the time and whenever I went nearby she would quickly change the screen to the homework she was supposed to be working on. She was using a form of "Computer Mediated Communication" (CMC) (Herring, 1996) called "Instant Messaging" (IM). In the early 2000s I started exploring how teenagers were using language on the Internet. The first step was to figure out how to do it.

The Toronto Instant Messaging Corpus: 2004–2006

The Faculty of Arts and Science at the University of Toronto offers a distinctive program that encourages secondary school students to join university professors in their research projects – the Mentorship Program. Between 2004 and 2006 I set up a research project entitled *Teen Talk in Toronto* that was specifically designed to tap into IM communication. Over the course of the two-year project two teams of Mentees from high schools within the Toronto District School Board worked on this project. They became co-researchers and participant observers and created an immense corpus of IM language. One of my senior undergraduate students at the time (Derek Denis) aided in the management of these projects as well as the training and supervision of the teenage Mentees. He also collected data from his own IM conversations from the summer of 2005, providing data from 17- to 20-year-olds. Together these materials form the Toronto Instant Messaging Corpus (TIMC).

The TIMC corpus was constructed from conversational histories – computerized records of the participants' IM interactions with friends. These substantial text-logs comprise thousands of individual conversations.[6] An extraordinary facet of this IM data is that the vast majority of the material came from conversational histories that had been saved well before the study began.[7] Thus, this corpus is extraordinary among data sets in that it has had little to no influence from the observer's paradox (Labov, 1972a: 209). This is exceptional because it means that the dialogue was entirely unmonitored – there was no parent over the shoulder! At the time that the interchanges occurred, none of the participants could have anticipated that they would someday be studied by a language scientist. This is a notable difference between this and any previous study of IM (Baron, 2004: 404) and makes it a unique documentation of IM communication among teenagers. I believe it may also be one of the most authentic pictures of teen language and interactive Internet discourse of its time. Moreover, and crucially, the corpora comprise data from the same interlocutors in spoken *and* written conversations. Each Mentee conducted a conversational interview with one or two of the same friends with whom they communicated using IM. This means we are able to directly contrast an individual's behavior in IM and in speech (SP).

In total, there are 71 individuals in the corpus, 31 male and 40 female, all born and raised in Canada, all between the ages of 15 and 20 in the years 2004–2006. I emphasize that the existence of this corpus was only possible due to the cooperation and generosity of my students and their friends who enthusiastically collected a wealth of data for study.

Following ethical guidelines, each individual signed standard consent forms and all names and screen names were changed in order to ensure anonymity. The SP data were transcribed and digitized and subjected to the same cataloguing techniques. Table 2.3 shows the size and distribution of these corpora.[8]

It wasn't long after this that teenagers started getting smartphones. Then yet another kind of rapid typing started happening. It is remarkable to see how fast thumbs can move.

Although the TIMC is a documentation of Instant Messaging communication alongside Spoken Conversation, it does not offer the perspective of how teenagers behave across different registers of written language, including Email, Instant Messaging, and Texting on phones. These registers are all distinct, but what differentiates them? There was still more exploration to be done.

Sali in email to an editor: You know I was joking, right? ;) Editor: Absolutely!! Emails are a bit hateful for making that clear, but I'm never too certain how confident authors will feel if they work with an editor who uses emoticons ... (5-12-12)

Table 2.3 *Toronto Instant Messaging Corpus (2004–2006)*

Register/media	2004–2005	Summer 2005	2005–2006	Total
Spoken Conversation [SP]	146,768	72,480	70,206	289,454
Instant Messaging [IM]	503,269	523,370	154,283	1,180,922
Total	650,037	595,850	224,489	1,470,376

The Toronto Internet Corpus: 2009–2010

In 2009 and 2010 I designed a first-year course called Language and the Internet, which in practice was a research project. Here again, my students became co-researchers and participant observers engaging in fieldwork, corpus construction, and data analysis.[9] This time we produced the Toronto Internet Corpus (TIC). The students ranged in age from 17–20 and both males and females are represented. Among the 45 individuals, most were born and raised in Toronto, Canada. The TIC is summarized in Table 2.4. Data were collected using assignments where samples of the students' communications on Email (EM), Instant Messaging (IM), and texting on phones (SMS) were submitted to a course database. The samples were required to be one-to-one, peer-to-peer interactions fitting the three different kinds of registers described below. The data were collected and each student was assigned a single-letter code to protect his or her anonymity. The corpus comprises 179,241 words. In addition, a sample of formal writing was collected from each student for comparison with the CMC data.

One of the most important contributions of this study is the data themselves. They comprise peer interactions across three different CMC registers and the number of data is large (see Table 2.4). Crucially, the corpus comprises data from *the same* speakers across four different written registers. This provides a large number of tokens such that both group and individual statistical analyses are possible.

For example, "Assignment 3, Instant Messaging" was described as follows: *Submit an electronic version of an instant messaging interaction with a friend your own age. Your contribution must be at least 1000 words.* This directive inevitably produced linguistic material such as in (5). Note that this was no deterrent to producing non-standard linguistic phenomena typical of the register.[10]

5.   a. [friend] yo, should we do 2000 words or 1000 words
        b. [b] only 1000 words
        c. [b] short and easy
        d. [friend] last time it was 2000 words wasnt it
        e. [b] yes it was
        f. [friend] ok it will end faster than last time
        g. [b] yeah omg im already so tired

Table 2.4 *Sample constitution, Toronto Internet Corpus (TIC)*

	Male	Female	Total
2009	11	13	24
2010	10	11	21
Total	21	24	45

Most submissions, however, were obtained from archived correspondence that had taken place previous to the course. Therefore much of the materials in TIC (like the TIMC) comprise interactions that had taken place with no observer present, a fact that makes these materials authentic in a way that far surpasses many corpora of Internet language (but see Tagliamonte and Denis, 2008a). Table 2.5 shows the constitution of the TIC in terms of the number of words in each register for both years.

The total word-count for this corpus is close to 200,000 words, including transmissions from both the students and their interlocutors. The TIC can be put into perspective with a comparison of CMC corpora from the same time period (Baron, 2004; Ferrara et al., 1991; Herring, 2003; Hinrichs, 2010; Jones and Schieffelin, 2009; Ling, 2005; Segerstad, 2005; Tagliamonte and Denis, 2008a; Thurlow, 2003; Yates, 1996), as in Table 2.6.

The vernacular, interactive, unmonitored interaction in TIC is substantial. An advantage to the TIC (in conjunction with the TTC and the Storytelling

Table 2.5 *Sample design of the TIC*

Year	Register				Total words
	Email	IM	SMS	Written	
2009	16,457	18,664	6,949	29,467	71,537
2010	27,109	41,910	9,930	28,755	107,704
Total words	43,566	60,574	16,879	58,222	179,241

Table 2.6 *Comparison of TIC with other CMC corpora*

Study	Register	No. of words
Ling, 2005	SMS	5,414
Thurlow, 2003	SMS	7,616
Baron, 2004	IM	11,718
Segerstad, 2005	SMS, questionnaire responses, user diaries (N=4)	17,024
Ferarra et al., 1991	E-messages/Interactive Written Discourse (precursor to IM)	18,769
Herring and Paolillo, 2006	Blogs	35,721
Paolillo, 2001	Internet Relay Chat (IM)	37,902
Hinrichs, 2010	Emails, blog posts, blog comments in Jamaican Creole	45,550
Jones and Schieffelin, 2009	IM	83,135
Tagliamonte and Denis, 2008	IM	> 1 million
Yates, 1996	Writing, speech, early news groups/message boards	2,222,049

Corpus (STC)) is the uncommon coverage of different registers of teen language. Unlike research that focuses on specific features in individuals or groups, the breadth of these data sets enables exploration of parallels and contrasts across a range of different ages and modes of communication. In so doing, it is possible to answer questions above and beyond those that are particular to individuals, social groups, or even one style or register. The same features may not be found from one age group to the next. Moreover, the types of change found in one register may not be found in others. It is important to situate such changes more broadly as part of ongoing innovation in English. From this broader perspective, it will be possible to assess whether the external influences on innovation in one age group or register are similar to that in another. Further, it then becomes possible to compare innovations observed in teenagers speaking English in North America to other varieties of English and other languages. Is there a common teen language or do features differ depending on the age or community of the teenagers?

What's a register?
"Register" refers to a variety of language used for a particular purpose or in a particular social setting. For example spoken vs. written language can be viewed as a register difference. I will use the term "register" to refer to many different written varieties of CMC.

A critical caveat is that the TIC is dated. It comes from a particular time – (2009–2010) – when the three CMC registers had distinct characteristics. The participants in these studies were not using their phones for email or web browsing. CMC on a phone in the TIC is limited to a single type of CMC – SMS. Of course, this fact also means that the study is circumscribed to a particular phase in the evolution of the Internet and cannot be replicated. It is no longer possible to tap the distinct registers documented in the TIC. Another distinctive characteristic of the TIC is that it contains a sample of formal writing from each individual who contributed EM, IM, and SMS. Each writing sample, before the study, had been submitted for educational assessment and stands as a representation of the students' most formal written language. This component of the TIC serves as a baseline and a control for the CMC sections. It is important to emphasize that the TIC offers insight on the *same* set of writers in *different* registers (written language, EM, IM, and SMS) making it possible to compare how the same individuals behave from one CMC register to the next.

Together, these corpora – the TTC, the TIMC, TIC, and the STC – provide one of the largest repositories of teen language in the world. They offer a vibrant documentation of the state of teen language in North American English at the turn of the twenty-first century.

The Toronto English Corpus

If I were to make recommendations for future study of the language of adolescents, I would ... argue that adolescents could benefit from more research on middle-aged adult speech.

(Eckert, 2005: 107)

In order to understand teen language, contrast and comparison with a wider range of age groups from the same speech community is necessary. The Toronto English Corpus (TEC) provides this critical baseline. It is the foundation (and control) for the teen language data. This corpus comes from a large-scale project of the entire Toronto speech community containing data from 267 individuals who were aged between 19 and 97 when they were interviewed in 2003–2004, as in Table 2.7.[11] All of them were born and raised in Toronto (Tagliamonte, 2003–2006).

The conversations with each individual are between one and three hours long and represent individuals born in the early 1900s to adolescents who were born in the 1980s and 1990s – a time span of approximately 100 years. The data are a rich resource of stories, reminiscences, and lively characterizations of life and times in Toronto. This type of socially stratified sampling can effectively model changes underway in the community (Labov, 1966, 1970, 1981).[12]

The Clara Corpus

One of the most critical issues in the study of language change is distinguishing between changes that are taking place in the linguistic system and changes that

Table 2.7 *The Toronto English Corpus, c.2011*

Date of birth	Age	M	F	Total
1991–1993	10–12	8	7	15
1990–1989	13–14	7	6	13
1987–1988	15–16	8	6	14
1984–1986	17–19	20	28	48
1979–1983	20–24	14	17	31
1974–1978	25–29	10	8	18
1964–1973	30–39	10	17	27
1954–1963	40–49	17	14	31
1944–1953	50–59	8	21	29
1934–1943	60–69	9	5	14
1924–1933	70–79	4	10	14
1914–1923	80–89	7	5	12
pre-1913	90+	1	0	1
	Total	123	144	267

Table 2.8 *The Clara Corpus, c.2015*

Age	Year of interview	Number of words (Clara only)	Number of words (Clara + her sister)
16	2002	13,365	14,055
17	2003	7,876	9,706
18	2004	12,871	15,115
19	2005	8,932	9,882
20	2006	8,126	10,325
21	2007	7,239	9,188
22	2008	10,058	11,367
24	2010	13,933	16,012
25	2011	12,124	14,484
27	2013	10,282	11,466
28	2014	10,019	12,663
Total		114,825	134,263

are associated with a particular phase in the life span. Do teenagers simply use a lot of weird words and expressions when they are teenagers and then lose those ways of speaking as they get older? The only way to scientifically test this is to follow someone across the years of her life and find out what she does.

I have been very fortunate to be able to follow one particular individual. She was born and raised in Toronto and has been recorded in casual conversations with her sister from the age of 16 to the present day, over the years 2002–2015. The woman, whom I call Clara Felipe, has changed from a high school student working in the library to a professional nurse with a graduate degree working in a large hospital in Toronto.[13] The corpus comprises 134,263 words, as detailed in Table 2.8.

This type of corpus is essentially a case study. It represents only a single individual. Had I been able to follow a group of individuals it would be called a panel study. When speakers of different ages are interviewed at the same time, it is called a "trend study." Despite the fact that a case study is small and individualistic, this material is precious in its perspective on language change across the life span. Further, although it is undersized on one level, it represents a substantial amount of language material. Using this corpus alongside all the others can help to disentangle changes that are actually affecting the language and phenomena that are transitory and tied to teenage life rather than the linguistic system.

Methods for analysis

The methodology I employ in my approach to the study of language is based on the quantitative techniques of Variationist Sociolinguistics (Fasold, 1972;

Labov, 1963, 1966; Tagliamonte, 2012; Wolfram, 1969). The basis for my investigations are large-scale corpora of vernacular speech from hundreds of individuals talking in relaxed circumstances guided by students and assistants trained to conduct informal life histories. Other research modes focus on different types of data, including social network studies (Milroy, 1980) and more ethnographic investigations, which permit the study of styles and social meaning (Eckert, 1988, 2000, 2005). In these approaches researchers are able to "uncover the social motivations for the kinds of linguistic emulation that lead to the spread of change through populations" (Eckert, 1988: 184). In contrast, my approach enables me to tap into broad currents of change, from which social meaning is made. Both large surveys and smaller focused studies are necessary and part of the whole. Here, however, I am providing the large survey perspective. In so doing, I utilize the major social categories that are known to be relevant for the study of language variation and change, namely sex of the individual (male and female) and age. This methodology is not meant to uphold the idea that the gender categories are homogeneous but to extrapolate beyond them in order to infer broader trends. In every study, the individuals were tabulated separately and checked against the group trends for anomalies. In my research program we employ what we refer to as "small-within-large studies" in order to focus in on social groups such as the GLBQ (gay, lesbian, bisexual, queer) community, Asian populations, stutterers, or snowboarders to observe and understand how smaller groups function within the complex of the greater whole.

Tapping the vernacular

The .wav files of these corpora represent many megabytes of data and the text files of transcriptions comprise millions of words. The variety is contemporary North American English as it is spoken in an urban setting. While there are undoubtedly certain formality effects operating within the context of the interview situation, these are significantly mitigated given the nature of the data collection situation. The interviewers engaged in much the same type of dialogue as they would normally have had with their interlocutors. The interviews reflect this in-group tone and unselfconscious style and expose the remarkable non-standard nature of teen language as well as the casual speech style of every other age cohort in the corpora.

Studying language change

Much of the rhetoric about teen language concerns the demise of "good" language. However, in order to determine whether there has, in fact, been language change, it is necessary to compare two points in time. The challenge becomes: how to access representative materials? To tap into what is going on now presents one type of problem. A trickier one is to tap historical states of a language. At the turn of the twenty-first century, it is possible to gain access to the past in a number of ways. Mega corpora of language materials are available from many different sources; however, one source that is readily accessible is Google Ngrams. The Google Ngrams Viewer enables anyone to type in a word and find out how frequent it is in published books from 1800–2012.[14] I will use this tool as a backdrop for analyses in this book.

The most important data source is real language from the speech community of interest – teenagers. However, observations of teen language use can only be fully understood in conjunction and in comparison with individuals spanning the entire age range. Ideally, the type of language data from two different points in time should be the same – in terms of representativeness, social make-up, ancestry, etc. In reality, two data points in time from wholly comparable data sources are impossible to find. The language scientist must use some other means to study historical change. In this case, we can use speakers of different ages, appealing not only to the relatively "older" participant observers in each project (e.g. the student interviewers in the TTC) but most importantly, the backdrop of the TEC which comprises people born from the early 1900s through to the early 1990s.

If a form steadily increases from oldest to youngest individuals, this can be taken as evidence that the form is incoming. Because change proceeds stepwise according to systemic patterns in the grammar, plotting such patterns by age may well reveal the mechanisms underlying the change. In addition, because the development of words and phrases is sensitive to social factors such as age and sex, these factors are key to the developmental process. The following testable hypotheses can be put forward:

(i) The frequency of forms may be related to their degree of development, i.e. stage of change.
(ii) Correlation of linguistic patterns with an individual's age can mirror this process.
(iii) Correlation of forms with broad social factors such as sex and education can be taken to tap into the social evaluation of the particular word or phrase within the community.
(iv) Through the examination of (i), (ii), and (iii) it may be possible to track the interrelationship between linguistic and social factors in language change and by extension the impact of these developments on teen language, language change, regional variation, etc.

Pattern vs. occurrence

A pattern is a series of structurally parallel occurrences that happen at a non-negligible rate in a body of language materials. These patterns reveal the organization and structure of the grammar.

An occurrence is an isolated token without reference to representativeness or recurrence. A token can be used as an illustration, but it cannot falsify a theory based on patterns.

Speaker age/birth date

Everyone notices that teenagers act and sound different from older people. A person who was born in 1991 will not speak the same way as a person born in 1911, or even 1960. Individuals of different ages in the same community will have different ways of speaking.

Sociolinguists refer to these age differences as differences in "apparent time." The construct of apparent time is an important and useful analytical tool for the analysis of language change (Bailey et al., 1991). Age differences are assumed to be a mirror for the passing of time, reflecting historical stages in the progress of the change. The technique has been in use since the early 1900s (e.g. Gauchat, 1905; Hermann, 1929) and has become a keystone of Variationist Sociolinguistics (Bailey, 2002; Bailey et al., 1991; Labov, 1963, 1966; Tagliamonte, 2012). A progressively increasing or decreasing frequency in the use of a linguistic feature when that feature is viewed according to speaker age can be interpreted as change in progress (Sankoff and Evans Wagner, 2006). This pattern has provided the basis for a synchronic approach to language change. Analytically, apparent time functions as a surrogate for chronological, or what sociolinguists refer to as "real" time, enabling the history of a linguistic process to be viewed from the perspective of the present.

Another issue that must be considered is the fact that teenagers represent an expanse from 13 to 19 years of age and individuals of these ages are not the same. Although there are many claims about teen language, which age group is under discussion? There is actually a dearth of conversational data from speakers in the late primary (10- to 11-years-old) and middle school (11- to 14-years-old) age brackets. Carefully stratified samples of teenage language are rare. Many of the linguistic features that are dismissed as features of "teen language" may be diffusing to these age cohorts from other members of the population, or maybe even have originated there, long before later adolescence in high school (the 15–17-year-olds). The question is which teenagers use the relevant forms? When do teenagers start using them and when do they stop, if at all?

On the assumption that language change is represented among people of different ages, I will use the age span of the adult TEC in order to assess how the putative innovations observed among the pre-adolescents and teenagers can be put in context with the rest of the speech community. Did the innovations arise *ex nihilo* or can they be traced back into the older generations of the community? Are the innovations being used haphazardly, representing language decay?

A whole different language has evolved. I'll hear the kids use words and I don't have any idea what they're talking about. They're not words that I've encountered or that I would use in that context. (Jake Ryall, 64)

Baselines for teen language

One criticism of teen language that inevitably arises is the vocabulary of adolescents. A lot of people think that teenagers stick in a lot of extra words that are unnecessary. In so doing, they are thought to reveal their lack of knowledge of other words. When you have millions of words available to you in a database, this type of claim is easy to verify. Do teenagers have less of a vocabulary than older people? Let's find out.

I took a random sample of 26 teenagers, male and female, from the TTC and a random sample of 40–50-year-olds from the TEC. Then I compared their use of distinct words. Table 2.9 shows the results.

There is little to distinguish the two groups in terms of vocabulary. The teenagers do pretty well in comparison to their adult counterparts. We can infer that a lack of vocabulary is not the explanation for the teenage linguistic patterns.

Among the most prominent features disparaged in teen language are a host of forms that are often referred to as pragmatic markers (e.g. Brinton, 1996) or discourse markers (Jucker and Ziv, 1998; Schiffrin, 1982) or more recently as "discourse-pragmatic" markers (Pichler, 2013). The term "pragmatic particle"

Table 2.9 *Comparison of vocabulary from teenagers and middle-aged individuals*

	No. of words	No. of distinct words	Proportion
13–20 years old	9,297	1,230	13%
40–50 years old	9,848	1,450	15%

is also used for many of the same forms (e.g. Erman, 1997; Östman, 1995). What is the difference between a "marker" and a "particle"? I will align with researchers who say that discourse markers (or pragmatic markers) are words that appear at the beginning of sentences while discourse (or pragmatic) particles are words that can appear inside sentences (Brinton and Traugott, 2005; see also discussion in D'Arcy, 2005; D'Arcy, forthcoming; Traugott, 1997). Consider the examples in (6) from several teenagers and (7) from a middle-aged man. There are markers and particles galore!

6.   a. *Like you know like* the snow crabs, *right*? (Clara Felipe, 16)
        b. *Like* African hand drum rhythms are completely different from *like you know* punk-rock regular drums. (Michael Llewellyn, 18)
        c. *Yeah*, because *it's like* everyone could *just* walk in. *Like* if you're in the room, then fine. (Rahim Vasanji, 19)
7.   *So* doesn't the bat hit me *like* right between the eyes. And I *just* felt *like you know* the gongs that "vibration sound" *you know* that just vibrate like that. *So* I put my head down and I *like* for *you know* a couple of seconds *or whatever*. And I lift my head up and everybody's like, "Oh my God Charlie!" *Well* it *just* swelled up *like* instantly. *So of course* they took me home, *right*? (Charlie Marietta, 40)

By the definition I have outlined above, *like*, *you know*, *yeah*, *well*, *of course*, and *so* are all discourse markers. Some words occur at the ends of sentences such as *right* and *or whatever*. Several words occur within the sentence. Some of the same words can occur within sentences such as *like* and *you know*. In addition there are others such as *it's like* and *just*. In the chapters that follow I will explore many of these words.

Taken together, discourse markers and particles comprise a wide range of phenomena typical of contemporary teenagers, but let's not forget Charlie Marietta's story above. Teenagers are not the only users of discourse markers and particles. Brinton (1996: 33; see also Schiffrin, 1987: 33) provides a list of characteristics of pragmatic markers:

a. high frequency
b. stylistically stigmatized
c. negatively evaluated in written or formal discourse
d. short, often unstressed or reduced
e. tend to occur sentence initially
f. have little or no propositional meaning
g. occur outside syntactic structure
h. no clear grammatical function
i. optional
j. multifunctional
k. more characteristic of women's speech than men's.

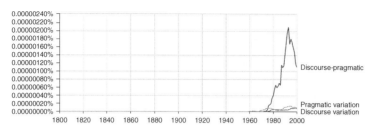

Figure 2.1 Trajectory of the term "discourse-pragmatic" in English

The increasing interest in discourse-pragmatic features can be graphically illustrated with the Google Ngrams graph in Figure 2.1, which shows that since the late 1970s the term *discourse-pragmatic* has emerged vigorously from what appears to be nothing.

The notable trajectory in Figure 2.1 illuminates a definitive trend. Obviously, the use of the term "discourse-pragmatic" reflects a renaissance of research studies on these phenomena; however, it also means that there is a rich reservoir of data containing these features. Many "new" discourse/pragmatic markers have gained considerable high-profile attention, from the media, educationalists, and linguists alike. They are conspicuous and typically associated with the younger generation. Consider the way discourse markers are described in the literature:

Linguistic Cinderellas: familiar, drab, hard-worked, and lacking morphological, phonological and etymological glamour. (Cited in Brinton, 1996: 1; Enkvist, 1972: 95)

Taking the reports in the literature as a starting point and the idea of the Linguistic Cinderella at face value, I scrutinized my corpora of teen language for the offending words that are part of the infamous discourse-pragmatic feature cohort. I also sought out other Linguistic Cinderellas in the data worthy of investigation.

To begin this discovery process, let's consider the top 50 words teenagers use in the TTC, as in Table 2.10. The top five words are shaded. Other words of interest are italicized.

The most straightforward observation to be made is that most of these words comprise the basic building blocks of the English language, including pronouns, *I*, *you*, *he*, *she*, *we*, *they*, and *it*, the conjunctions *and*, *but*, *or*, articles *the* and *a*, preposition *to*, negation *no* and *not*, the verb *be* and its various renditions, *'m*, *is*, *are*, *was*, as well as *have*, *think*, *know*, *go*, etc. There are also a few words that stand out, including *like*, *so*, *just*, and *really*. Let's compare this count to the top 49 words in COLT.[15] Once again, the top five words are shaded (Table 2.11).

Table 2.10 *Top 50 words by frequency in the TTC,*
c.*2002–2006*

1	42,931	i
2	37,441	*like*
3	30,007	and
4	25,405	you
5	23,639	the
6	22,649	it
7	19,619	to
8	17,802	's
9	16,500	a
10	16,003	that
11	13,672	*so*
12	12,158	yeah
13	11,785	of
14	11,710	was
15	11,012	't
16	9,675	in
17	9,450	but
18	8,723	they
19	8,553	know
20	8,000	he
21	7,902	then
22	7,874	do
23	7,838	my
24	7,468	we
25	7,397	um
26	7,395	*just*
27	7,330	have
28	6,871	what
29	6,101	*really*
30	5,822	don't
31	5,799	is
32	5,457	no
33	5,410	she
34	5,288	there
35	5,149	or
36	5,128	for
37	5,094	not
38	5,013	oh
39	4,643	on
40	4,204	all
41	4,181	one
42	4,137	go
43	4,102	me
44	4,063	with
45	4,027	this
46	3,971	at
47	3,948	'm
48	3,808	think
49	3,796	be
50	3,643	are

Table 2.11 *Top 49 words in the Bergen Corpus of London Teenage Language* (c.1993)

1	15,337	you
2	15,076	i
3	11,102	the
4	9,839	and
5	9,066	it
6	7,528	a
7	7,478	to
8	7,446	yeah
9	6,195	*that*
10	4,930	what
11	4,850	no
12	4,163	in
13	4,160	know
14	4,002	he
15	3,957	of
16	3,800	it's
17	3,791	oh
18	3,742	is
19	3,555	*like*
20	3,537	on
21	3,372	do
22	3,295	was
23	3,252	don't
24	3,184	got
25	2,977	have
26	2,861	*just*
27	2,759	*so*
28	2,655	but
29	2,616	she
30	2,591	they
31	2,554	not
32	2,526	me
33	2,525	this
34	2,433	my
34	2,366	well
35	2,345	one
36	2,269	i'm
37	2,159	go
38	2,109	up
39	2,105	erm
40	2,079	get
41	2,076	your
42	2,063	all
43	2,003	we
44	1,994	are
45	1,950	be
46	1,921	with
47	1,919	for
48	1,918	that's
49	1,847	can

Let's also compare this count to the top 50 words in each of the Multicultural London English (MLE) corpora (Cheshire et al., 2007–2010).[16] Two London boroughs were selected for this corpus in order to contrast inner city (Hackney, Table 2.12) and outer city (Havering, Table 2.13). The idea was to find out if there was ongoing divergence between Londoners and London periphery residents. A crucial part of this project was to tap the influence of ethnic minorities in the inner city, because the perception at the time was that ethnic minority speakers, particularly Afro-Caribbeans, were leading innovations in London teenager speech. The Multicultural London English Corpus represents the "ethnically neutral language of the youth of London." This time the top six words are shaded in each case.

Despite the different years of data collection (1993–2007), the different countries (Canada/England), the different varieties of English (North American/ British), the most frequent words in each corpus are effectively the same: *I*, *you*, *and*, *the*, and – conspicuously in TTC and MLE – the word *like*. Among the top words are also the most frequent verbs of English, *is/are/'m*, *do*, *go*, *have*, *know*, and the multifunctional grammatical word *that*. Remarkably, all the teenage corpora contain *like*, *just*, and *so* among the top 30 words. In the chapters to follow these words will figure prominently.

An increase in an item's text frequency is an important concomitant of its grammaticization. (Hook, 1991, cited in Traugott and Heine, 1991b: 319)

A very interesting fact from the standpoint of a language scientist is that frequency is a red flag for linguistic change. Language is always changing. It changes all the time and there is nothing we can do to stop it. But how do you know when language is changing? One of the most important bits of evidence is how many times a word occurs vis-à-vis other words. When a feature of language starts turning up a lot more often than it ever did before, this is usually a good indication that something is going on. The language is on the move; something is shifting from one state to another.

At the same time, adolescents are well-known extremists. This means that the way they speak might be something that they "grow out of" eventually. Therefore, it is always difficult to balance the passing frivolities of youth with the imperceptible currents of language change. Which words are here to stay and which will fall to the wayside as teenagers get older? We cannot know for certain what the teenagers in the TIC will do as they age; however, we can compare them to their elders. Table 2.14 tabulates the top 50 words for the over 60-year-olds in the TEC.

The vast majority of the very frequent words retain more or less the same ranking regardless of whether the individual is a teenager or a senior citizen. In fact, 7 of the top 10 are identical in both corpora. Some of the words that are suspected of change are present as well, but they have not reached the high

Table 2.12 *Top 50 words in the Multicultural London English Corpus – Hackney (c.2004)*[17]

1	18,638	i
2	16,259	you
3	14,995	and
4	14,741	sue
5	12,941	the
6	11,932	*like*
7	11,020	to
8	8,685	it
9	8,642	a
10	8,053	that
11	6,887	of
12	6,705	was
13	6,513	in
14	6,246	my
15	6,153	yeah
16	6,065	*so*
17	6,064	they
18	5,752	but
19	5,584	*just*
20	5,388	yeh
21	5,325	do
22	5,115	he
23	5,046	what
24	4,535	mm
25	4,315	no
26	4,158	it's
27	4,078	know
28	4,010	don't
29	3,849	name
30	3,593	then
31	3,529	me
32	3,431	is
33	3,386	with
34	3,330	she
35	3,316	got
36	3,155	on
37	3,105	we
38	3,096	go
39	3,087	all
40	3,084	have
41	3,056	oh
42	2,976	not
43	2,964	there
44	2,909	that's
45	2,898	your
46	2,746	them
47	2,744	get
48	2,720	for
49	2,647	cos
50	2,477	i'm

Table 2.13 *Top 50 words in the Multicultural London English Corpus – Havering (c.2004)*

1	17,151	i
2	15,582	and
3	13,400	you
4	12,777	sue
5	12,510	*like*
6	12,037	yeah
7	10,622	the
8	9,132	to
9	7,828	a
10	7,742	it
11	7,481	that
12	5,914	in
13	5,849	was
14	5,636	*just*
15	5,597	of
16	5,332	*so*
17	5,321	but
18	5,290	my
19	4,926	they
20	4,753	do
21	4,692	mm
22	4,587	what
23	4,181	it's
24	3,983	he
25	3,447	got
26	3,338	is
27	3,303	then
28	3,289	no
29	3,148	unclear
30	3,142	don't
31	3,023	me
32	3,019	on
33	3,015	all
34	2,996	know
35	2,919	we
36	2,885	go
37	2,845	she
38	2,814	there
39	2,753	with
40	2,698	cos
41	2,498	have
42	2,449	oh
43	2,380	not
44	2,377	get
45	2,376	really
46	2,366	for
47	2,357	or
48	2,291	er
49	2,280	name
50	2,233	your

Table 2.14 *Top 50 words in the Toronto English Archive,
age 60+, c.2002–2006*

1	12,477	the
2	11,101	I
3	10,938	and
4	7,799	a
5	7,468	you
6	7,355	was
7	6,895	to
8	6,249	it
9	6,239	*that*
10	5,366	of
11	5,301	's
12	5,198	in
13	4,022	they
14	3,660	't
15	3,566	And
16	3,343	we
17	3,258	know
18	3,220	there
19	2,511	ah
20	2,465	he
21	2,408	were
22	2,341	had
23	2,185	Yeah
24	2,092	on
25	2,048	*so*
26	1,809	at
27	1,806	for
28	1,762	but
29	1,754	have
30	1,685	my
31	1,637	yeah
32	1,563	*like*
33	1,539	all
34	1,460	when
35	1,453	is
36	1,422	or
37	1,395	up
38	1,366	then
39	1,359	um
40	1,348	Oh
41	1,289	*So*
42	1,279	*just*
43	1,271	go
44	1,264	think
45	1,263	with
46	1,252	what
47	1,216	would
48	1,195	one
49	1,177	But
50	1,173	this

levels of frequency as in the teenager data; these include *like*, *so*, and *just*. This exercise has been useful in identifying what features are the best for tapping into teen language.

It's usually young females when every other word is "like" and it drives me insane. I just like I hate it. (Gabrielle Prusskin, 55)

Which linguistic features to study?

Building on insights from extensive study of the corpora described above, each chapter in this book will examine a different linguistic feature or expression of teen language that shows evidence of being involved in ongoing linguistic change. These features must also fulfill my personal cheering code, the Principle of Curiosity: linguistic phenomena sufficiently intriguing and interesting so that lengthy study under tiresome circumstances (counting, coding, analyzing) can be weathered without fear of boredom. In other words, this book will investigate the most frequent, funky, infamous words of teen language. Questioning whether they are actually exclusive to teen language, were invented by teenagers, or are a hallmark of language decay will provide points for discussion.

Brinton (1996: appendix A) lists 34 separate words as "pragmatic markers":

Actually, after all, ah, almost, and, and (stuff/things) like that, anyway, basically, because, but, go (as a quotative), if, I mean, I think, just, like, mind you, moreover, now, ah, okay, or really, right/all right/that's right, say, so, sort of/kind of, then, therefore, uh huh, well, yes/no, you know, you see.

Like   The second most frequent word used by teenagers in Toronto is *like*. It occurs more than the word that has long been upheld as the most frequent word in the English language – *the*. This does not come as a surprise. Teenagers are well known to be using *like* a lot these days. However, how much is "a lot"? Is it every other word as Gabrielle Prusskin suggests above? Although *like* stands as the second ranked word in Toronto, it is the eleventh ranked word in the London corpus. Does this mean London teenagers don't use *like* as much as Toronto teenagers? This discrepancy may simply be due to the fact that the Toronto data were collected ten or more years later (*c*.2003–2006) than the London data (*c*.1993). Notice that the word *like* is among the top ten words in MLE teenage data regardless of borough. However, the fact that it is more frequent even than *and* in Toronto is a bit of a shock. What are teenagers doing with the word *like*? Consider the excerpt in (8):

8.   I worked *like* two shifts, just by accident. *Like* I went in for a training shift
       like Tuesday the week before Frosh Week, and *like* within fifteen they're
       like- it was *like*- I got in during *like* a shift change, and it was *like*, "Can you
       work tomorrow? Can you work tomorrow?" And no one could work, and

they look at me, "Can you work tomorrow?" And I'm *like*, "Seeing as I have
no idea what I'm doing so far, sure." So I worked *like* two shifts and *like*
I haven't gotten any shifts since. *Like* they hired too many people. (Elizabeth
McKinley, 19)

I have taught hundreds of undergraduate students between the ages of
17 and 30 at the University of Toronto. In order to enter the university every
student must have achieved a high average in high school. These are not by
any stretch of the imagination dull or stupid human beings. Yet one day in
class one of my undergraduate students stood up in the lecture hall in front of
several hundred other students surrounding her and said: *"I can't stop saying
'like.' I've tried I can't. Why can't I?!"* I provide some answers to this question
in Chapter 4.

[Interviewer] I had a lady, an elderly lady, she was in her eighties, and she corrected me
on my use of "yeah" and for the life of me, I was trying so hard to say "yes" instead of
"yeah" and I couldn't do it. [077] No, and it's just slang and actually I have a friend who
I had dinner with last night and he said you say "yeah" all the time, and it's just sloppy,
sloppy language isn't it, eh? (June Watson, 49)

So Another word that is among the most frequent words in all the
corpora is *so*. Among the teenagers it is the eleventh most frequent word in the
TTC and the 27th in COLT. Another frequent word is *really*, which is 29th in
the TTC but a little further down the list elsewhere. These words have a variety
of different uses in English. Let's first consider the one function they have in
common. They can both be used to "boost up" another word, as in (9) and (10).

9.   a. Hop's *really* cool though. (Amanda Levy, 12)
        b. Sometimes my marks are like *really* high so I was *really* happy.
            (Kevin Lam, 15)
10.   a. Then guys, when it comes to talk about girls, it's *so* funny. They freak out.
            (Catherine Hui, 19)
        b. It's because we're all like *so* close. (Lina Delmonico, 16)

In fact, teenagers use *so* and *really* as boosters in ways that are different
from the rest of the population. I'll tell you more about this feature in
Chapter 5.

The word *so* can also be used as a sentence starter, as in (11).

11.   a. *So* like if you cut off the zombie's head, yeah it's still a live head.
            It will just try to bite. (Trevor Klinke, 20)
        b. *So* I ran back into the truck and *so* I was honking to scare away the bear,
            but I was just too scared to get out of the vehicle. (Katrina Wilson, 18)

Teenagers use a multitude of words at the beginning of sentences, including
oh, ah, yeah, like, and others, as in (12). I'll tell you more about sentence
starters in Chapter 6.

12.   a. And *ah* he tried to get people so pumped up for it but it usually- *like* it
            usually sucks. *Like* people usually just laugh at him. *Like* "penny wars!
            Whoo! I love penny wars!" (Erin Gadek, 16)
        b. [Interviewer] *So*, what does that do to the team? [026] *Ah, well*, it kind
            of split us up in like clicks. (Caleb Stine, 16)
        c. [Interviewer] That's awesome. What games? [006] *Ah you know* just
            like- she always like those RPG games, like Final Fantasy stuff like
            that, Lord of the Ring or anything. Yeah. (Kirk Pollock, 18)
        d. *Yeah so but I mean* it's not like he actually bit him (Joanna Lunche, 19)

If teenagers use a lot of different words at the beginning of sentences, what
do you think they do at the ends? In fact, the many words that teenagers use at
the beginning of sentences are mirrored in the wide range of words and
expressions they tack on at the finish. In fact, there are probably even more
sentence enders than starters, including *you know, or anything, and stuff, or
whatever, right*, and *so* in (13). So, you may begin to realize that the same
word can have a variety of uses.

13.   a. And I was like, "come on like look at them" *you know*. (Craig
            Thompson, 18)
        b. See, but we wouldn't go into smoking *or anything*. (Catherine
            Hui, 19)
        c. Yeah and there was like a store and a casino on the boat *and stuff*.
            (Randy Mantle, 11)
        d. He like slapped him across the face *right*. (Stephen Hardwick, 15)
        e. The acrobats they had like fancy dress outfits *or whatever*. (Tina
            Mancini, 11)
        f. So he doesn't do that *so*. (Ian McCready, 13)

That   Another word that is among the top 50 words in each of the
corpora is *that*, another supremely multifunctional word. It can be used as a
pronoun as in (14a), or as a relative pronoun, as in (14b).

14.   a. Whoa, *that*'s cool. So, *that*'s my story. (Clara Felipe, 16)
        b. There were a bunch of other colleges *that* used to do it (Shannon
            Ermak, 19)

However, an interesting role that *that* plays in English is to form part of a
group of words that are used at the ends of sentences, as in (15). I'll tell you
more about this feature in Chapter 7.

15.   a. It's a gifted school *or something like <u>that</u>*. (Michael Llewellyn, 18)
        b. [Interviewer] Do you go to many parties *and things like <u>that</u>*? (DF)

Stuff   The word *stuff* is not among the top 50 words, but it is used
frequently as well, sometimes as a pronoun, as in (16), but also as part of a
sentence ender, as in (17).

16.   After school was done, I'd come home, drop off all my books, grab my
        stuff, and then bike down to paddling. (Craig Thompson, 18)

17.   We'd just go to arenas and play that *stuff*. It was pretty good. I mean we tried
        a lot of different things. We had two camps during the year. We had a fall
        camp, you know, where we went on the trip to Algonquin, which was a lot of
        fun, and then we had a winter trip as well. But like we were staying in cabins
        and *stuff*. And yeah we did a lot of activities. Snowshoeing, and like orien-
        teering, and cross-country skiing, all that kind of *stuff*, which I really like.
        Cross-country skiing was a lot of fun. And um, the snowshoeing is pretty cool
        too. That year there was an awful lot of snow up there and *stuff*. (Craig
        Thompson, 18)

In Chapter 8 I'll tell you more about *stuff*.

Just   A surprisingly frequent word is *just*. It is the 26th most frequent
word in the TTC and even more frequent in the MLE, both Hackney
and Havering. To get the full flavor of how *just* is used consider the excerpts
in (18).

18.   a. I'm like *just* playing around, doing nothing. Same thing over and over
            again. And then, every once in a while me and my friend who plays the
            bass. Like, whenever somebody would come in, we'll like *just* stop and
            play 'Another One Bites the Dust'. It's really funny. And then we're
            going to try and learn like *just* to piss him off, really. We *just* do, 'cause
            it's more fun. (Vivian Bustamante, 16)
        b. My dad gets them [hockey tickets]. Like, he *just* gets them from his work.
            And then we *just* go and then I guess usually it's *just* me and my dad.
            And then sometimes my dad and my mom and I *just* stay home by myself.
            And then my brother, we *just* watch TV until they come back around
            twelve or eleven and then we go to bed. (Christopher O'Neil, 11)

In Chapter 9, I will explore what is going on with the word *just*.

Focusing on the top 50 words in a corpus is a good starting-point for
discovering potential features undergoing change; however, this method has
limitations. There are many words and meanings in language that may be
undergoing change, but are not necessarily frequent. Another way to probe a
large corpus of language data is to use computation tools. With the help of
collaborator Julian Brooke, I probed the TEC using some basic techniques in
computational linguistics to identify features that might serve as ideal linguistic features to target for investigation (Tagliamonte and Brooke, 2014).
A *feature* consists of any computationally identifiable linguistic form or
construction that may be undergoing change or doing interesting social work.
For instance, if a word patterns by speaker age then we go looking for how
speakers of all ages might say the same thing. For example, an older person
might use the word *terrific* where I would use *fantastic* whereas teenagers will

probably say *sick* or *dope*. All these words together form what is referred to as a "structured set" (Labov, 1972a: 127), a group of alternates in the language that mean more or less the same thing. Once we know the set and the contexts in which the words in the set are used, the variants can be studied as a linguistic variable. Then, we can find out if the language is changing and if so, how and why.

The advantage of using computational tools is that they facilitate automatic exploration of a huge array of possibilities, and provide a statistical measure to identify the promising ones (Brooke and Tagliamonte, 2012). In a corpus the size of the TEC (approximately 1.2 million words) (see Tagliamonte, 2006b), there are hundreds of thousands of potential words and constructions that could unlock the mystery of language change. How do computational tools identify promising ones? The first step is to automatically remove extremely rare features (those appearing fewer than five times across the corpus), since these are unlikely to lead to viable phenomena to analyze quantitatively. The second step is much more complex: assessing whether the remaining features can predict the various sociolinguistic factors that are present in the corpus (e.g. age, sex). The metric used for this is called *information gain*, which measures the change in entropy (predictability) between a situation where there isn't any knowledge about the presence or absence of a feature, and one where there is. One advantage of information gain over raw feature counts is a preference for common features that distinguish factors but that are well spread among the individuals in the corpus; a single person who uses one feature incessantly will not cause it to be ranked high according to information gain, since one individual represents a small portion of the overall probability. Information gain is employed by machine learning models such as decision trees, and is used generally for feature selection. Note that information gain is mathematically distinct from the notion of statistically significant differences in distribution, though the two will often agree.

Table 2.15 shows the top-ranked features from the TEC by information gain using the WEKA machine learning suite (Witten and Eibe, 2005). In this case the algorithm shows the top three-word contenders for predicting whether an individual is +/– 30 years of age (I have omitted some repetitive features).

Notice some of the same words identified in the corpora word lists in Tables 2.10–2.13 also turn up in Table 2.15, in particular *like* and *just*. Several others emerge, including *weird*, *cool*, and *really*. This is just a small sample of the most highly ranked features (as measured by information gain). There are actually thousands of word collocations that have positive information gain (though the vast majority have less than 0.2). The word *like* and associated expressions are by far the most useful words for distinguishing age; this is no surprise given the extensive research on *like* in contemporary English

Table 2.15 *Top three word constructions in the TEC by information gain: < or > 30 years old*

Feature	Information Gain
like	0.5844
really *adjective*	0.4663
just *adjective*	0.4113
I was like	0.4110
is pretty *adjective*	0.3411
friends	0.3386
weird	0.3275
adverb cool	0.2908
hang out	0.2832

(e.g. Blyth et al., 1990; Brebieri, 2009; Buchstaller and D'Arcy, 2009; Cukor-Avila, 2002; D'Arcy, 2005, 2007, 2008, forthcoming; Durham et al., 2012; Macaulay, 2001). The sociolinguistic characteristics of intensifying expressions (*really, just, pretty* adjective) have also been investigated with a notable story of linguistic change (e.g. D'Arcy, 2014; Macaulay, 2007; Méndez-Naya, 2003; Stenström, 1999; Tagliamonte, 2008; Van Herk, 2009). The second ranked individual word, *friends*, highlights a danger of this approach. The word is a useful distinguisher of young versus old because of differences in the preferred topics and recounting of actions (see also *hang out*) of each group, but not because the word is of any real sociolinguistic or dialectological interest. This foregrounds a critical and foundational axiom – although a statistical method may help bring new variables to the awareness of researchers, they are not a substitute for a thoughtful, linguistically informed analysis. Information gain gives no direct information about whether a feature was preferred by one group over another. It only identifies features (forms or words) that are relevant to the task of distinguishing one group from another. It does not make an explicit connection between features (forms or words) and sociolinguistic factors even though this may be intuitively apparent. In order to conduct the type of analysis that would substantiate the connection, a different method is required, as I will describe in due course.

The third most important individual word for distinguishing age (and thus suggesting change in progress) is the word *weird*, which is often used as an adjective. We might have predicted that an adjective like *cool*, with its colloquial associations, would appear high in this list (and in fact it does), but *weird* is even higher, despite having no strong stylistic biases. This result tells us that young people in Toronto are using *weird* much more often than the older population. This was a surprise and the catalyst for the exploration of adjectives of strangeness in Chapter 10.

Other phenomena of interest that emerged from the information gain analysis included expressions that involve several words, including *I don't know*, *what do you mean*, and *whatever*. The collocation *I don't know* together occurs well over 2,000 times. Why do teenagers say *I don't know* so much? Is it due to ignorance? Not exactly. And you know what, there's another group of words that teenagers are also using a lot these days too. You guessed it. The expression *you know what* occurs 401 times. Why do teenagers say this so often? You can't get too far in a discussion with a teenager these days without hearing the word *whatever*. What does *whatever* mean? Are these phenomena the product of adolescent slang and the bemoaned lack of vocabulary among teenagers? You know what? I don't know, whatever! Just kidding. We will find out more about these expressions in Chapter 11.

In Chapter 12, I'll take a completely different approach and bring you on a journey into the world of Internet language among teenagers online using the TIC. Reports in the media say this type of communication is the "linguistic ruin" of the generation (Axtman, 2002). Is it really?

Finally, in Chapter 13, I will summarize the findings for all the features I have explored with you. Then, as many people wonder, I will address the question: What will teenagers do as they get older? We'll find out by providing a synthesis of the comparisons between teenagers and everyone else in the community.

In summary, my overarching goal is to explore the origin, pathways, and impacts of these words among teenagers but also to find out where they fit in with everyone else. So far, little is known about the origin of these words in the places where they are used so much or about their trajectory of linguistic change in contemporary English. Let's try to find out what is going on.

By the end of the book, I hope you will find yourself listening intently to the teenagers around you and hearing some, or all, of the features I have investigated, as well as many more. If so, you will have developed an enviable vantage point. Teen language is one of the most creative forms of talk and a key source of what is coming in the future, specifically the future of the English language.

[Interviewer] Like when I was interviewing you, were you trying- were you paying attention to the words you were saying and stuff like that. Were you like conscious of it? [011] I think near the beginning 'cause you said it was a language thing, but two minutes into it I just forgot and just started talking. (Jason Levine 17)

Activity

Examine the quips and quotes more closely. How many of the features identified and studied in the book can you find? How many others warrant investigation? Notice the construction 'a x thing', *a language thing*. Can you find other examples?

Language puzzle

Lists of words compiled from corpora are a great place to begin examining language. For this puzzle consult the WORDLISTS for the TTC and the TEC that can be found on the CUP website. I have already introduced some of the frequent words that will be the subject of investigation in this book. Let's take a look at some others.

a. Sort the wordlists by frequency of occurrence. What frequency of word makes up the bulk of the data?
b. What is the most frequent verb in the TEC and in the TTC?
c. What is the most frequent hyphenated word in the TEC and in the TTC?
d. Find the word "basically." How often does it occur in the TTC and in the TEC?
e. Among the words found by information gain in Table 2.15 are *friends* and *hang out.* Find these words in the TTC and TEC. How often do they occur?
f. Notice all the different variations on the word "hang." I have made a list of examples of the entry *hangs* from the TTC and TEC below. How many meanings are there?
g. What co-occurrence pattern do you notice with the verb "hang"?

Let your curiosity guide you in discovering some other interesting facts about language corpora by further scrutiny of the WORDLISTS.

1. ... and ties them to a rope and *hangs* them over the building. (Gordon Combs, 17)
2. Then she just *hangs* up on him. (Janice Hu, 9)
3. He like *hangs* up all the Flyer pictures. (Tina Mancini, 11)
4. There are all those different groups that everyone *hangs* around with. (Vittoria Delmonico, 16)
5. She *hangs* around with that other group ... (Vittoria Delmonico, 16)
6. She's like, "Oh I'll talk to you later" and *hangs* up the phone. (Bridgitte Santino, 20)
7. Nick *hangs* around here. (Linda Palantini, 25)
8. There's this big black cloud that *hangs* over these people. (Darina Stobart, 53)
9. There's sort of one father that kind of *hangs* around. (Macy Griffo, 43)
10. He *hangs* out with my kids. (Timothy Arnett, 47)

Answers
a. *Most words occur only once. These are called singletons or "hapax legomena."*
b. *The verb "to be" in its past tense form, "was."*
c. *The most frequent hyphenated word is "you-know." TTC = 1,416; TEC 8,209.*
d. *"Basically/basically-" occurs 217 + 5 times in the TTC and 443 + 14 times in the TEC. This seems like a lot. What might this word be doing in the language? Note: The hyphens at the end of the word signal false starts in the orthographic transcription.*

(cont.)

e. *The word "friends" occurs 874 times in the TTC and 760 times in the TEC. The word "hang-out" (with a hyphenated spelling) occurs 7 times in the TTC and 25 times in the TEC.*
f. *The different meanings for "hang" are: (i) be suspended; (ii) disconnect a phone connection; (iii) put up; (iv) mark time.*
g. *The verb "hang" often occurs with small words called "particles," including "around," "up," "out." Notice how the meanings correlate with different phrases: "hang around" means "to mark time," while "hang up" can mean "hang up a phone" or "hang up pictures."*

3   Methods

How to tap teen language?

> And these are all girls who are pretty smart, and they have some of the little
> you know idiosyncrasies of youth language, but they're pretty articulate.
> They can express an idea, provide an opinion and are pretty self-assured
> and yeah.
>
> (Candice Yuranyi, 40)

Imagine you overhear a person say: *That's like so random* and another person
say: *That's very unpredictable.* Which person is almost certainly younger and
which older? Which one is using "proper" English and which one is using
slang? You might feel you could guess the correct answer to both of those
questions. But there's another question that's more interesting: why do young
people and old people use language so differently in the first place?

Let's consider three basic facts about language:

1. Language is always changing.
2. No one can stop language change – not teachers, not parents, not the prime
   minister.
3. Age has a huge impact on how a person uses language.

In our culture, young people usually try to set themselves apart from the older
generation – through clothing and appearance, preferences in music, and
acutely through language. That's because language is a very important symbol
of social solidarity. The ways we use language let other people know who we
are and where we belong. As teens gain independence and come in contact
with a wider circle of friends, they are exposed to an increasingly rich range of
new language uses. When these new uses spread among more and more teens,
new expressions enter English, and sometimes they even influence English
grammar. This is how young people become the driving force behind language
change. You might also be interested to know that girls are far more likely to
use new features of language than boys are, which means that girls are the
primary transmitters of new usages.

Where do the "new" features of language come from? Young people do not
create them out of nothing. As we shall see, young people take the materials
already available in the language and modify them in new ways. Here's an

43

example. An older person will almost always use the word *very* when emphasizing something: "That's *very* fine." A middle-aged person will be more likely to use *really*, as in "That's *really* nice." And an adolescent today will undoubtedly say, "That's *so* cool." In this case, the "new" feature is simply a different word to perform a familiar function. However, language change is not always that straightforward.

One of the most interesting changes occurring in English right now is the evolution of the word *like*. As we have seen, a single word can have different meanings and functions. *Like* is no exception. Some uses of *like* are standard and banal, such as "I *like* pizza," "There's nothing *like* pizza," or "I feel *like* pizza." But young people are using *like* in other ways that are sweeping through the language and are non-standard. Consider the examples in (19).

19.   a.   "My mom*'s like*, 'Here's your pizza,' and I*'m like*, 'Thanks!'"
        b.   "Pizza is *like* awesome."
        c.   "Pizza is *like* my favorite."

The first kind of *like* is used instead of *said* to introduce words that someone else spoke. Young Canadians (especially girls) choose *like* over *said* and other similar words nearly two-thirds of the time. People over 40 hardly ever do. Language scientists wonder what will happen as teens get older. Will they keep using *like* this way? Will the boys catch up to the girls? Will the older generation start using this *like* too?

Young people between 9 and 19 use *like* a lot. About 4 percent of an individual's average conversation consists of the word *like*. Although that might not sound like much, it means that *like* shows up more often than any other word, even *the*, *a*, and *um*! (See for example Table 2.10.) Older people use *like* far less often – about 0.05 percent of the time. People typically think that teens use the word *like* whenever they don't know what to say next. They worry that this habit is leading to a decrease in vocabulary. And they're sure this trend is new and bad. Interestingly, even 60 years ago grammarians were complaining that people were using *like* too much, therefore it is not a new trend. Young people are also pushing the boundaries of where *like* can be used, i.e. not just before a noun or adjective, but also before a verb, as in "I *like* ate the whole pizza," and "I'm *like* eating it all up." These uses follow a definite pattern and suggest that *like* is beginning to take on new roles in the grammar. Which roles will stay and which will disappear?

The only way to find out is to study teen language in a way that is scientific and replicable. This is where a variationist approach to sociolinguistics comes in.

Well, their language has changed obviously. They use a lot of words that weren't around fifty years ago and I was trying to think of some of them but. [Interviewer] "Like," maybe? [099] Well yes I mean you would have students who would throw "like" into practically every second sentence as they went along. (Dirk Brooks, 73)

The linguistic variable

The key to a scientific approach to language behavior is the observation that speakers make choices when they speak. In variationist sociolinguistics, these are called "linguistic variables." A linguistic variable in its most basic definition is "two or more ways of saying the same thing" (Labov, 1982: 49). Examples of different words for the same thing are easy to find in daily life, e.g. *truck, lorry*; *candy, sweets*; *pail, bucket*. There are also different ways of pronouncing the same word, *to-may-to, to-mah-to*. When you meet someone in the street do you say *hi, hello*, or *hey*? This type of variation is everywhere in language from sounds to service encounters to storytelling styles. In (20) two different ways of saying the past tense of the verb "got" are visible as a sister asks her younger brother a question. In (21) Janet uses two different intensifiers to boost her adjectives. In (22) Michael uses two different syntactic constructions for mailing a letter to a group of people: a double object and a prepositional phrase using *to*.

20.   a. [Interviewer] Okay, I have another question. What's the worst thing
            you've ever *got* in trouble for? (Gloria Fraute, 20)
        b. I haven't really *gotten* in trouble. Like worst- they've all been the same
            like when I stretched my ear. (Steve Fraute, 15)

21.   We're actually *very* close so it's *really* good 'cause if I ever need anything,
        she'll help me out. (Janet McDonald, 19)

22.   I emailed *them a letter*. . . . I wrote *a letter to them*. (Michael McGuigan, 32)

Alternative forms with comparable meaning in running discourse enable the language scientist to probe the linguistic system, the grammar (Sankoff, 1988a: 142–143). The analysis begins with a search for all the possible forms and the contexts where a choice between one and the other is possible. It is possible to study the full range of environments in which a word or phrase occurs in a particular body of data (distributional accountability) or to study a particular discourse context where the forms are prevalent (sequential accountability) (Schiffrin, 1987: 69). Whichever approach the language scientist takes, the critical point is to include in the investigation each of the possible words or phrases people use within the data. The analysis must include each time a speaker or writer uses a form *and* each time a speaker or writer does *not* use a form in a context where she might have. Doing this ensures that all possibilities are taken into account. The next step is to determine why one form is used more often in one place over another. Perhaps a word or phrase will be used more by women than men or more at the beginning of a sentence than at the end. Discovering the many patterns underlying the use of words and phrases enables the language scientist to understand the linguistic system and ultimately the group, community, or society that uses it.

Variants in language typically differ subtly in meaning and distribution but these patterns can only be discovered by methodical procedures. Once an adequate number of choices has been tabulated, the selection of one variant or another can be tested for the influence of one factor or another (Cedergren and Sankoff, 1974; Labov, 1969). This is where the quantitative approach differentiates itself from many other methods for understanding language – counting and accounting for where words are used, who uses them and why.

Frequency

When people make claims about teen language, they often frame their argument in terms of frequency, i.e. teenagers use certain words "a lot," "everywhere," or "every second sentence" as in the quote above.

Counting the number of times a person uses a particular word or phrase is not as easy as it sounds. First, you need to be able to record a person talking or writing for a long period of time so that you have a reasonable body of data. Second, you have to count things accurately. Third, you need to know what to count. If it's true that students insert *like* into practically every second sentence, then we can easily test to see if this is true. Consider the following excerpt from an interview with Clara Felipe (age 16) being interviewed by her sister:

23. a. [Interviewer] So is there anything else you want to like shop for?
  b. Shop for? Oh man! There's so many things that I want. I want like that hat. You know that hat *like* that we were looking at? The one that you tried on in Hawaii when we did our thug picture? That's a really cool hat. But I don't know, there's not really anything. I want new boots. I'm still looking for boots. And *like* you can never have enough *like* winter sweaters and stuff. Or *like* a fall jacket. I want a fall jacket. *Like* I dunno. A fall jacket and boots. That's what I want and a hat. But the hat's not really necessary, so. Yeah, but I dunno. I think I have enough clothes for now. And *like* pants. But *like* yeah, I can scrap up enough outfits. So, oh, I dunno what I'm going to be for Halloween though. I don't know. I was contemplating a princess today, but that's kind of prissy. And I wouldn't know. *Like* I would have *like* 'cause I have *like* my little tiara thing, right? I don't know. 'Cause last year I was a witch, but there's only so much you can do. 'Cause I don't want to be ugly. *Like* who wants to be ugly on Halloween? (Clara Felipe, 16)

How many times does Clara use *like*? Eleven times. Is it a lot? Without further investigation the number of tokens, N=11, is meaningless. We need to be able to assess how frequent 11 is. One of the easiest ways to do this is to count how many *like* tokens occur out of the total number of words in the sample. In this case, the excerpt contains 207 words. The number of *like* tokens and the total number of words from which those *like* tokens were uttered can be calculated as follows: 11/207, which is a rate of 5.3 percent. Is this a lot? Now, we need to do something else – compare.

Let's consider the use of *like* by a woman who is much older, but born and raised in the same city, Flora Valentin, age 83, as in (24).

24. a. [Interviewer] Is that the groceries or?
     b. [022] There was grocery, wholesale groceries. Except one boy was a French Canadian and to me, it was a bit different because the people who worked in the warehouse, I hadn't seen people who worked *like* that you know. They were all nice. We all got along and you know we'd go uptown and shop and go to the Severn and have a cocktail then go across to Eaton's and buy funny hats. Auntie Lil and I used to do that and I still see her. And she's, she's technically blind and not very well so if I want to bring her out of something I say, you know, "Remember when we went to the Severn and we'd have a couple of cocktails and we'd go over and buy hats?" you know. That always gets her going. And we used to go on trips you know. You could go by bus. We used to go over to Buffalo to shop and down to Rochester. Just you know not too often 'cause there wasn't that much money. I think when I left there I was making twenty nine dollars and some odd cents. And that was supposedly good pay. For a week. (Flora Valentin, 83)

The excerpt contains 200 words. There is one token of *like*. Taking into account the number of *like* tokens and the total number of words from which those *like* tokens were uttered gives 1/200, which is a rate of 0.05 percent. This seems low in comparison to 5 percent. But how can we tell if this difference makes the two samples distinct? Maybe the difference is simply due to chance. This is where statistics is helpful. A basic measure, the chi square statistic, can offer an assessment that this difference is meaningful. In fact, it is significant at the $p < 0.05$ level.

What's chi square?
This is a statistical test used to compare expectations to results in order to determine if the results are due to chance or not.

We could use Clara's rate of *like* to compare her to any other individual simply by applying the same methods. We can even compare her to herself. The excerpt in (25) comes from an interview with Clara when she is 28. Has her rate of use of *like* changed? Let's find out.

25. a. [Interviewer] 'Cause then you'll feel like you're stuck?
     b. Well, that condo is tiny. *Like* even now I haven't moved in, I don't know what I'm going to do with my stuff. I have so much clothes that he totally underestimates how much crap I have. He's *like*, "I made some room in the closet." And it's *like*, "Aw that's very nice of you but that's not

enough." (laughs) That fits my T-shirts. And he doesn't have that many things so he has *like* a four-drawer-chest-thing and his walk-in closet is very spaced-out. So he has his dress clothes basically for work and then he has *like* a few sweaters 'cause he doesn't really *like* sweaters. And then his four drawer chest has *like* his boxers, his socks, um and his T-shirts, and then he has a drawer for towels. So he has *like* no clothes! So I think we might put the towels somewhere and then I'm going to take that and then he's going to move his things, he's going to buy this *like* little Ikea thing, it's almost *like* a night stand. But he thinks his stuff will fit in there and I'm *like* "It probably will" And I'm *like*, "I have so much stuff." I don't want to break it to him. (Clara Felipe, 28)

Once again, let's count the *like* tokens. There are 12. Calculating the frequency of *like* out of the total number of words gives us 12/207. This is nearly identical to Clara's description of shopping in (23b). We do not need a statistic to tell us that there is no meaningful difference between Clara at 16 and Clara at 28. Her frequency of *like* has not changed.

Given these demonstrations, you can easily see how numbers help us to understand the use of words. However, there is more to understanding words than simply counting them. We must also take into account the function the words have, i.e. their meaning. Notice that not all the *like* tokens are the same.

You might think to yourself that *like* does not have any meaning at all most of the time, but that may not be true. Let's consider the environments in which *like* is used. In many cases, Clara uses *like* at the beginning of a sentence, as in (26a). She also uses it just before a noun, as in (26b). In (25b) she can also use it to introduce a quote, as in (26c). The fact that there are no tokens of *like* as a quotative in (24b) is probably due to the nature of the discourse as description rather than storytelling. More data from each of the interviews could confirm this. In the next step, let's compare Clara's tokens of *like* to the single token in Flora's excerpt, as in (26d). Here, *like* is used as an adverb, a use that is part of Standard English grammar. Notice too that Clara uses *like* in its perfectly standard function as a verb as well, as in (26e).

26.   a. *Like* who wants to be ugly on Halloween?
       b. I have *like* my little tiara thing, right?
       c. And I'm *like* "It probably will"
       d. I hadn't seen people who worked *like* that you know
       e. He doesn't really *like* sweaters

A more in-depth examination of *like* would take into account these differences in function (see D'Arcy, forthcoming). It may well be the case that Flora has fewer functions of *like* than Clara does. If so, then we have started to uncover a linguistic change in progress.

Principle of accountability

A foundational concept in the quantitative approach to studying language is the Principle of Accountability (Labov, 1972a: 72). This principle stipulates that it is necessary to include all tokens in the relevant sub-system of grammar in one's analysis, not simply the variant of interest. This means that while we may be interested in the use of *like* in particular, in order to understand its meaning and present course of development we have to examine how it functions within the grammar. Putting the *like* where it appears at the beginning of a sentence, as in (26a), into the same analysis as *like* where it functions as a quotative, in (26c), or where it functions as a verb, as in (26e), would be mixing apples and oranges. The language scientist must narrow down the data that is relevant to the investigation.

As an exercise, let's focus on Clara's use of *like* in its quotative function (26c) (see also Chapter 4) and track the number of tokens across Clara's teenage years as in Table 3.1. First, we will simply count the tokens.

These numbers make it look like Clara's use of quoting *like* rises and falls erratically over the four-year period. As we saw earlier however, bare numbers do not offer an informed perspective on language use because they do not take into account the proportion these *like* tokens represent out of the relevant contexts where this type of *like* might have been used in the data.

Distributional analysis

The next step for studying and understanding linguistic features is to find the appropriate context in which the forms are used. In some cases, language scientists examine the proportion of a form out of the total number of words in a sample, as in (23–24). However, in order to understand the grammar of a language you need to study linguistic forms as part of the system in which they function. In the case at hand, quoting *like* is one of a set of quotative verbs. The relevant question is: out of all the quotative verbs that a person uses, how often does the person use *like?*

Table 3.2 now compares all the quotative verbs Clara uses in each interview and shows the proportion represented by *like*.

You can now see why the number of quoting *like* tokens rises and falls. It is the result of the total number of quotative verbs found in each interview.

Table 3.1 *Number of quoting* like *tokens per year for Clara*

Year of interview	2002	2003	2004	2005
Age	16	17	18	19
Number	191	81	203	92

Table 3.2 *Proportion of quoting* like *tokens out of total number of quotative verbs by year*

Year of interview	2002	2003	2004	2005
Age	16	17	18	19
Proportion of *like*	64.1%	66.7%	78.8%	73.9%
No. of quotative verbs	125	54	160	68
Total quotative verbs	**192**	**81**	**203**	**92**

In 2002 and 2004 Clara simply told more stories. Moreover, the results in Table 3.2 represent the totality of Clara's quotative verbs. Although quoting *like* dominates, there is a cohort of additional forms, including the verbs *tell*, *think*, *say*, etc. as in (27a–d).

27.   a. It's not like he doesn't trust me but he *says*, "I don't think you want to drive my car."
      b. So then I *'m* like *telling* her, "Well, tomorrow I have a paper due."
      c. I *was thinking*, "Yeah, oh maybe."
      d. He *said*, "hi."
      e. And I *was just like*, "Oh my gosh," *like* "Who do you not go out with?"
      f. But it's nothing special *like*, "Oh wow, it's good that he's back!"

This provides a much more informed perspective of Clara's use of quoting *like*. It represents the majority of her quotative verbs in each interview. The proportional perspective also enables us to observe a slight increase in quoting *like* in real time.

This demonstration exposes a fundamental component of the scientific approach to analyzing language – knowing the *distribution* of forms in the data, not simply their number. The counting procedure must be tempered by meticulous attention to: (1) where variation is possible; (2) where variation is not possible; and (3) inclusions of only those tokens where the targeted function is constant throughout. This is the starting point for studying any feature of language. Each analysis in the chapters that follow will utilize this method.

Once you know how frequent a form is in the relevant context, the next step is to try to find out how the choice of each variant is influenced by different aspects of the contexts in which it occurs (Sankoff, 1988b: 985). Many social, stylistic, and contextual factors influence the frequency of one variant over another. Sometimes it is the social context, sometimes the formality of the situation, sometimes the person you're talking to, etc. Sometimes it has to do with the linguistic context, the words that are surrounding the form, the type of clause, whether the sentence is a question or a statement, whether the subject is a noun or a pronoun, etc. For example, if the tokens of *like* in (25b) are examined more carefully, the astute reader may notice that there is a tendency for *like* to occur before a noun, as in (28).

28.   a.   ... he has *like* a four drawer chest ...
        b.   ... has *like* his boxer shorts
        c.   ... this *like* little Ikea thing
        d.   It's almost *like* a night stand

This observation is a preliminary hypothesis that gives us a hint as to how the form may be patterning. We can test this out in the data. Is it actually the case that *like* occurs more before nouns? Once we've noticed that *like* tends to occur in this context we need to prove that it does. Taking into account all the contexts where *like* could have occurred but did not provides a means to assess not only the overt tokens of the variable (i.e. *like*) but also the tokens of the alternative variant, the same type of context but no marker. These slip past because they are unremarkable (Labov, 1984), as in (29a). This is the negative evidence.

29.   And then Ø his four drawer chest has *like* his boxers, Ø his socks, um and Ø his T-shirts, and then he has Ø a drawer for towels

While the noun "his boxers" is marked with *like*, none of the other nouns are. Which of them *could have* had a *like* in front of it? (For a detailed discussion about the scientific investigation of *like* see D'Arcy, 2007, 2008.) The task of deciding which of these contexts to count, which ones to leave aside, and what types of contexts to treat as categorical, exceptional, or indeterminate is yet another part of the language scientist's job. In fact, all these procedures combined require scrupulous investigative abilities. Studying language in this way is like being a language detective.

An important methodological point is necessary here. Sometimes when people discuss linguistic forms they report how many times a context occurs in the data instead of how the context influences the choice of form. Consider the results in Table 3.3 which come from Clara, ages 16–28.

Table 3.3 makes it look like most quoting *like* tokens occur in speech contexts. But the reason for this is because speech represents the bulk of the examples where quoting *like* occurs (N=873 tokens, 73 percent). While this information is interesting, it says nothing about how the quote's context

Table 3.3 *Number of contexts in the data where quotative* like *occurs by quote type*

	Speech	Internal thought	Sound/gesture	N
be like	73%	24%	21.5%	
	873	281	41	1,191

Table 3.4 *Distribution of quoting* like *by quote type*

Quote type	% like	N of like	N of quote type
Speech	73	873	1,191
Internal thought	83	281	337
Sound/gesture	84	41	49
Total N			1,577

influences which quotative form is used. Only a distributional table as in Table 3.4 will provide this information. It is based on all the tokens of each quote type. The percentages reveal the proportion of *like* for each quote type. When we compare across quote types, this influence on the choice of form is revealed. Quoting *like* occurs more often in contexts of internal thought and sound/gesture than in speech.

Table 3.3 makes it look like quoting *like* occurs with internal thought only 24 percent of the time but that is not the case. Instead, what the table shows is that 22.7 percent of the quoting *like* tokens occur with internal thought. It does not reveal which quotative form occurs most often or least often in contexts of internal thought. Table 3.4 provides this information. Here, we can see that quoting *like* occurs very frequently when the content of the quote is internal thought (83 percent of the time). The difference here is between: (1) the distribution of quote types in the data (Table 3.3) and (2) the influence of the quote type on the choice of form (Table 3.4). Only Table 3.4 uncovers the hidden patterns of quotative use – *be like* is highly correlated with internal thought and sound/gesture, as in (30a) rather than in (30b).

30. a. He's riding his camel and he's *like*, "What am I doing in this desert?"
         (Finnegan Connor, 17)
     b. I *was like*, "Awww!" (Clara Felipe, 16)
     c. Your dad *says*, "Oh no, Einstein already thought that up." (Finnegan
         Connor, 17)

Language has many intricate patterns but you have to know how to look for them. You can scour the literature for observations, reports, and claims about the forms of interest. What are the claims in the press, the literature, the dictionary? Some patterns can be discerned from observation. If you look carefully at where and how words are used, you can usually spot one pattern or another. In sociolinguistics, factors that influence where one form or another is used are called "constraints." Some constraints are social. Some are stylistic. Many are the results of how the grammar is organized. When contextual tendencies such as these remain constant regardless of the frequency of a word or construction they offer insights into the nature of the language (Poplack and Tagliamonte, 2001: chapter 5). In taking an analytic approach, a language scientist can determine which of the factors that are hypothesized to condition the use of words and phrases actually *do* condition them in some meaningful way by using statistical modeling. This will expose the significance, relative strength of constraints, and the way different contexts are ranked, all of which can be used as evidence to infer the underlying system of the grammar.

Basic principles

Why would adolescents have so many non-standard language features? In adolescence social networks expand both geographically and socially and individuals are exposed to a wider range of language behaviors. This leads to learning new words and phrases from peers. Adolescents are seeking an identity that will mark their separateness from their elders (Chambers, 2003a: chapter 4). These are the two most powerful forces that govern language use in adolescence: (1) solidarity with peers and (2) separation from adults. They combine to make adolescence the focal point for linguistic innovation and change.

The foremost factor bearing on language change is age. Evidence for generational differences is easy to come by. Older people simply do not talk like younger people. However, as discussed earlier, there is always the possibility that these differences are the result of age-grading, i.e. that certain linguistic behaviors are typical of an individual at different stages in their life. The fact that one generation differs from the next is obvious: each generation retains, to some extent, the language patterns that were learned early in life, and each new generation may learn new and/or different forms. Which features come and go as people go through certain life stages and which features are bona fide language change moving the language down the currents of time? Sociolinguists still do not have an ideal way of distinguishing language change from linguistic features that are typical of a certain age. Romaine and Lange (1991: 269) suggest that young people's casual conversation may actually provide an important potential source for disentangling these dual aspects of language change.

A factor that has played a central role in the study of linguistic variation and change is social class, which has typically been derived from a composite of characteristics such as income, status of employment, and type of housing. When change starts happening and spreads without anyone being consciously aware of it, the source is typically the middle of the social spectrum, not the extremes. Neither the highest classes nor the lowest class are leaders when it comes to changing language (Labov, 1963; Trudgill, 1972). Labov formulated this insight as Principle 1, as in (31).

31.   *Principle 1*: Change from within the community comes from the internal sectors of the social continuum.

However, pre-adolescents, teenagers, and young adults are difficult to place using the standard measures applied to adults like education and job type. Teenagers do not have these attributes.

A more endemic factor in linguistic variation and change as it relates to the pre- and adolescent phase of the life span is the contrast between men and women (or girls and boys). One of the most pervasive findings in sociolinguistics is that women lead linguistic change (Labov, 1963; Trudgill, 1972). The contrast between men and women is central to Principles 2, 3, and 4, as in (32a–c) (Labov, 1990: 210–215, 2001: 266–293). Principle 2 states that for stable sociolinguistic variables (those that are not changing), women show a higher rate of prestige variants than men. Principle 3 states that when linguistic change comes from people adopting forms that they think are prestigious, women adopt these forms at a higher rate than men. This type of change is also called "change from above." Principle 4 states that in linguistic change that comes from people adopting forms that they think are trendy (but not necessarily prestigious), here too women use higher frequencies of innovative forms than men do. This type of change is typically called "change from below." Note that in every case, the contrast between female and male is primordial.

32.   a. *Principle 2*: When a variable is stable, women use more of the prestige variant.
         b. *Principle 3*: When a feature is innovative and prestigious, women use more of it.
         c. *Principle 4*: When a feature is innovative and stigmatized, women use more of it.

Women and men are influenced by social factors such as prestige, attitude, and social identity, but in very different ways. Women are more sensitive to the pressures of norms imposed from the standard language, education, and social media. Change introduced in this way tends to involve the introduction of respected words and features. Young women who are socially mobile are particularly sensitive to these pressures. In contrast, men are more sensitive to local, in-group values, particularly men in the lower social strata (Schilling-Estes and Wolfram, 1997). Language in local networks tends not to change and it is under pressure (albeit covert pressure – see example in Trudgill, 1972) to be maintained. This contrast in the way men and women respond to language can tell us a lot about what is happening with language, what is changing, and what is staying the same. In the chapters that follow I will always test for the effect of sex on forms and patterns.

Change from below
This type of change comes from within a community, arising from social, cognitive, or physiological pressures from within the language variety that is spoken therein. Change from below emerges without overt commentary, below the level of conscious awareness.

These aspects of language are also linked to the source of linguistic change. Sometimes change comes from outside a language or a community. The origin can be another country where the same language is spoken (think of British influence in the Caribbean) or even another language (think of French influence on English during the Middle English period). The cause of external influence is often linked to social change, revolution, war, or famine. Sometimes such influence arises from mobility. For any number of reasons people move from place to place, influencing the language of the new locale or being influenced by it. When changes come into a community from elsewhere they tend to be noticed. Language change can also come from within a community as language is passed on from one generation to the next. When change comes from inside a community, it is typically unconscious because it happens through normal processes of acquisition from parents and development along with peers via incrementation.

Language change is not just influenced by social factors. It is deeply embroiled in the mechanisms of the language system, the grammar (Labov, 1994: 2–3). The linguistic facts are multi-dimensional involving the sounds and pronunciations of words, the way words are put together, their order in sentences, and where words are used in interaction.

Most research on the internal factors of linguistic change has focused on the sound system of language, the way people pronounce words (Eckert, 1988, 2000; Labov, 1994; Trudgill, 1974). The structure of language has been widely studied using historical texts (Kroch, 1989; Pintzuk, 1995; Pintzuk and Kroch, 1989). These studies have produced important and insightful principles of language change that may be tested on changes in progress. However, comparatively little quantitative research has been done on discourse level changes. Discourse focuses on how words and phrases get tacked on or inserted into sentences without apparent meaning. Pragmatics focuses on how these words and phrases are used to convey meaning. The exciting thing for the study of teen language is that many of the changes that are going on among teenagers involve discourse-pragmatic phenomena. So, the question is: are these phenomena superfluous or part of the ongoing evolution of the language?

The dearth of quantitative studies of discourse-pragmatic change is undoubtedly due in part to the early debates questioning the extension of the variationist sociolinguistic enterprise to levels of grammar above phonology (e.g. Lavandera, 1978; Rickford, 1975; G. Sankoff, 1973). More recently, these earlier concerns have resurfaced as cautionary notes on quantitative methods in the study of discourse-pragmatic variation. There is also a con-comitant unease that generalizations about the nature of change in phonology, morphology, and syntax – including a constant rate of change (Kroch, 1989), layering effects, phonetic reduction/erosion, and analogical leveling (e.g. Hopper, 1991; Hopper and Traugott, 1993) – will not apply in the same way to discourse-pragmatic phenomena (see e.g. Pichler, 2013: 13). The best early models for the quantitative study of syntactic change come from empirical work on developing creoles (Sankoff, 1980; Sankoff and Laberge, 1980). This work attests to the salience of discourse-level strategies as the source of and input to linguistic change (Cheshire, 1998, 2003). How discourse strat-egies develop into grammatical phenomena has only begun to be explored (e.g. Cheshire, 2007; Pichler and Levey, 2011; Tagliamonte and Denis, 2008b). These studies have determinedly opened up this area of grammar to quantitative investigation.

I would say it's education's fault. We swung a little bit too too much to being loosey-goosey to now we're coming back and saying, "No, there are proper ways of- of doing things." (Stacy Ryall, 55)

How to catch language changing

Changes in language are always happening and there are different types of change. Some changes move slowly; some are quicker. How quickly a change moves depends on the nature of the change and the social and cultural circumstances in which it is happening. Change in language can happen at many levels: at the level of the word (lexicon), sound, parts of words, ordering of words, or meaning of words. When there is a lot of upheaval going on in a society, there also tends to be a lot of language change going on too.

The most captivating process in language change is the evolution of words into grammatical devices (Meillet, 1912: 131). When such changes take place, they proceed in long series of transitions that are like a path in the linguistic time continuum (Hopper and Traugott, 1993: 3). Content words with referen-tial meaning evolve into the functional components of grammar: verbs, pro-nouns, adverbs, etc. The process of grammatical change can be identified by various diagnostics (Fischer and Rosenbach, 2000: 8–9). An often-used example is the development of tense/aspect features, in particular the *going to* future. Here, let's consider a different example, the word *will*. It has changed from a lexical item (a word) meaning "desire, wish, longing," into a grammat-ical meaning indicating future, which has coalesced with surrounding words (e.g. *I'll*) in the progression sketched in (33a), explained in (33b), and illustrated in (33c) (Hopper and Traugott, 1993: 3). At the point of writing, a further projected step, that of becoming an inflectional affix, has not yet materialized.

33.   a. WORD   > GRAMMATICAL > CLITIC   > INFLECTIONAL
                            ITEM   AFFIX
       b. verb "to want" > future intention > future general >
       c. *will*   > *will go*   > *I'll go*   >

As words become grammatical devices, they undergo various changes (see details in Hopper, 1991; Hopper and Traugott, 1993). As a word changes, it, and other forms with similar meaning, coexist in the language (layering). As the word develops new meanings, it diverges from the meaning of its source (divergence). In the process the number of variants meaning the same thing decreases and one form assumes a more general meaning (specialization). However, through this process the word undergoing change tends to retain hints of its earlier lexical meaning (persistence). At the same time, these words also tend to lose morphological markers and syntactic co-occurrence patterns that were typical of their original lexical source (decategorization).

Because grammatical changes may go on for centuries, the same form can have different functions at any given stage of a change. Consider the common word *will* in contemporary English. The original meaning of the word remains active; however, this use has receded. I found only a single example in my North American corpora, as in (34a). The word *will* also has other uses, as in (34b–c). It can be used as an adjective, as in (35a), as a verb for bequeathing something to someone, as in (35b), or it can mean the faculty by which a person decides on an action, as in (34c).

34.   a. The price is so big for the fence and for what you get out of your cattle
           now, it don't pay. Just the *will* to quit. (Otto Reinhart, 84)
       b. Its true history lay, not among things done, but among things *willed*.
           (*Tess of the d'Urbervilles*, Thomas Hardy, 1891)
       c. Marilla would have given much just then to have possessed Anne's power
           of putting her feelings into words; but nature and habit had *willed* it
           otherwise. (*Anne of Green Gables*, Lucy Maud Montgomery, 1908)

35.   a. I don't know if it's sure of what they want or unsure of what they want
           or just more vocal more *strong-willed*. (Ernest Spencer, 35)
       b. It was the farm that my grandparents bought when they came to
           Canada and it was you know, *willed* to my dad. (Alexander Auer, 40)

The point I am making here is that words can have many different meanings at any given point in a language's history and these meanings and uses shift over time. Taking into account the different ways words are used provides evidence for understanding what is taking place in the language. If you hear someone say, "I will you to understand," you'll know they must have time-travelled from the fifteenth century!

Grammatical change

Grammatical change can be identified by a number of different patterns or trends (Heine et al., 1991). First, words may lose a strict hold on their original meaning and become broader in their usage. Second, words will lose their original collocation patterns. Both these processes happened when the verb meaning "to want" gradually became a future marker, as in (33b). Third, words may get shortened in some way, contracted or merged with other words, as in the case of *I'll* above. In the final stage, words may turn into affixes, but this has not happened for *will*, at least not yet.

What's an affix?
An affix is a small word that attaches to another word to mark a grammatical meaning. An affix can appear before a word, as a prefix, or after a word as a suffix. English has suffixes such as *–s* that marks plurality, e.g. *cats*, and both prefixes and suffixes such as *–ish* or *un–* that change one word into another, e.g. *fool* ➔ *foolish;* *happy* ➔ *unhappy.*

These tendencies in grammatical change are diagnostics for interpreting trends in the evolution of forms.

As changes are taking place, the variation among forms provides a dynamic representation of the degrees of grammatical development. If *will* is used in the majority of future temporal reference contexts, we can infer that it is more developed. However, it may always retain a nuance of "desire, wish, longing" from its original meaning.

At any stage of a grammatical change, linguistic patterns can be correlated with the evolving grammatical morphemes. A linguistic pattern can be any tendency for a word to occur in a particular context, with specific other words. These associations offer crucial keys to viewing the diachronic process of grammatical change in contemporary language materials (Traugott and Heine, 1991a: 6). One of the best ways to track language change is to find out how words were used in the past. When language patterns in contemporary data can be traced to the historical record, they can be interpreted as persistence of earlier meanings or patterns. Such information can then provide insights into what earlier points in the development of these areas of grammar may have been like. Similarly, if words are taking on new grammatical functions, it is often possible to observe shifts and re-weighting of contextual effects. This evidence provides the language scientist with the means to detect how a language change is progressing.

Not all changes in language involve words changing into the grammatical apparatus of the language. In fact, most changes are lexical changes.

Lexical change

Lexical change is the most common, most rapid, and most obvious type of linguistic change (Chambers, 2003a: 193) as "lexical use is always changing" (von Schneidemesser, 2000: 420). This type of change is in operation when one word is substituted for another word, or when a word changes its form and meaning, e.g. *adore, adoring, adorable, adorbs, dorbs.* Lexical variation has been studied extensively from a typological perspective as it relates to language contact and borrowing (e.g. Harvey, 2011). It has also been useful in measuring correspondences between and among languages (e.g. D. Sankoff, 1973). Lexical variation is also the cornerstone of dialectology where shifts from one word to another in the same semantic field are notoriously socially, regionally and ethnically delimited (Chambers, 2003a; von Schneidemesser, 2000: 420). People tend to be supremely conscious of words, especially when a common lexical item differs from one place to another, e.g. British English *WC, loo*, American English *restroom, toilet*, Canadian English *washroom*. Such word choices are even more notable when there are generational differences. For example, Canadian English *chesterfield* (the piece of living-room furniture that seats more than two people) was avant-garde in the early twentieth century, but is so rarely used at the beginning of the twenty-first century that young people do not even know what it is.

Sometimes lexical developments can be eclectic and unusual, e.g. *pissed off* ➔ *pissoffedness* (see example 142a), alternative ➔ alternativish (see example 158b). Notice that by adding different endings (i.e. *-ing, -able, -s*) words can shift categories in the grammar, e.g. verb ➔ adjective. In some cases, words remain in the same category, but take a different form. Words can be shortened, blended, and compounded and all manner of different transformations may obtain, e.g. television ➔ tv ➔ MTV. The task of the language scientist is to figure out what kind of change is actually going on, how, and, if possible, why. Is it regular and widespread or is it off the cuff and idiosyncratic?

Simple appropriation of a word happens easily through limited personal contacts. For example, if you were to travel to England you might learn the word *brilliant* as a lexical item to refer to something "good" rather than the corresponding North American word *awesome*. This is lexical change; one word with a particular meaning is substituted for another word with the same meaning. However, even many years in England may not enable you to learn the complex system for using the present perfect instead of the past tense. In

British English, it is typical to say at noon: *I haven't had lunch yet*, whereas a North American can say *I didn't have lunch yet*. In other words, some changes can be learned easily and quickly but others require sustained exposure (Meyerhoff and Niedzielski, 2003). Milroy (2007) has argued for a differentiation between changes that are "off the shelf" (i.e. do not require sustained contact) and those that are "under the counter" (i.e. require repeated social interaction). As we shall see, the type of change – lexical vs. grammatical – has important ramifications for how changes evolve in the community.

The best way to study changes in language would be to have a representative sample of language over centuries, but this would only be possible: (1) if we had recordings from every stage of a change across time, or (2) if time travel were possible. Neither choice is tenable. Language scientists have come up with a practical solution.

Let's return to the topic at hand – teenage language at the turn of the twenty-first century. There is a tremendous amount of change going on in this period. Many of these changes are readily evident in an efflorescence of language phenomena, including many of the words I have discussed up to this point – *like*, *just*, *so*, etc. The difficulty in studying these words is that they comprise many different variants with potentially diverse functions. Take for example the word *like*. In present-day English it functions as a main verb, adverb, conjunction, and quotative verb and is possibly developing additional new functions (D'Arcy, 2006, 2007, 2008). Approaching the study of these words scientifically requires examination of the structural aspects of the linguistic context and the meaning of the words (e.g. Dubois, 1992, 2010, 2013; Vincent, 1992; Vincent and Sankoff, 1992).

First, assess the frequency of the word in question along with the other words that mean the same thing. Examine how the frequency of each of the words correlates with speaker age. Where does the word occur with high frequency vs. low frequency? The level of use can be used to interpret a change as an early, mid, or late stage in the history of the change. Second, examine the linguistic contexts associated with the word to determine if any patterns exist. If so, examine the nature of these patterns and their strength. For example, one particular linguistic context might strongly correlate with a word. Another linguistic context may rarely exhibit the same word, but tend towards another. Contextual factors can be correlated with the different variants in the data using quantitative techniques such as distributional analysis. This is the procedure that I will apply in the remaining chapters of this book.

I refuse to say oxymoron. It's a stupid awkward word. If I'm ever in a situation where I'm talking about something that contradicts itself like that I say, "oxzimirant." (Finnegan Connor, 17)

Outline of method

In each of the analyses in this book, my goal is to provide a scientific assessment of choice words and their uses by teenagers and other members of the community using the procedures of variationist sociolinguistics (e.g. Labov, 1970; D. Sankoff, 1988a; G. Sankoff, 1974). This method is documented in Tagliamonte (2012):

1. Extract all words and variants of words where they occur in contexts of comparable meaning. These comprise the locus of variation in the grammar.
2. Seek out the historical background by consulting the *Oxford English Dictionary* (OED),[1] Google Ngrams,[2] and other sources. This offers a broad perspective on usage patterns and trends.
3. Count and code the forms according to social factors such as age, sex, and linguistic factors. This provides a substantive means to understand the system and its mechanisms.
4. Analyze the frequency and distribution of words and phrases according to social and linguistic factors. These correlations will determine the nature of the variation and offer evidence for linguistic change.

A note on baselines for speaker age

Most of the language materials that will be subject to analysis in the following chapters were collected between 2002 and 2006. The research that was conducted on the corpora over the subsequent ten years was based on the age of the individuals at the date of interview – pre-adolescents, teenagers, and adults of various ages – with a categorization of age groups replicating established studies (e.g. Labov, 2001). However, this does not provide grounding in real time for the studies reported in this book. In order to provide a unified perspective for understanding and interpreting the linguistic analyses that follow, I have re-categorized the individuals' ages by year of birth with a baseline of 2003. This is accurate within one year for the adult data, which was collected between 2003 and 2004. For the "teenagers" in the sample, their actual birth years will vary somewhat more broadly than this schema, as schematized in Table 3.5.

Every change must be put in context with time and place. This categorization for individual age will be used so that the analyses in the book will have a dependable baseline. As discussed earlier, the Bergen Corpus of teenage language collected in 1993, COLT, is already visibly dated compared to the MLE data collected in 2004.The storytelling data I collected in 1995 are now rather old-fashioned compared to the TIC collected in 2007–2008. Every change is rooted in its milieu. This schema offers readers a baseline for

Table 3.5 *Baselines for individual age and date of birth*

Age at interview	Year of birth baseline (2003)	Data collection 2002–2006	Year of birth categorization
9–12	1991–1994	1990–1997	1990–1994
13–16	1987–1990	1986–1993	1985–1989
17–19	1984–1986	1983–1989	1980–1984
20–29	1974–1983	1973–1984	1975–1989
30–39	1964–1973	1963–1974	early 1970s
40–49	1954–1963	1955–1964	1960s
50–59	1947–1953	1946–1954	1950s
60+	1910–1943	1909–1944	1910–1940

comparison should they wish to embark on a study of any of these features in their own data.

These corpora, which represent real language in use across approximately 100 years in apparent time, will provide the raw materials from which we will explore linguistic variation and change among teenagers within the milieu of the community in which they live.

[Interviewer] Well what other words do other people say that don't mean anything? [003] Okay. [Interviewer] So, you think when people say "okay" they're not even listening? [003] Yeah. That's what I do. [Interviewer] People say something to you and you don't even listen? [003] Sometimes. [Interviewer] And then you just say "okay"? [003] Yeah. (Tony Griffo, 13)

Language puzzle

Approaching language as a scientist requires: (1) being attentive to linguistic forms as well as their function; and (2) considering both positive and negative evidence. In sociolinguistics the former is referred to as *circumscribing the variable context* and the latter concerns the *Principle of Accountability*. Let's explore these key concepts in practice.

Circumscribe the variable context:

> Find all the words and constructions that mean the same thing. Exclude forms that are a different category, formulaic utterances, anomalies, or invariant contexts.

Principle of Accountability:

> Include in your analysis *all* the forms that mean the same thing, even if one of those forms is zero.

In Table 3A are all tokens of the word *brilliant* in the TEC and TIC. If you were going to conduct a study about adjectives meaning "good":

(*cont.*)

a. Which examples in Table 3A would you exclude from your study? Why?
b. Looking at Table 3B, who uses which types, Old vs. Young? Is there a trend?
c. Thinking back to the discussion of methodology, are the data in Table 3A sufficient for study?

Table 3A *Examples of* brilliant *in TTC and TEC*

No.	Example	Age
a	and he was just like he was BRILLIANT actually	O
b	a criminal lawyer in Toronto, now dead, who had a BRILLIANT and tumultuous career	O
c	he had a BRILLIANT streak, got addicted to cocaine, got cancer, died	O
d	great, BRILLIANT location, you can get anywhere, you can get downtown	O
e	my parents did a BRILLIANT thing. They bought me a pass to the swimming pool	O
f	BRILLIANT kids- um, he decides to go with the ten-year-old	O
g	Another BRILLIANT [graduate student]	O
h	the graduate students there are all uniformly BRILLIANT	O
i	they never thought us- of themselves as BRILLIANT	O
j	they had really cool sayings like, "Oh that's BRILLIANT!" [in England]	Y
k	Freud had some BRILLIANT concepts. Unfortunately they weren't right	Y
l	it's not that they weren't BRILLIANT. His concepts are very ingenious and they appear	Y
m	and then BRILLIANT idea to tan topless	Y
n	It's BRILLIANT [a quote by a politician]	Y
o	The drag-queen challenge was BRILLIANT	Y
p	I'm like "woah, BRILLIANT deduction there," right. So he says it's stolen	Y
q	Oh my god. It's BRILLIANT [a song]	Y
r	being the BRILLIANT people that we are-	Y
s	BRILLIANT. Like it touches me in all the right places [music]	Y
t	and then we realized how BRILLIANT we are, we're supposed to be the best in Canada	Y
u	he just comes into class late and like, says BRILLIANT things and leaves	Y

Table 3B *Distribution of reading of* brilliant

	Smart/successful	Very good	Total
Old	7 78%	2 22%	9
Young	5 42%	7 58%	12

(*cont.*)

Answers
a. *Exclude a, c, d, f, i, k, l, m, r, t, u. They all mean "smart" or "successful."*
   Exclude token "j" which is meta-linguistic commentary. Include b, e, g, h, n, o,
   p, q, s.
b. *See Table 3B. Older people use more of the meaning "smart/successful";*
   younger speakers use more of the meaning "very good."
c. *No. We need to include all the other adjectives that are used for the same*
   meaning.

4   Quotatives

I'm like, "Oh my God!"

> I'll wake up and I'll be like, "Oh my God! Oh my God! Oh God!" And
> then I'll start thinking about the leprechaun.
>
> (Craig Carvalheiro, 19)

Telling stories is one of the most intrinsic aspects of human experience. We
like to share our lives with our friends, our colleagues, and our families.
Storytelling is as old as language itself, but the way people tell stories has
changed with the times. Individuals who were born in the 1970s spearheaded a
change that has completely transformed the way people tell stories.

When people tell stories they usually want to tell you about something that
happened to them at an earlier point in time. Much of what they say will
involve what they (and others) were thinking or saying. The Standard English
way of doing this is to use verbs to introduce the dialogue or inner thoughts.
I will refer to these as quotative verbs.

Here are some examples of the quotative verb "think," which self-evidently
introduces a thought, as in (36).

36.   a. I *thought*, "Whoa these are hilarious." (Finnegan Connor, 17)
        b. I was *thinking*, "You're not from Toronto." (Alyssa Sailner, 29)
        c. You shake your head and *think*, "God, I grew up in this nice little
           comfortable country." (Flora Valentin, 83)

Here are some examples of the quotative verb "say," which typically
introduces dialogue. Note that when there is an exchange between protagon-
ists, as in (37b–c), this function is transparent.

37.   a. He *says*, "Don't worry about it. I'll build you a house." (Matt Latimer, 84)
        b. Then you *say*, "Oh, it's right there." They *say*, "No, you know, just
           wash it when you get home from school." (Charles Lee, 15)
        c. We said, "okay, let's go back." And they said, "No, let's keep going."
           (Ronald Street, 35)

Of course in written language any number of verbs, such as *scream, fret,* and
growl, can be used to quote in storytelling. You may remember exercises in
grade school in which the task was to change all the *say/said* verbs of quoting
to other, more illustrative verbs, as in (38).

38. a. She *was whimpering,* "We're gonna die out in the hallway."
         (STC, Carrie Johns, 19)
     b. So one of them they just *asked* him, you know, "Which way is it to Queen
         Street? And can you give us a ride there?" (STC, Ash Chan, 16)
     c. And he *answers* me, "Yes." (STC, Herman Drutz, 50)
     d. And my friend *responds,* "Well, you have to know how to have sex!"
         (STC, Nadia Jenk, 19)

Until the 1970s *say* and *think* were the primary forms used for direct quotes
in spoken English. A few others were also used, such as *go* or *tell,* as in (39).

39. a. The guy wakes up to it and he *goes,* "Oh my God." (Parvati Prakesh, 14)
     b. He was *telling* everyone "Yo, I got a cell-phone." (Charles Lee, 15)

Yet another way of presenting dialogue in stories is with no introducing
verb at all, as in (40b–d) and (41b–e).

40. a. Three people phoned me one night,
     b. Ø "You're being an idiot."
     c. Ø "What?"
     d. Ø "You're being an idiot."
     e. Three people.
     f. I was like, "I better stop being an idiot." (Antonio Silvaggio, 16)
41. a. I'll come back and she's like, "So Jason, how are things with Pearl?"
     b. Ø "Good."
     c. Ø "Am I still the number one woman in your life?"
     d. Ø "Yes."
     e. Ø "Okay, good to know." (Jason Levine, 17)

This type of quotative can also occur within a single speaker's dialogue, as
in (42):

42. I mean, we also were the typical divorce kids. I mean, there's always the, you
     know, Ø "Well, Dad said I could." Or you know like, Ø "Dad, could I have
     fifty dollars? I need to pay for like this." (Chloe McDoungall, 23)

For most of the history of English the inventory of quotative verbs was the
same – *say, think, go,* and zero. But listen to a teenager or adolescent tell a
story today. You will hear something quite different. A typical example is
shown in (43).

43. a. And I'*m like,* "Hey what's your name? My name's Lana."
     b. And he'*s like,* "Um ..."
     c. I'*m like,* "What?"
     d. He'*s like,* "I'm Sida"
     e. I'*m like,* "What's that? It's not a name. I've never heard a name that's
         Sida."
     f. He'*s like,* "Sida"
     g. I'*m like,* "OK, I'll just call you Sailor Moon." (Lana Sivasubramaniam, 16)

Lana is telling a story about when she met a new friend, Sida. Notice the conspicuous use of *like* in the places where she introduces what she said and what he said. There is no *say* or *tell* here. There isn't even a *think* or a *go* – only *like*.

Where did this use of *like* come from? Why are teenagers using it? Many linguists have studied quoting *like* in a variety of different dialects, including American English, African American English, British English, and others. Quoting *like* entered North American English in the early 1970s (Tagliamonte et al., 2014a). By 2006 it had taken over to the point where young people hardly use any of the standard forms anymore. The fact that this change is happening so fast has provided an unprecedented opportunity to figure out how language changes. Let me tell you the story of how I think this change has come about.

Early days of quoting with *like*

The received wisdom in the world at large is that the way young people use quoting *like* comes from California and the Valley Girls. Whenever I talk about quoting *like* people always say, "Wasn't it something that came from that Frank Zappa song?" While it may be true that quoting with *like* originated among a certain sector of the population in the United States, it is not the case that the song started it. Rather the song epitomized a trend that was already going on. Let's look at the quotative verbs from the original song ("Valley Girl"), which appeared in 1982, as in (44).

44. Excerpt from ... "Valley Girl," Frank Zappa
    a. Anyway, he *goes* "Are you into S and M?"
    b. I *go* "Oh right ... Could you like just picture me in like a leather Teddy?"
    c. And the lady like *goes* "Oh my God, your toenails are like so grody!"
    d. It was like really embarrassing
    e. She *'s like*, "Oh my God, like bag those toenails"
    f. I *'m like*, "sure ..."
    g. She *goes*, "Uh, I don't know if I can handle this, y'know."
    h. I was like really embarrassed ...
    i. It *'s like*, "Barf me out..."

There are three tokens of quoting *like* along with four tokens of quoting *go*. In addition, you may notice a few other features associated with teenagers introduced earlier, such as *like*, i.e. it was *like* really embarrassing, or *just*, e.g. Could you like *just* picture me (Chapter 9), or intensifier *really*, e.g. *really* embarrassing (see Chapter 10).

In the same year as the Zappa song was released, quoting *like* was reported in *American Speech*, one of the most widely read academic journals in North America (Butters, 1982). These early attestations point to the fact that quoting *like* had begun to attract some attention. By the early 1980s quoting *like* began a massive flow into the language. The earliest research, not surprisingly, was based on American English and pointed to teenagers and university students as the primary users. By the early 1990s it was claimed to be a prevalent American phenomenon (Ferrara and Bell, 1995; Meehan, 1991; Miller and Weinert, 1995; Romaine and Lange, 1991). But I could also hear it in my university students in Canada and England.

In the mid 1990s my students at the University of Ottawa in Ottawa, Canada (1995), and in 1996 at the University of York in York, England (1996), collected stories told by their friends who were between 18 and 28 years of age at the time. These teenagers and 20-year-olds represented the same age cohort that had been studied earlier in American English. Did they have quoting *like*? Just barely, but it was there. Consider a snippet of complicating action clauses from a story about an acid trip, as in (45). At the point of writing, some 20 years later, notice how the use of quotative verbs in this story seems a bit old-fashioned.

45. a. So, I called Joe at home
     b. And I*'m like*, "Joe man, how's the truck?"
     c. And he*'s like*, "Oh, Clarky man, I fucked my truck up. Were you with me?"
     d. I*'m like*, "Yeah, man."
     e. He *goes*, "No way man. What was I doing?"
     f. I*'m like*, "Rabbits man that's all I remember was rabbits."
     g. He *goes*, "I'm short man, I'm short like eighty bucks man. Did we do those tabs?"
     h. And I*'m thinking*, "Yeah, I think we did bud."
     i. And he*'s like*, "Oh man, I'm so fucked."
     j. And he *goes*, "but I gotta go."
     k. And he hung up.

Evidently, quoting *like* had spread to Canada and England. However, at that time it was relatively infrequent, representing less than 20 percent of the data (13 percent in Ottawa and 18 percent in York). In other words, the young people were still using a lot of *saying*, *going*, and *thinking* verbs for quoting as you see here in (45e, g, h, and j). The interesting thing was that even at this early stage, speakers were already using quoting *like* in the same way (i.e. with the same patterns) as had been reported in American English.

They used it when they were referring to sounds, as in (46).

46. a. It's just *like*, "Drip, drip." (Clara Felipe, 16)
     b. Every five seconds he*'s like*, "(panting noise)." (Jared Jamil, 13)
     c. I *was like*, "Nnnrrrggh!" (YRK/G1)[1]

They used it when referring to themselves, using the first-person pronoun, *I*, as in (47c).

47. a. And she came back and *told* me, "No! There's no way he's gonna call you."
     b. "He wants you ta' call him"
     c. And *I'm like*, "Oh my goodness!"
     d. She *says*, "you're calling him – whether you like it or not." (OTT/K, Kim K)

They also used it for describing the inner thoughts of the storyteller, as in (48).

48. a. Because I was really upset.
     b. I *was like*, "Oh my God everybody's let me down." (YRK/G1)
     c. I *was like*, "Yeah, right!"
     d. By that point I *was like*, "Are you sure? I'm thinking something else is going on here." (Alyssa Sailner, 29)

Another characteristic of quoting *like* is its use with the existential pronoun *it*, as in (49).

49. a. But there's this something, this noise outside our door.
     b. It's *like*, "[breathing sound repeated 3 times]" (Heather Mitchell, 20)

Notice that this is a unique feature of quoting *like* that does not occur with any other quotative verb. No one ever says *it says* or *it thinks* unless they are referring to some object or thing. This means that the *it* in the collocation is referential – it refers to a non-animate entity, as in (50a–b). This is a different function from the form in (49b) with quoting *like*.

50. a. There were um ads that were like, it said, they had a picture of a person and they had like an image of a different place in their head, and it *said*, "I'm so there." (Amanda Levy, 12)
     b. There was a poster ... and it *said*, "See what diving can do?" (Alyssa Sailner, 29)

In summary, the early traits of quoting *like* are the following: used with sounds, gestures, and expressions, first person, inner thoughts. A good example is the title of this chapter, *I'm like, "oh my God!"* Or one of the quotes in the Frank Zappa song: *I'm like, "sure ..."*

In the 1990s American youth were using quoting *like* in these ways and so were both the Canadian and the British young people. As far as the rest of the quotative verbs were concerned, there were some small differences between the two groups. The British young people used more *thinking* quotes than the Canadians and the Canadian guys were using more *go* than anyone else. These contrasts show that when you look at the details of how different varieties of English use language features, you start seeing how each variety is unique unto itself. Another interesting finding was that the girls were using more quoting *like* than the guys, but this was more pronounced in Canada than in England.

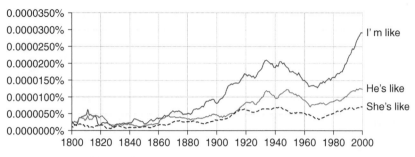

Figure 4.1 Google Ngrams search for collocations of quoting *like*

As we shall see over and over again, when the girls are in the lead, you can expect a change to take off.

From an article on the Linguistics of quoting "like": "Eventually the people who hate this kind of thing are going to be dead, and the ones who use it are going to be in control." (Tricia Cukor-Avila, 2015)[2]

To put historical and contemporary observations into perspective, Figure 4.1 shows the frequency of collocations typical of quotative *like* over the last two centuries of written documents using Google Ngrams. Do not be beguiled by the acceleration visible in the early 1900s. This is an upswing in adverbial *like*, as in (51). By the 1970s a new acceleration takes place for all collocations, especially *I'm like*.

51.   "If she's *like* this to start when she's hot," he screamed to Barbara, "you can imagine what she's *like* when she's cold." (Charlotte Arthur, *Poor Faun*, 1930, p. 9)

Entering the twenty-first century

Let's now move forward in time to 2002–2003. Students in my undergraduate research courses at the University of Toronto interviewed members of their families and social networks (see Chapter 2). The stories they collected were by design comparable to the earlier Canadian (1995) and British (1997) stories, but this time they came from a broader range of speakers in terms of age. The individuals were between 10 and 19, coming from distinct education levels within the Canadian educational system (primary school, middle school, high school, and first-year university). The questions were: how far had quoting *like* spread and were the pre-adolescents picking it up?

As had been found in earlier research, the young people were using the same four quotative verbs – *say, go, think, zero,* and *like*; however, by this point in time, quoting *like* had increased considerably, representing nearly 60 percent of all the quotative verbs. This means that quoting *like* had increased by more than four and a half times in seven years! Conversely, the traditional quotative verbs, *say* and *think* and even the more casual forms, *go* and *zero* had all waned in frequency. Once, *say* was the most frequent quotative verb in the English language. Among these young people, it represented just 11 percent of quotative verbs overall. Moreover, quoting *like* was unmistakably used more by girls than by guys. In fact, girls were using it so much more that people in Canada began to think of quoting *like* as a "girl thing."

Rocketing change

Quoting *like* was mushrooming. My own kids were using it most of the time and so were my students. However, I also noticed that there was a big difference between my own use of quotative verbs (mostly *say/think*) and that of my graduate students, typically in their 30s (*say/think* and *like*). As far as I could tell, no one my own age was using quoting *like*. Yet, from the 30s on down through the age groups everyone was using quoting *like*. I started to wonder what the age limit on quoting *like* was. How old did you have to be to *not* use *like* and how young did you have to be to use it? Another question that occurred to me (and to a lot of other people) was: are the tweens and teens and 20-year-olds who are using *like* now ever going to stop using it? The next step was to do a study of the whole age range. By then, the TEC was substantially transcribed so I had the ideal corpus in which to test out these questions.

Quoting *like* across generations

The following study was conducted with Alexandra D'Arcy who came to Toronto in 2001 to begin a PhD. The analysis is based on stories told by nearly 200 people aged between 9 and 87 in the years 2003–2005. Each person was born and raised in the city. Figure 4.2 shows how often people of each age group use quoting *like* in contrast to quoting *say* (Tagliamonte and D'Arcy, 2007a: 205, Figure 2). You can see that a person over 40 in the early 2000s is very unlikely to use quoting *like*. Instead, this is where you will find lots of quoting *say* or *said*. In fact, the graph exposes an impressive crossover, or "X" pattern. As *like* rises, *say* falls.

Is this a case of the under 40-year-olds substituting a new term (*be like*) in place of the standard form(s) (*say, think*) used by the older generations? As it turns out, this isn't the case. How can we tell? You have to look closely at how the quotative verbs are used. When I did, I discovered that the under 40-year-olds were using quoting *like* in a different way than the older generations were using quoting *say* or *think*. Recall that the characteristic uses of quoting *like* are

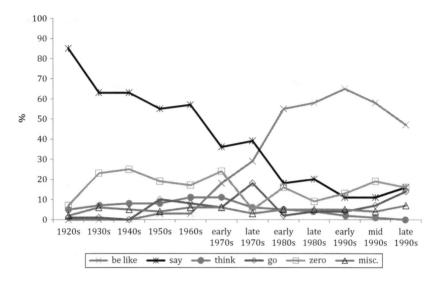

Figure 4.2 Overall distribution of quotative verbs by speaker date of birth

for quoting oneself (the pronoun *I*) and when quoting inner thoughts, sounds, and exclamations. In contrast, when older people quote with *say/said* they use it more often for quoting other people, as in (52). This is an excerpt from Wilbur Carlsberg, aged 82, talking about his experiences in a lecture course in university.

52.   a.   He *said*, "there are too many of you here gentleman, too many of you."
       b.   He *said*, "I like to see a class of about a hundred and twenty-five."
       c.   So, he *said*, "look at the person on your right and the person on your left, because only one of you is going to be here at the end of the term." (Wilbur Carlsberg, 82)

Although the over 40-year-olds may use *say* to talk about their thoughts, as in (53a), they more typically use *go* or *think*, as in (53b).

53.   a.   You just sit back and well, after ten years, you *say*, "Well, geez I'm unhappy" (Cory Davin, M, 49)
       b.   You just throw up your hands and *go*, "Well, there's not a darn thing you can do." (Amy Sinkic, 41)
       c.   So I *thought*, "Wow, this is cool." (Antonia Silvera, 40)

However quoting *say* is most often used for introducing dialogue, as in (54).

54.   a.   So I *said* to him, "I'm sorry."
       b.   He *said*, "That's perfectly all right." In his big loud voice. (Flora Valentin, 83)

This means that the system of quotative verbs used by the over 40-year-olds has a distinct patterning from the one used by the under 40-year-olds. Once, people used *say* for speech, *think* for thoughts, and *go* for either one and/or sounds. Now, not only has the incidence of dialogue, thoughts, and sounds in storytelling changed, but the quotative verbs are no longer organized in the same way. *Be like* can be all of the above, but most especially for first-person inner dialogue. When people talk about a "generation gap" they do not know how right they are!

Who were the first users of quoting *like*? Although it is tempting to blame the current tweens and teens, it was definitely not them. They are using a form that has been in the language for at least 20 years. If anyone can be blamed for the origins of this form, it's the 30-year-olds, the generation who were born in the 1970s and became teenagers in the 1980s. If you look back at the graph you can see that this is the generation that shows the first spike in use of this feature. The 30-year-olds are also a generation in flux. They use quoting *like* but also *say*. Here is Jill MacIntosh. She provides a good example of how a 30-year-old in Canada tells a story. Look at the mix of quotative verbs in (55).

55.   a. The guy *said*, "Sir, you haven't ticked off this box."
       b. And he *said*, "Well you tick it off for me."
       c. And he *goes*, "it's not my job to tick off the box."
       d. So he *said*, "Okay, give me a pen."
       e. And he *goes*, "it's not my job to give you a pen" right?
       f. So he's going to lose his place in line and be another like five hours in line.
       g. And he said he just grabbed the bars and *went*, "I'm not leaving until you give me-" he just like lost it.
       h. And that they respected 'cause everyone in line was *like*, "Here, have a pen." (Jill MacIntosh, 30)

The important question is how are these 30-year-olds using quoting *like*? Are they using it in the same way as the tweens and teens? It is one thing to use a word; it is another thing to use it appropriately! Everyone knows an older person who tries to sound hip by using a young person's word, but ends up using it in the wrong way. As my kids tell me, "Don't try to be cool, mum! It's so not cool!"

Recall that when quoting *like* started being used in the 1980s it was typically used for quoting oneself (i.e. *I*), but also with existential *it*, and for quoting sounds and gestures, as in (56).

56.   a. It's just *like* "Snap, snap, snap, snap." (Jillian Clarin, 26)
       b. It's *like*, "(sighs)." Which is frustrating. (Noreen Jalna, 39)
       c. The thing's *like* (sound effect), gone. (Daniel Friesen, 26)

Example (57) provides a good example of an older person's storytelling style. This is a story told by Alexander Menegol, aged 51.

57.   a. He *goes* "it's me."
       b. I *go*, "yeah, I kind of figured it was you."
       c. It was *like*, "great."
       d. I *says*, "let them open their Christmas presents."
       e. And my wife *goes*, "No. We don't open them 'til Christmas morning."
       f. I *go*, "well at my house we open them up Christmas-Eve after midnight."
          (Alexander Menegol, 51)

Alexander uses a mix of *say*, *go*, and in one case *like*, which is used with existential *it*. If you listen to older people using quoting *like* they probably use it in this way. Moreover, the quoting *like* tokens are mixed in with the other quotative verbs. When *like* occurs, it tends to be in the contexts where *like* first appeared many years ago. Now you know why people of this age sound old-fashioned to teenagers.

Look back at Figure 4.2. Who are the people who are using quoting *like* the most? It is the speakers born in the early 1990s, the pre-adolescents. They are the speakers who are on the leading edge of change for this feature. They use quoting *like* a lot more than anyone else and further, they use it differently. Instead of a specific set of patterns, such as for quoting oneself (e.g. *I'm like*) and quoting what one is thinking about (e.g. I'm like, "wonder what I should do about that"), younger people now use *like* to quote everyone. They also use quoting *like* for every type of quote, whether inner thoughts, gestures, sounds, or speech. In other words, the younger generation has not simply replaced one form with another. Instead *be like* is sweeping the system.

But why did these generations of young people do this? One of the strongest patterns of the *like*-using generations is to quote their own inner thoughts. I wondered when people started telling stories by performing what they were thinking at the time. Consider the typical examples in (58) and (59).

58.   a. I'*m like*, "Oh my God!"
       b. I'*m like*, "He's going to get wet. I give it ten seconds."
       c. Sure enough, Ø "Boom!"
       d. I *was* just *like*, "Oh man, you guys are so predictable." (Alyssna Sailner, 29)

59.   a. I'*m like*, "Shit, my parents are going to wake up 'cause of that."
       b. I'*m like*, "Oh shit."
       c. I'*m like*, "Okay, I gotta pretend like something happened, think something, think something," right? (STC, Daniella Loca, 17)

This storytelling style is a new development in English. People in their 40s and 50s had already started telling stories in this way just before quoting *like* took off in the 1980s. Examine the story in (60) told by Rose Cooper, aged 48, about her boyfriend Dean, who later became her husband. Notice how much of the story consists of what she was thinking at the time, but here the quotative verb is always *think (thinking)* or *thought*.

60.   a. So, at the three year period I *thought* "enough of this man"
        b. And my dad at one point *said*, "well can I talk to Dean? Would that help?"
        c. And I, Ø "no way!"
        d. I *said*, "if you talk to him,"
        e. I *said*, "then what good is our relationship if I need someone else to intervene for me?"
        f. So I *thought* "no that won't work"
        g. So I *suggested* "is it possible that we can go away?"
        h. And I *thought* "that's it, I'm away from this man for at least 10 days"
        i. And I *thought* "this is good"
        j. Then I started to kind a sneak around myself *thinking* "what are they up to?"
        k. And at one point I *heard* my dad say, "he's not there, he's not there"
        l. And I *thought* "what are they talking about?"
        m. And I *thought* "well the only person they could be thinking about – could it be Dean?"
        n. I *heard* them say, "do you think he's changed his mind?"
        o. Well I *thought* "this is unbelievable! Is it possible that this fantasy is really coming true?" (STC, Rose Cooper, 48)

At the time, this was probably a trendy new way of telling stories. Rose may well have been on the leading edge of her generation. This storytelling style had already started *before* quoting *like* came on the scene, hence Rose's use of *think/thought*. However, this new narrative style set the stage for quoting *like* when it was picked up by the next generation of adolescents in the 1980s. Noreen Jalna, in (61), is just ten years younger than Rose, at age 39. Her story is about the Northern American Blackout of 2003. Notice that she tells her story with the same style as Rose but instead of using *think/thought* she uses *realize* and *like*.

61.   a. It's *like* "This is really weird."
        b. And it's *like*, "Oh, this is really weird, power's still not on,"
        c. Ø "Oh I can't reach this person on cell, this is really weird."
        d. And then you *realize*, "Oh the lights are out there, the lights are out. Wow this is really big,"
        e. It's *like* "Whoa."
        f. And then, you know you *realize* "Okay barbeque" (Noreen Jalna, 39)

Now the question is, why did teenagers in the 1980s pick up on quoting *like* so quickly and why did it spread? We know that innovations in language are driven by both linguistic and social factors. Teenagers, in particular, pick up on new features of language when those features have positive value, either because the features are associated with a desirable social group or because they encapsulate a style that teenagers aspire to emulate. The feature, in this case quoting *like*, is not a feature you will find in a grammar book, but in the

1980s it was what the in-crowd was using. Street cred is a good way to describe this. At the time, the desirable social category was young, urban, savvy, e.g. *Valley Girl* and the place was *California*. As part of the preppie movement of the 1980s, quoting *like* gained prestige as a fashionable and socially desirable way to voice inner experience. This is how language changes. It begins because the language itself provides a hospitable environment, and then a social force drives it forward.

To this day, quoting *like* continues to increase in use and is spreading far and wide. At the same time, it is evolving and as it does it transforms. Where once quoting *like* tended to be used for quoting oneself and quoting inner thoughts, now you can hear teenagers using it in ever more expanding ways. For example, for quoting email messages and instant messaging conversations, as in (62).

62.   a.   And e-mail that'*s* all *like*, "Okay," then we'll reply later. (Catherine Hui, 19)
      b.   . . . we were talking on-line, and then she'*s like* "Hey, do you wanna go to CNE?" (Kevin Lam, 15)

Quoting *like* is also used for expressing intentions and speculations, as in (63).

63.   a.   I'm trying to *be* more *like*, "Oh, hi, I'm Clara!" (Clara Felipe, 16)
      b.   I thought she would just *be like*, "Euh! These are so small! Oh, couldn't you find more?" (Clara Felipe, 16)

Eventually another quotative verb will come in and take over from quoting *like*. A number of others have appeared in the last few years, including *just*, as in (65a), *all* and *be* (as in 65b–c).

64.   a.   I *was just*, "You're a jerk!"
      b.   Sarah's friends, they're *all* like, "Yeah, I'm cool." (Clara Felipe, 16)
      c.   And then I'd go up to her and *be*, "What?" (Parvati Prakesh, 20)

In London, where quoting *like* constitutes only 24 percent of the total quotatives in the inner city borough of Hackney, a new quotative is developing, namely *this is*, e.g. *This is my mom, "What are you doing?"* (Cheshire and Fox, 2007). In California, quoting *all* was reported to be on the rise, as in "She's *all*, 'Oh my god!'" (Rickford et al., 2007); however, although it showed promise, the development was short-lived (Buchstaller et al., 2010).

Given the alleged Valley Girl connections to quoting *like*, it was expected that this new Californian feature might spread and the whole cycle would start again. Interestingly, even though I keep looking out for it, quoting *all* has not taken off, at least not in Canada and as far as I know it is not present in the MLE (Cheshire and Fox, 2009). I found only a handful of examples in millions of words of Canadian English. This shows that it is not simply the place of origin (e.g. California) that determines whether a feature will be successful in a language change. The development of quotative verbs is specific to certain social or ethnic groups and to particular varieties at specific points in time. This provokes at least two compelling questions for the future: what other community-specific quotatives might there be and what does it take for such local developments to spread?

It is possible that tweens and teens who use quoting *like* a lot will drop it as they get older. It could be that tweens and teens learn quoting *like* and then keep using it. It could even be that older people, wanting to sound hip or cool or "with it" might start using quoting *like* for the first time. It will be interesting to see how things evolve in the years to come. Meantime, I have been following a single person, Clara Felipe, since she was 16 in 2002. Has her use of quoting *like* changed as she gets older? Let's find out.

Figure 4.3 plots the frequency of quotative *like* as a proportion of all quotative verbs in Clara's interviews from 2002 to 2015, which tracks her from age 16 to age 28. In this time frame she has gone from a shy 16-year-old working in the public library to a high level professional (a nurse) with a graduate degree.

Clara's use of quotative *like* increased to age 18 and then does not change very much over the following years. Thinking back to Figure 1.1, which illustrated Labov's prediction about the course of linguistic change across the life span, recall that the prediction is that individuals will increase their use of an incoming form until late adolescence/early adulthood (incrementation) and

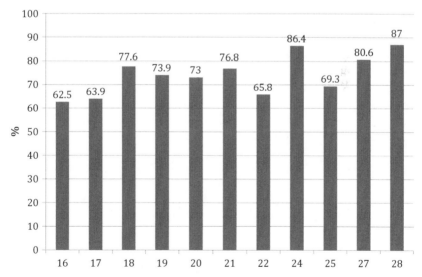

Figure 4.3 Proportion of quoting *like* used by Clara by age at time of recording

then remain at the same level for the rest of their life (stability). Figure 4.3 provides evidence that this is exactly right. Incrementation in adolescence is followed by stability in adulthood. Although Clara's use of quotative *like* varies somewhat across time, the dips and rises are not significant. This provides strong evidence that quoting *like* is part of her grammar.

When we interviewed Clara at the age of 20, we asked her if she thought her language had changed. Her reply is in (65):

65.   Oh yeah sometimes I really wonder if my vocabulary has improved. 'Cause really I don't think it has. Maybe. But I don't think so. I still have the same things like I start my sentences with "ands" and then I end with like "so yeah!" I still do that. But I can't help it.

Take note of the way teenagers tell stories and you may spot the next new trendy quotative verb. Teenagers use playful forms of language all the time, but whether or not those features take root in the language depends on having just the right set of circumstances – a hospitable spot in the grammar and a socially desirable group that starts using it.

What does the use of quotatives tell us about teen language?

Let's put young people's use of the quoting *like* in perspective. Since the 1970s quoting *like* has accelerated across time and space and is now found in every continent and even the most remote island where English is spoken (i.e. Tristan da Cunha, Schrier, personal communication). Yet quoting *like* has not spread from one place to another based on geographic proximity. (Recall that in 1995–1996 quoting *like* was more frequent in British English, much farther away from the United States than Canadian English is.) Instead, quoting *like* appears to have spread by different pathways, perhaps by way of television, perhaps by way of virtual networks on the Internet. Its expansive spread is also tied to the increased global mobility of youth beginning in the 1970s (Tagliamonte et al., 2014a). By whatever means, quoting *like* has eclipsed storytelling quotation, at least in urban centers among middle-class speakers.

It will be interesting to see what will happen next. Will the uses of quoting *like* continue to increase and change and if so how? Will all social groups and varieties of English pick up this innovation in the same way? Will the tweens and teens of today keep using quoting *like* as they go to university and into the workforce? The 30-year-olds certainly do and have been using it for the last 20 years. Will the grandparents of tomorrow be using quoting *like*? In fact, they already do.

There's little groups and each little group has their own kind of slang or way to talk, or whether they're formal about it or whether they're a little bit more lackadaisical in how they say stuff, you know. (Antonio Silvera, 40)

Language puzzle

Consider the stories below.
a. First, we have to establish a basis for our investigation. To facilitate this, the stories have been divided into lines corresponding to the utterances of the stories.
b. How many quotative verbs are there in each story?
c. Compute the proportion of each quotative type (e.g. *say, go*) in each story.
d. What is the frequency of quoting *like* in each story?
e. Given the evidence in the data has there been a change in quoting *like* between 1995 and 2004?
f. What is speaker A's favored quotative verb?
g. Identify some words and expressions that are the same across stories.
h. Identify some words and expressions that are different.

Answers
a. *Speaker A = 31; Speaker B = 17.*
b. *Speaker A = 12; Speaker B = 4.*
c. *Speaker A = say = 1/12; go = 11/12; like = 0/12; Speaker B, like = 4/5; zero = 1/5. The zero quotative is tricky. While this token may look like a quotative "like" token, this type of construction is a token of a zero quotative, which just happens to have discourse marker "like" in the same construction.*
d. *Speaker A = 0 percent; Speaker B = 100 percent.*
e. *Yes. 0 → 100 in 9 years.*
f. *The quotative "go."*
g. *Discourse "so," "and then," discourse "like," future "going to," indefinite "this," double subjects, "my friend, he."*
h. *Speaker A uses "anyways," "pretty" as an intensifier, sentence ender "right"; Speaker B uses "and stuff," "so" as an intensifier, sentence ender "you know."*

Speaker A: Male, 23, 1995

Encounter

Okay, I go out the other night, right?
Sitting there we go to uh where'd we go?
We went to the Entwhistle that's where it was.
So we're sitting there.
We're having a good time alright
We're there for a while.
Anyways near the end of the night I end up talking to this girl.
So I'm talking to her you know,
Things are going pretty good.
I'm talking to her for about twenty minutes.
She asks me where I'm from.
So I say, "Petawawa."

She goes, "Oh Pet."
She goes, "Oh, I got relatives up there."
I go, "Oh yeah, who you related to?"
She goes, "Oh do you know so and so?"
I go, "yeah, yeah."
I go, "they used to live on the street behind me."
And anyways she goes, "They're not my relatives."
She goes, "I'm related to these people named Robinson."
I go, "holy woah!"
I go, "well you're not going to believe this."
I go, "Here let me show you something."
I give her my driver's license, "my last name is Robinson."
So we end up talking.
We figure it out her grandfather and my grandfather were brothers.
So that makes us like what fourth or fifth cousins.
So nothing happens anyways right.
But pretty weird,
Pretty neat
But pretty weird.

Speaker B: Male, aged 23, 2004

The guitar

One time I was in grade nine.
My friend, he got this guitar body.
And I was like, "oh you got this guitar body."
And it was all this crazy, spiky, BC rich style guitar.
And I thought it was so cool
And I was like "he's not even a guitar player why doesn't he give it
to me?"
So he lent it to me,
And then, he came over,
And then we were fighting over it.
And then I got mad at him like, "you bastard."
And then he's like, "well no one's going to have it."
Then he smashed it.
And I was like, "you bastard I'm going to kill you."
And then kind of like started fighting and stuff.
But it wasn't like serious fighting
It was just more or less, you know.
And I stopped hanging around with them in grade ten because they
were just idiots.

5   Intensifiers

Upping the ante – super *cool!*

> If I was talking to you on an ongoing basis I wouldn't use a swear word
> necessarily, but it seems to me the young people do that to a certain extent.
> Now I don't know whether that's more anecdotal. As a teacher you don't
> really hear that 'cause they don't swear in front of you.
>
> (Dirk Brooks, 73)

Even though language is always changing, it is actually difficult to catch
language change in action. This is because many of the changes language
undergoes take place slowly over a very long period of time, sometimes
thousands of years. However, some parts of a language change constantly –
so continuously in fact, that sometimes you can stand a good chance of
catching them while they are happening. This is a story about how I caught
another language change in progress.

Some of the best places to look for language change are those where people
use words imaginatively. Slang terms are a good example. Most changes in the
selection of words are lexical changes. If you want to tap into more systemic
changes in progress a better place to look is within the grammatical devices of
the language. In this study, I examined adverbs. Adverbs are words that add
further meaning to other words. They can act to tone words down or boost
them up. In the latter case they are called "intensifying" adverbs. Take for
example a day that is colder than usual. How would you describe such a day?
You can "up the ante," so to speak, and say that it is *very cold*. You can also
diminish the quality of an adjective as well. You could say, for example, *it is
kind of cold . . . sort of cold . . .* or *moderately cold.* The words that tone down
the nature of the *cold* are also adverbs, but in this case they are called down-
toners, as in (66).

66.   a.   That's *kind of* funny but, ah, it was good fun. (Craig Thompson, 18)
       b.   So the neighborhood's changing a lot but it's still *fairly* well mixed.
             (Shannon Ermak, 19)
       c.   It was *kind of* confusing but a lot of fun. (Cheryl Choi, 12)

Listen out on days that are either bitterly cold or burning hot. You may hear
all kinds of adverbs.

In this chapter, I'm going to focus on adverbs that boost up the meaning of adjectives, either to the highest degree, as in (67), or to some unspecified extent, as in (68).

67.   a. I think my mother would find your coming out story *absolutely* hysterical. (Lauren Welsby, 18)
        b. My mom's *completely* different. (Greg Parkinson, 16)
        c. As of two days ago, this room was *entirely* full of boxes with no furniture. (Emma Timbali, 19)
        d. I guess it was … *exceedingly* difficult to just like understand that it had happened. (Nina Swanson, 18)

68.   a. The Grand Canyon is the most boring place in the world. People think it's fun there just 'cause it's cool but it's *really* boring. (Eleanor Colum, 14)
        b. I'm *very* active in sports and stuff like that. (Janet McDonald, 19)
        c. So it was *pretty* cool. (Shannon Ermak, 19)
        d. Batman. Yeah, it was *so* cool. (Kevin Lam, 15)

When studying intensifiers, it's important to remember that the vast majority of the time people don't use intensifiers at all, even though they could. These unintensified adjectives pass by without you realizing it most of the time, as in (69).

69.   a. She thought it was Ø *interesting* but I think it's Ø *boring* 'cause it's all on evolution. (Dana Naskauskaas, 17)
        b. He's got a Ø *good* life, Dan's Ø *smart*. (Katherine Berazzi, 18)

The fact that most adjectives are not intensified of course makes a lot of sense. Intensifiers wouldn't be capable of intensification if they turned up all the time. When people use these words their intention is to heighten the meaning of the adjective beyond the norm, oftentimes to exaggerate and sometimes even to be original. Why say that it is "cold" outside, when it is possibly the coldest temperature you have ever experienced and you are freezing? Another aspect of using intensifying adverbs is that they permit people to demonstrate their verbal skills. If you want to be captivating, especially in telling stories, intensifying adverbs are an ideal place to be inventive and interesting. That's why they're one of the best places to catch language change. People need to change their intensifiers often in order to be fresh and new.

> **Consider the intensifier *totally*.**
>   When does it have its original meaning "entirely," when does it simply boost the meaning of an adjective, and when does it mean something else? Check the examples in the book! (2, 25b, 75g, 155a, 201ℓ)

In fact, competition, change, and recycling among intensifiers have been going on in English for thousands of years. You might think that the Standard

English intensifier *very* has always been the proper way to boost the meaning of word. However, *very* is actually one of the newer intensifiers in English. If you go back to Old English, the favorite intensifier was *well*, as in *it's well cold outside*. Then came *full*, as in *it's full cold outside*. *Full* was replaced by *right*, and then *right* was replaced by *very*, followed some time after by *pretty*, and then *really*. Today *very* is still the Standard English intensifier. In the early twentieth century *really* was grouped among the other non-standard intensifiers, but these days it is said to be the most frequent intensifier in North American English.

Use of intensifiers is associated with casual speech and non-standard varieties. In the early twentieth century *pretty*, *really*, and *so* were even deemed vulgar. Use of intensifiers in general has typically been associated with women. Why? People say women are more emotional and talk about more emotive topics. Apparently, intensifiers go along with such exaggerated states of being and of expression. The intensifier *so* in particular has long been associated with women (e.g. Stoffel, 1901). However, which intensifier(s) you use can also tell people where you come from and even your social connection. These days your favorite intensifier tells everyone something more: it reveals how old you are!

To put historical and contemporary observations into perspective, Figure 5.1 shows the frequency of intensifier *really* in the collocation *really good*. I have chosen to search for this collocation in order to limit the search to intensifying adverbs and because *good* is the most frequent adjective in my archive and therefore expected to be robust in Google Ngrams.

Figure 5.1 makes it apparent that the intensifier *really* increased steadily from 1800 to the late 1970s, then it reached a plateau. It dipped in the 1950s only to begin an upward swing in the early 1960s and has been increasing more markedly after that. How does such a longitudinal perspective pan out in vernacular speech?

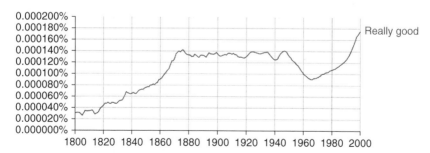

Figure 5.1 Google Ngrams search for collocation "really good"

British English, *circa* 1990s

In the late 1990s I conducted a study of intensifiers in British English. The data came from people born and raised in the city of York, a small city in the northeast, between the ages of 17 and 97 (Ito and Tagliamonte, 2003). Given previous studies of British English, *very* should have been the favored form in the data. However, I discovered that there were actually many different intensifiers in use. The two most frequent ones were *very* and *really*, as in (70). Yet the same speakers using these forms also used older forms, such as *right* in (70c). A number of casual forms were also present, as in (70d–f). Occasionally a younger person used *very* among the other intensifiers, as in (70g).

70.   a. It was a *really* old building . . . and one night the old one burnt down . . .
          It was a *very* old rambling mess of a building. (Samuel Watkins, 37)
       b. We must have been *bloody* mad. (Samuel Watkins, 37)
       c. He was a *right* old character. He's passed on now. (Samuel Watkins, 37)
       d. You're *flippin'* cold in an alley wagon. (Samuel Watkins, 37)
       e. Oh we were *blimmin'* terrified. (Robin Jones, 50)
       f. He'd be there in his overalls at the hospitals, oh *dashed* attractive!
          (Nicky Bond, 34)
       g. It's *so* difficult to get over that barrier . . . It's *very* difficult to say,
          "How about doing it this way?" (Nicky Bond, 34)

When all the potential intensifying adverbs were taken into account, it became clear that the way people used these forms was a lot more complex than previously thought. In fact, the study showed that intensifiers that had been around from as early as Old English, e.g. *well*, were still in use, albeit at a very low frequency. Apparently, old intensifiers do not fade away, but endure across centuries, as in (71).

71.   It's *well* weird. (Nicky Bond, 34)

At the same time, the intensifiers used by the York inhabitants were changing. Figure 5.2 shows the frequency of *very*, *really*, and *so* for three age groups: those over 66, those between 35 and 65, and those between 17 and 34 around the year 1997.

Notice that, as expected, the overall rate of intensification is modest. Note that the scale on the Y axis is 20 percent usage only. The vast majority of adjectives are not intensified. However, when an intensifier is present, which one is it? *Really* occurs sporadically among older individuals (72a), but surges to be the most frequent intensifier among the youngest speakers, as in (72b–c).

72.   a. It's *really* crazy! (Samuel Clark, 75)
       b. My mum was terrified 'cause Clifton had a *really* bad name. (Sandra
          George, 22)
       c. But I was *really* scared, you see. (Nick Hudson, 17)

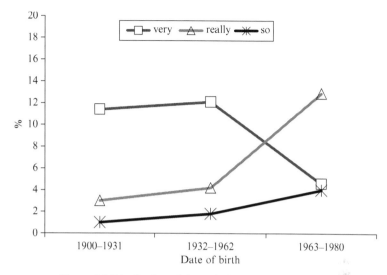

Figure 5.2 Distribution of the main intensifiers in British English (York) by speaker date of birth

Notice too that there is a new intensifier on the horizon – *so*, which was just beginning to be used by the youngest speakers, the under 35-year-olds, as in (73).

73.   a. He looked *so* rough and mean it was unbelievable. (Paul Gregory, 23)
        b. I was *so* nervous. (Ivy Robinson, 28)
        c. They always think they're *so* small, don't they, and they're *so* big like. (Daniel Davis, 20)

I had discovered a true generation gap. Use of the intensifier *very* was the mark of being over 35, while using *really* openly identified a much younger speaker.

I also discovered that the traditional assumptions about intensifiers did not hold up. First, the educated speakers rather than the less educated speakers used intensifiers more. This means that educated individuals were leading the change towards *really* in British English. Second, although earlier commentators had suggested that women are "notoriously fond of hyperbole" (Stoffel, 1901: 101) or that "the fondness of women for hyperbole will very often lead the fashion with regard to adverbs of intensity" (Jespersen, 1922: 250), it was not true that the women in York were using more intensifiers than the men. Moreover, the young women were not the only ones responsible for the change from *very* to *really*. The younger educated males used *really* as much as the women.

In the past, when men had been found to use a lot of intensifiers they were referred to as "ladies' men" (Stoffel, 1901: 101). I wondered if they had simply been the educated men of that time period. Alternatively, I wondered whether the finding that men and women were using the same frequency of intensifiers in the 1990s might reflect the more equal roles of men and women in the late twentieth century in Britain.

The question was: were these trends specific to British English? To what extent would they be replicated in English elsewhere? Research on London teenagers conducted about the same time (in the COLT corpus) also noted that *really* was on the rise among teenagers (Stenström, 1999). This supported my idea that the favored intensifier of British English was changing from *very* to *really*. In contrast, teenagers in Glasgow, Scotland, were using a different intensifier altogether, *pure* (Macaulay, 2007). Unfortunately, I had no data from tweens or teenagers in York in order to corroborate these findings because the sample of York English I had collected had not included anyone younger than 17. However, in those years I had three young children entering pre-adolescence. I started noticing that their use of intensifiers was reflecting the trends I had found in the York intensifier study. Not only were they using *really*, they had begun to use *so* as well.

About the same time, I had started watching a television sit-com called *Friends*. My kids were just at the age to enjoy it and I was thankful to be watching something other than Barney the Dinosaur.[1] As we watched the show together I realized that the *Friends* characters were using a lot of intensifiers. Guess which ones? *Really*, and most interestingly for me, *so*. It was not long before I had embarked on another study.

I think there's a fair bit more of American usage – now in Canada because of TV. (Sheila Shapley, 63)

Television

A lot of people think that television is influencing the way we talk. Sociolinguists have typically believed that this is not possible. They believe that interaction between people is a critical component for language change to occur. Television, however, is passive. You just sit there and watch it. Therefore, how can it influence your grammar? For animated discussion about these issues see the *Journal of Sociolinguistics, Media and Language Change* (2014).

Despite the received wisdom in the field that television cannot cause language change (e.g. Milroy and Milroy, 1985; Trudgill, 1986: 55), I noticed that the actors and actresses on *Friends* were all using *so*, as in (74).

74. a. No ... oh, I feel *so* stupid! (Rachel)
    b. Oh my God. This is *so* exciting. (Phoebe)
    c. That was *so* lame. (Chandler)
    d. This guy is *so* stupid. (Joey)
    e. He is *so* sexy. (Monica)

I was suspicious. There was an increase in intensifier *so* in the York study. There was an increase in use of *so* among my children. What was going on? Was the use of *so* by the *Friends* characters leading the way in ongoing changes in the intensifier system in English? Or was the language being used on TV influencing the way my kids were talking? I set out to find out.

Among the lay population, the received wisdom is that television must surely be influencing the way we talk. If so, then television shows which: (1) reach an extensive audience and (2) command widespread attention across diverse populations might be targets for modeling. *Friends* was the ideal example of a long-running, enormously popular television series. It seemed the ideal candidate for investigation.

Friends

Friends was a sit-com about six friends living in New York City – three men and three women. The comedy follows these characters (Monica, Phoebe, Rachel, Ross, Joey, and Chandler) through the ups and downs of American life. This series was all the rage in North America and worldwide. In any given week it drew an average of 24.5 million viewers in the US alone. *Friends* was also an influential cultural phenomenon with Internet fan sites and merchandise and the actors became focal pop-culture personalities. While television is actually scripted talk, the *Friends* dialogue was well known to have been a joint effort between screenwriters and cast. As I mentioned earlier, intensifiers are subject to the whims of fashion. Speakers want to embellish their stories in such a way as to hold the attention of their audience. What better place to study this than in television where the need for new and interesting entertainment is not only relentless but an imperative for success. I guessed that the talk on *Friends* might provide a glimpse at North American English and an informative window on the changes going on in the English intensifiers.

Using transcriptions of all the *Friends* episodes from seasons 1–8, which were available on the Internet in the mid to late 1990s, I replicated the York study. Like the people in York, the *Friends* characters used lots of different intensifiers, as in (75).

75. a. I think it is *pretty* exciting. (Chandler)
    b. Oh, Janine, the *really* hot dancer girl. (Monica)

    c. Oh, come on man. You can dance with my partner. She's *real* uh- mellow. (Joey)

    d. Trust me, it was actually- it was *very* funny. (Rachel)

    e. And this is *so* weird. (Joey)

    f. Well, Frank has to quit college because his *super* fertile sister is having three babies! (Phoebe)

    g. Oh, you're *totally* welcome! (Monica)

    h. Well, actually, she only did it the one time. But it was *pretty* weird. (Phoebe)

    i. Look, it is not my fault that your chairs are *incredibly* ugly! (Joey)

The interesting thing was that the same three intensifiers as in York were the most frequent – *very, really,* and *so.* But there was at least one critical difference. In the York data *very* and *really* were the most popular intensifiers. In the *Friends* data *so* was by far the out-runner, representing nearly 50 percent of all the intensifiers used, far more than the 38 percent in York! If both data sets could be taken to represent the way people talk in Britain and the United States, then there was clearly a change going on. American English was in the lead.

To support this possibility it was necessary to examine the data in more detail. Women are known to use incoming forms more often than men (Labov's Principles 3 and 4). Which characters were using *so* more? Figure 5.3 shows the six *Friends* characters and how often they use intensifier *so.*

All three girls are well ahead of the guys, suggesting that they are leading the change of intensifiers towards the form *so.*

I argued based on this and other evidence that media language actually does reflect what is going on in language, at least with respect to this feature – intensifiers (Tagliamonte and Roberts, 2005: 296). The *Friends* data had the

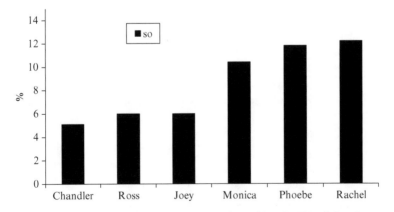

Figure 5.3 Distribution of the main intensifiers in *Friends* by character

same overall rate of intensification as similar studies of contemporary English *and* the same intensifiers occurred most frequently – *really, very,* and *so.* However, *so* was occurring at frequencies well above any other study. The *Friends* data seem to provide a kind of "preview" of a more advanced state of mainstream language. In fact, the television data appeared to be paving the way for *so* to be the new favorite in American English. The female *Friends* characters regularly intensified using *so* more often than males. This result is consistent with earlier observations that *so* is a "female" intensifier (Stoffel, 1901). It is also in line with Principles 3 and 4 that women lead linguistic change.

At the same time, the results suggested that the intensifier system was undergoing rapid change, apparently being led by American English and moving towards *so.* Intensifier *so* was not completely new. Its use "in affirmative clauses, tending to become a mere intensive without comparative force" is reported in the OED from as early as *Beowulf*, as in (76), and then at time points thereafter, e.g. (77).

76.   a. þæt we hine *swa* godne gretan moton
       b. that we might be allowed to address him, he who is *so* good

77.   a. My Face ... was hid in my Bosom, and I looked *so* silly! (Richardson, *Pamela* III.168, 1741)
       b. My dear brother is *so* good. (Dickens, *Pickwick Papers* IV, 1837)

Nevertheless, its heightened frequency in *Friends* suggested that it was undergoing a period of advance.

But of course the *Friends* data were from television and from characters who were in the 20-something age bracket. What would North American teenagers be doing? Would they be following the trends found in British English and apparent from the *Friends* study? Let's find out.

Canadian English, *c.* 2000s

In the early 2000s I conducted a study of the intensifying adverbs in the TEC, which enabled me to include the full range of the population in the study. The results showed remarkable consistency with the earlier studies. The very same main intensifying adverbs were found: *very, really,* and *so.* However, there was a complication. Another frequent form, *pretty,* as in (78), was also present. It was being used at about the same frequency as *very* and *so.* Although *pretty* did not have the same degree of intensity, it still boosted the meaning of the following adjective upwards.

78.   a. I guess I was *pretty* naïve. (Amanda Levy, 13)
       b. I didn't think I would 'cause I'm usually *pretty* quiet. (Jason Levine, 11)
       c. I'm *pretty* excited about it. (Clara Felipe, 16)

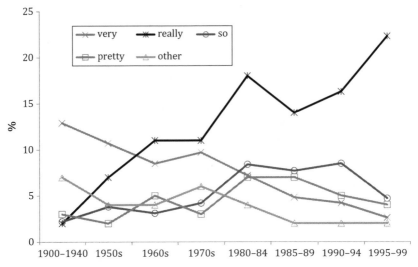

Figure 5.4 Distribution of the main intensifiers by speaker date of birth

The next question is: which speakers used what intensifiers? Figure 5.4 shows the distribution of the main intensifiers by speaker year of birth.

Figure 5.4 shows that the Standard English intensifier *very* drops from being the most frequent intensifier among older speakers to being the least used form among teens and tweens. This contrasts markedly with *really* which is rare among older people, but skyrockets from the 50-year-olds on down. Notice too that among the teens and tweens yet another trend is apparent. Both *so* and *pretty* are relatively frequent, but only in these age groups.

These findings lead to at least two other questions: First, are the young women leading this change? Second, why are the Canadian teens and tweens using *two* new forms, not just one? In order to answer the first question we must separate the girls and guys and compare their use of intensifiers, as in Figure 5.5.

The dark lines are female; the light lines are male. There is marked change visible among the individuals born in the 1980s. The young women show a major increase in *so*, but the use of *pretty* is stable for all women across all ages. Contrast this with *pretty*, which rises sharply among the young men. Yet the male population across age groups shows a relatively level proportion of *so* across the board. In other words, not only is there a generation gap in the use of intensifiers in Toronto, but there is also a salient sex effect. Using *so* is the mark of being young and female. Using *pretty* is the mark of being young and

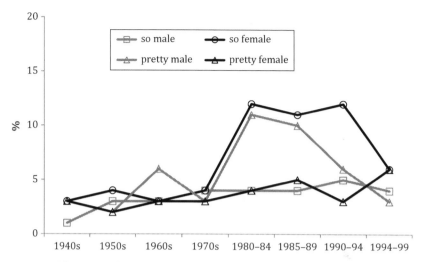

Figure 5.5 Distribution of *pretty* and *so* by speaker sex and date of birth

male. Canadian teenagers are marking their age and gender by which intensifiers they use. Why would Canadian teenagers do this? Perhaps because *so* has always been an intensifier associated with women/girls, the guys have had to find their own. By the time the guys are 17–19, they are using *pretty* about as much as the girls are using *so*. As far as I know, neither the girls nor the guys realize they are doing this. This is one of those strange things about language. While the need to mark our identity as being a part of the groups we want to belong to is endemic, sometimes distinguishing ourselves from the group we *don't belong* to is just as important. This is an exemplary empirical corroboration of Eckert's theory of the heterosexual market in adolescence (Eckert, 2011: 88). In adolescence "gender differences ... emerge just at the point when male–female separation gives way."

You may wonder if these male teenagers were mimicking the characters from *Friends*. I went back to the *Friends* data and checked. Although the frequency of *pretty* is much lower than in Toronto, the guys in *Friends* used a lot more *pretty* than the girls. I also went back to the British data, but there the incidence of *pretty* is rare. It may be the case that the *so/pretty* sex split is a North American phenomenon. We will need more studies to find out for sure.

By 2012, I started wondering about how intensifiers were being used on another North American sit-com, the television series *How I Met Your Mother*. The show is similar to *Friends* in that it has several male and female characters who are all friends and young adults. Would intensifier *so* still be

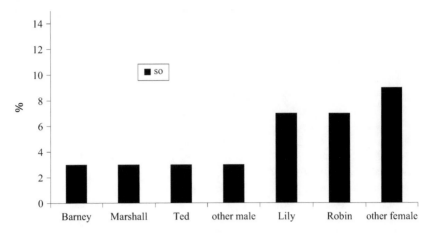

Figure 5.6 Distribution of the main intensifiers in *How I Met Your Mother* by character

prominent and would the female characters be using it more? Figure 5.6 shows the five central *How I Met Your Mother* characters and how often they use intensifier *so*.

The results are parallel to the earlier study of *Friends*. The main female characters (Lily and Robin) as well as other female characters are well ahead of the guys. The pattern of females using more *so* has persisted. The findings show us that although social patterns of language can diverge from one community to the next, once a pattern of male/female contrast has been established, it tends to be maintained.

What does the use of intensifiers tell us about teen language?

Intensifiers in English are a mark of the times. Your grandmother, wherever she may live in urban Britain, America, or Canada, may use *very*. The middle-aged baby-boomers use *really*, but if you were born in the 1980s you probably use *so* too.

By their very nature, intensifiers cannot have staying power since their impact is only as good as their novelty. If you overuse an intensifier it will lose its value. This is why speakers must reinvent them from time to time. Right now *really* is the dominant form in spoken English across the generations in Britain, Canada, the United States, and undoubtedly elsewhere. In the early 2000s *so* was in an upswing, especially among teenage girls. What will be the next intensifier to come on the scene? Listen out. I'm sure there will be a new one soon.

Language puzzle

Let's take a preliminary look at the adjective *random* in the TTC. All 32 tokens in the corpus are listed in Table 5A. The DOB column records the decade of birth in

Table 5A *Tokens of* random *in TTC by date of birth and sex*

#	Sentence	Individual	DOB	SEX
1	So sometimes you'd roll like a *random* number and it'd be-	mbeaulieu	8	M
2	Just say another *random* thing, kind of like that.	bremmington	8	F
3	Anywhere . . . *random*.	jwang	9	F
4	'cause she does it as this complete *random* draw	cchoi	9	F
5	and every *random* time that my grandma says that	nswanson	8	F
6	like when you get *random* things like that it's just like	kberazzi	8	F
7	How *random* is that?	gparkinson	9	M
8	sorry, this is *random*.	kpaul	8	F
9	like just *random* and they wouldn't stop.	egriffo	8	F
10	Just *random* things. Movies and games and stuff like that.	gcombs	8	M
11	I think it was just *random*.	kpaul	8	F
12	like just *random* stories and they make me crazy. A	ljackov	8	F
13	I'm tired of you coming home with like *random* bruises all over your body	bremmington	8	F
14	I say like *random* things	gsimatovic	9	F
15	I make *random* e-mails	gsimatovic	9	F
16	if you go into town, you like, make *random* comments as you pass by people.	nhardwick	8	M
17	It's a lot of just my like my *random* friends.	vwilloughby	9	F
18	It's so sad but that was kind of *random*.	ljackov	8	F
19	It was also pretty *random* but my family is very strange.	ljackov	8	F
20	like I just do it because it's *random* money	kberazzi	8	F
21	variable, such as color, or whether or not it's *random*	kvanspilt	8	M
22	You'll see *random* people you've met	ljackov	8	F
23	and they ask me these *random* questions and make me crazy	ljackov	8	F
24	and all of my ice cream to *random* people on the street	edaneva	8	F
25	I took them from my house and gave them to *random* people.	edaneva	8	F
26	I'm not scared of like speaking to *random* people,	edaneva	8	F
27	Some total *random* stranger.	jlevine	8	M
28	something totally *random*	gsimkovic	8	M
39	Totally *random*, almost.	kpaul	8	F
30	'cause like you'll look up *random* stuff,	gsimatovic	9	F
31	Or I just mix up *random* stuff	ljackov	8	F
32	I did it in school a couple times with *random* people and I won most of the time.	jlevine	8	M

(*cont.*)

the 1980s, 8, or 1990s, 9. The sex of the individual is male, M, or female,
F. Examination of forms is the first for understanding the patterns of *random* in
the data.

a. Who uses it more, the guys or the girls?
b. Who uses it more, the younger or older individuals?
c. Which individual uses it the most?
d. Is *random* used more as a predicative adjective, e.g. *That's so random*, or an
   attributive adjective, e.g. *That random guy is hot?*
e. There are at least two patterns in the data. Identify one.

   Try a Google Ngrams search (https://books.google.com/ngrams) for *totally
   random* or *random people*. Which generation is responsible for these uses?

Answers
a. *The number of tokens by females is 24, 75 percent of the data.*
b. *25 tokens come from individuals born in the 1980s.*
c. *L. Jackov uses it 6 times.*
d. *More as an attributive adjective, N=23/32.*
e. *(i) "Random" occurs 40 percent of the time with the words: "like, just, totally."
   These are adverbs. (ii) "Random" modifies the word "people" quite a few times,
   N=5.*

6   How do you start a sentence?

Oh okay well okay then I guess that is my destination.

(Trevor Klinke, 20)

When a person starts a sentence, which words come out first? According to the grammar books of English, you start a sentence with a subject, e.g. *I*, *she*, *Sali*, *my daughter*, in order to get sentences such as, e.g. *I̲ like cats*, *Sa̲li̲ likes cats*, *My̲ daughter likes cats*. But that is not what happens in spoken language. Sentences do not always unfold with a subject first. What typically happens is more like: *You know, I like cats*, *So, I like cats*, or even *So, you know, I think, I like cats*. Everyone thinks that it is teenagers who do this, and if not teenagers, people who are uneducated or inarticulate.

In this chapter, I explore the words that come before sentences, including words such as *so*, *well*, *you know*, *uh*, as in (79). I will refer to these words as "sentence starters," SS.[1]

79.   a. *So uh. Well* I really loved it. *You know uh* I enjoyed it. (William Carlsburg, 82)
        b. *Oh okay yeah so because* you grow up with it, you just don't even hear it. (Ken Smuckers, 53)

In the literature, these words have been included under the general umbrella of "discourse markers" (DMs) (e.g. Jucker and Ziv, 1998; Schiffrin, 1987), "pragmatic markers" (e.g. Andersen, 2001; Brinton, 1996; Erman, 2001), or "discourse-pragmatic markers." A question that arises is: Are these all the same *type* of markers? Why are such words sometimes referred to as "discourse markers," at other times "pragmatic markers," and sometimes as "particles"? Aside from being words and phrases that have been disparaged as meaningless and bad, what else can be said?

Traditionally, the words in (79) were thought to be empty, meaningless fillers. In the mid 1970s Longacre (1976) referred to them as "mystery particles," in part because at the time no one really knew what function they served in the language. As we shall see, these words are actually a multifarious set of phenomena and an important part of the grammar of spoken language.

There is a great deal to be learned yet, then, about the interrelations that exist between syntax and semantics, and about the way in which the syntactic structure of informal spoken language can best be analyzed. (Cheshire, 1987: 278)

Historical perspective

Brinton (1996: v) noticed how difficult it was for certain words of Old English to be translated. Consider – as she did – the first word in the first line of the famous epic poem *Beowulf*, as in (80a), *hwæt*. What does it mean?

80. a. *Hwæt!* We Gardena in geardagum þeodcyninga.
     b. *Lo*, praise of the prowess of people-kings.
     c. *Listen!* We – of the Spear-Danes ...
     d. *So*. The Spear-Danes in days gone by ...[2]

A cursory search on the Internet for different versions of *Beowulf* provides at least four different translations of the original with *hwæt*. One translation is *lo* (80b), another is *listen* (80c). Notice that the choice in (80d) is a word we are already familiar with. All this is to say that these types of words have a long history in the English language. They can be found as far back as *Beowulf* (Old English) and they have been studied extensively in historical corpora of written English.

Brinton (1996: 278) concludes that while the particular forms may have changed from *Beowulf* to Modern English, the pragmatic functions they encode are preserved. Regardless of time or form, the words serve to introduce an utterance. Language is continually renewing itself. New words may emerge to replace already existing words. New functions may emerge which require new words. In the latter case, the expressive needs of speakers change as language evolves. The question is how to tell which type of change is in evidence.

Synchronic perspective

Early research on DMs targeted words and phrases and analyzed them in terms of how the expressions were used to "provide contextual coordinates for ongoing talk" (Schiffrin, 1987: 41). The forms were abundant in the available data and the nuances of meaning they encoded offered a cornucopia of new findings demonstrating how DMs were instrumental in organizing discourse (e.g. Fraser, 1988; Schourup, 1985). Using the concept of "unit of talk" rather than sentence, Schiffrin (1987) outlined a number of functions of DMs. She discovered that there were several types. Boundary markers function to signal the beginning and end units of talk. These include forms and phrases such as *I mean, you know*. Continuity markers serve to indicate ongoing discourse, including particles, adverbs, and connectors. Sequential dependency markers make connections across sentences, such as *and, then, still*. Anderson (2001: 40) points out that DMs have a "high degree of context sensitivity" while at the same time being optional syntactically (Pichler, 2013: 4). This characteristic of optionality means that quantitative investigation is important in order to grapple with the trends in the data. It has also become increasingly clear that DMs straddle the boundaries of syntax and pragmatics. While syntax considers the position of the word in sentence structure, pragmatics focuses on how context contributes to meaning. In essence, DMs are Janus-faced phenomena because they require reference to the structure of the language, i.e. the category and position of the word in the sentence, but also the subjective, interactional, and textual information that is conveyed by their use in the context of the discourse.

Systematic examination of talk in conversation reveals that far from being meaningless, DMs serve as key signposts of the unfolding discourse. A conversation devoid of DMs would actually be awkward. I wanted to illustrate this for you, but once words are written down, the absence of DMs does not seem unusual, only curt. You will have to experiment with this in real life. Stop using DMs of any kind. Record how long it takes for someone to say: *Are you okay?*

Markers allow speakers to construct and integrate multiple planes and dimensions of an emergent reality: it is out of such processes that coherent discourse results. (Schiffrin, 1982: 330)

As we shall see, every sentence starter (SS) also has a function in discourse. Consider two excerpts representing an older speaker (Bud), as in (81) and a younger speaker (Jason), as in (82). I have italicized all the words and phrases that come in pre-sentence position, including the ones that come at the beginning of quoted speech.

81.   a. *And* <u>one time</u>, I remember my brother came home with a cabbage.
       b. *And* my father said, "Where did you get that?"
       c. He said, "*Oh* there's a whole bunch of them in a field up there."
       d. *And* Dad said, "*Okay*, you come and show me it."
       e. *And* he took my brother right back
       f. *And* said, "*Now* put it down and don't you ever take any of these again."
       g. Never did.
       h. Neither did I. (Bud Combdon, 83)

82.   a. <u>One time</u> I tried to call a friend of mine, Ella.
       b. She goes here too now.
       c. I've only bumped into her once since school started.
       d. *But* I called her house
       e. *And* I spoke to her brother.
       f. *And* I'd gotten her number from four-one-one or something,
       g. *So* I spoke to her brother

    h. *And* I left a message for her,
    i. *So* I decided I'd leave my phone number, "***Oh***, okay, what's your phone number?"
    j. "***Oh***, it's uh, nine-O-five."
    k. *And then* I left her number.
    l. *So*, he laughed at me. (Jason Levine, 17)

It is immediately apparent that although *and* is technically a conjunction – a grammatical device used to combine words, phrases, clauses, and sentences – it functions here as a DM of sequencing (see Schiffrin, 1982: 39). Researchers have noted that "the idea units of discourse are held together by *and*" (Chafe, 1984: 38; cited in Culpepper and Kytö, 2000: 300). Notice that *and* prefaces many parts of the storyline, both the action sequences (e.g. *took*, *called*, *left*) and the quoted speech. Indeed, *and* neatly segments the story into events. Further, notice how the two stories begin with adverbs, underlined (i.e. *one time*), that bracket the story beginning. Stories are remarkably structured in this way and as we shall see so is conversation. A study of *and* in storytelling and spoken discourse would be a very interesting undertaking (see e.g. Culpepper and Kytö, 2000). Notice too that the story told by the elderly man comprises sentences marked by *and* but the story by the younger man is mixed with *and*, *but*, and *so*. At the same time, quoted segments of the elderly man are varied, *oh*, *okay*, *now*, while the younger man only uses *oh*. Leaving aside the fact that these samples are very small and are being used for illustration purposes only, these could reflect a changing pattern. Only detailed investigation could confirm this to be true.

Method

One of the pitfalls of studying discourse-pragmatic features is that most studies in the literature focus on the salient and interesting forms without considering the contexts from which they came or the other forms with which they vary. In this chapter I will begin the investigation by describing all the words in the TEC, TTC, and for this study only, the Ontario Dialects Corpora (ODC), which comprise data from communities all over the province of Ontario (Tagliamonte, 2010–2013, 2013–2018). In essence, this study examines the left periphery of canonical English utterances in Ontario English. What is the inventory of forms in this position? How often do they occur and in what combinations? Given the stories in (81) and (82), people might think that sentence starters happen frequently or "all the time," but in actuality how often do people use SSs? Which ones do they use and under what conditions? Is there a particular age group that uses them more than others – could it be the teenagers? Let's find out.

In order to study the ways teenagers start sentences we have to begin by documenting all the possible ways sentences begin. Then, we need to compare the sentences of teenagers to those of pre-adolescents, middle-aged, and elderly people. If teenagers are special, different, or aberrant, this will be apparent in the data. In order to begin to understand sentence starters I first extracted from the TEC/TTC *every* reasonably well-formed sentence from a sample of 12 individuals, teenagers, middle-aged, and older. The reason for the "well formed" condition is that in conversation there are many starts and stops as people pause, reconsider, reformulate, and start again. I excluded sentences preceded by false starts and sentences that were broken several times. In these cases it was impossible to determine what the actual structure of the SS conglomerate might have been. For example, consider (83).

83.   a. *You just like- you know* you watch your step. (Joseph Tayles, 26)
         b. *So- so* she follows him … (Joseph Tayles, 26)

Crucially, false starts obscure the underlying structure. In (83a) what is the underlying structure of the sentence? It could either be "you just like you watch your step" or "you know you watch your step." However, because there is a break and a re-start, i.e. *you just like-*, and then *you know you watch your step*, we cannot second guess the structure. Therefore such sentences were excluded. However, when there was simply a repetition of the same word I included the sentence. In (83b), I assume the sentence is: *so she follows him.*

In order to focus on declarative sentences, I also excluded sentences that introduced direct speech, as in (84a), and the answers to yes/no questions, as in (84b).

84.   a. 'Cause they were *like*, "I never associated much with Timmins people."
         b. [Interviewer] So, there's no like drama? [074] *No.* And you know that's interesting because the last place I lived there was real drama, and there was only two other girls. (Annie Muscat, 22)

To understand how this procedure worked in practice, consider the excerpt in (85). The SSs are indicated with italics on the SS, e.g. *well, yeah* and *so*.

85.   a. *Well* my grandmother got kicked by a cow once.
         b. [Interviewer] How?
         c. *Yeah* she was uh- she was working um with the cows
         d. *And* she was milking them
         e. *And* one of them started being stupid
         f. *And* ah my grandmother just stabbed it 'cause it was like- it was kicking her and stuff.
         g. *So* she- she just stabbed it. No big deal. (Erin Gadek, 16)

Notice that sentences often begin with "and" as in (85d–f). There are run-on sentences, many cases of stopping and starting, as well as other anomalies. However, once the false starts are accounted for (as above), and repetition and hesitations, e.g. *uh* and *um*, are ignored, it is relatively straightforward to find the SSs. Every sentence meeting the criteria above was included in the analysis enabling me to collect thousands of sentences and determine the inventory and patterning of SS usage. The following inventory is based on a sample of 13,516 sentences.

What is exciting and amazing is that I discovered that there is a tremendous amount of regularity to both the forms used in pre-sentential positions and their positioning vis-à-vis other forms. In fact, these words are remarkably fixed and ordered. In what follows, I will first describe the inventory of words and phrases that people use before they start a sentence. Table 6.1 displays an exhaustive summary of these words and their positions.

Each column in Table 6.1 lists the words that are possible in each position or slot. The columns are labeled from A to P showing the order of the words. Notice that *uhm* and *uh* can occur in virtually any position. The most frequent locations are indicated here in columns E, I, K, M. While *uhm*'s and *uh*'s are interesting in their own right (e.g. Tottie, 2015), I will ignore them here in order to focus on the other phenomena. In the examples that follow I will italicize all the SS words and use underlining to highlight the feature under discussion.

Let's begin with what I will refer to as the "Outer Rim" slots. These are words that occur first. An interesting collection can occur in these positions, including *oh*, as in (86a), *ah*, as in (86b), and *yeah*, as in (86c).[3]

86. a. *Oh* it's okay. I just wanted to hear your voice. (Clara Felipe, 18)
     b. *Ah* they met through friends. (Katrina Wilson, 18)
     c. *Yeah so* we're going- going up in the world again. (Kayley Dupuis, 19)

The Outer Rim has three slots. The first slot is to attract attention; it serves the purpose of saying "I heard what you said." The second slot serves the purpose of acknowledging a previous statement. The third slot is to agree or disagree. Consider the example in (87). Ken and the interviewer are talking about accents. Ken grew up with a father who had a British accent but he says he could not hear his father's accent because he grew up with it. The interviewer is attempting to explain how and why this happens. Notice how Ken responds in (87b).

87. a. [Interviewer] Some people start hearing- yeah, they get more self aware. It's one of those-
     b. *Oh okay yeah so because* you grow up with it, you just don't even hear it. (Ken Smuckers, 53)

He uses all three Outer Rim words. First, he uses, *oh* to get the attention of the person he wants to address, in this case the interviewer, and let her know he's about to reply. Second, he acknowledges what the interviewer has told him just beforehand with *okay*. Third, he says *yeah* in order to agree with her.

Table 6.1 *Template for words and phrases that come before a sentence*

A	B	C	D	E	F	G	H	I	J	K	L	M	N	O	P
OUTER RIM			DISCOURSE MARKERS									INNER RIM			
ATTENTION	ACKNOWLEDGE	AGREE/ DISAGREE	UH 1	CONJ 1	ADVERB 1	SLOT 1	SLOT 2 (rare)	UH 2	CONJ 2	UH	AGREE/ DISAGREE	UH	ADVERB 2	PARENTHETICAL	ADVERB 3
ah															
oh (boy)	*okay*	*yeah*	*uh*	*and*	*then*	*so*	*you know*	*uh*	*if*	*uh*	*yeah*	*uh*	*then*	*I guess*	*then*
gosh	*yes*	*yes, yeah*	*um*	*because*	*now*	*well*	*like*	*um*	*when*	*um*	*no*	*um*	*basically*	*I mean*	*basically*
wow	*oh*	*no*	*ah*	*but*	*actually*	*like*	*I dunno*	*ah*		*ah*		*ah*	*now*	*I think*	*now*
golly	*right*	*nope*			*basically*	*you know*							*whatever*	*I believe*	*whatever*
see		*yeah, exactly*			*then again*	*I dunno*							*actually*		*actually*
hey		*yeah, yeah*				*anyway(s)*							*maybe*		*maybe*
look						*anyhow*									*probably*
geez						*of course*									*meanwhile*
sure						*see*									*currently*
man						*you see*									*eventually*
yeah						*mind you*									*finally*
no															*hopefully*
															occasionally
															technically
															again
															sure
															you know
															what

Then he begins his sentence. It is remarkable to see how this all works when you put the linguistic magnifying glass to work.

The same pattern can be observed in (88). In this case, Trevor Klinke is engrossed in a long monologue in response to the interviewer's question: *So, what are you going to school for?* In this part of the discussion he is describing how he works with a software package called *Dragon*, a speech detection package that he uses to write his essays.

88.   a.   When I tried to do the scribe thing, it didn't work out too well … when I'm trying to put it up and they're writing it down, I feel as though that was like the final copy and it was kind of- kind of like,

b.   *Oh okay no* that doesn't work, go back, go back. (Trevor Klinke, 20)

Notice how Trevor frames his own response to a previous action. He uses all three Outer Rim positions. First, he uses, *oh*, the attention getter. Second, he acknowledges what he himself has done. Third, he disagrees with his earlier hypothesis. Then he begins his sentence.

The case of all three positions filled at the same time does occur frequently in the data. However, every time all three slots are filled, they follow the same pattern of attention, acknowledge, and agree/disagree, as outlined in Table 6.2.

Note too that the same word can occur in different slots. For example, consider the sequence in (89). In (89c) the Outer Rim comprises three of the same word repeated. Look more closely to see how each one serves a separate function:

Table 6.2 *Slots and contents of the Outer Rim*

ATTENTION	ACKNOWLEDGE	AGREE/DISAGREE
ah	*okay*	*yeah*
oh (boy)	*yes*	*yes, yeah*
gosh	*oh*	*no*
wow	*right*	*nope*
golly		*yeah, exactly*
see		*yeah, yeah*
hey		
look		
geez		
sure		
fine		
man		
yeah		
no		

89.   a. The house on the corner of the schoolyard, on the north-east corner the
             schoolyard, north-west corner, was a woman had all these critters.
         b. [Interviewer] She had a garden, and she had chickens and, and ducks
             and-things, and she had a donkey!
         c. *Yeah, yeah, yeah* this is Yonge-Eglinton. This woman's got a donkey.
             (Jim Lear, 51)

The interviewer, (89b), is incredulous that someone living in a suburban
neighborhood in a large city would have farm animals and expressly a donkey.
Jim replies in (89c) with an attention-getting *yeah,* an acknowledgement, *yeah,*
and an agreement, *yeah.*[4]

It is important to put these Outer Rim phenomena into context. While a variety
of words and combinations of words are possible (and notice how steeped in
meaning they are!) they occur in only 3.2 percent of the sentences. Recall that
I first probed the data by extracting every single canonical sentence in the data.
This is the only way I could find out the overall frequency of these left periphery
features. In sum, the Outer Rim forms are rare, but key components of interaction.

After the Outer Rim comes a slot for a conjunction, e.g. *and, but, because,*
followed by a slot for an adverb, e.g. *then,* as in Table 6.3 and illustrated in
(90). In this example, the three Outer Rim slots are empty and the sentence
begins with a conjunction, *and,* followed by an adverb, *then,* both items which
Schiffrin (1982: 37–39) considers sequential dependency markers.

90.   *And then like* five minutes later a nurse comes to help me. (Alicia Karan, 24)

The words that come next are what I will refer to as discourse markers
(DMs). These words are italicized in (91–92). Notice how they are positioned
between Outer and Inner Rim words. These forms are the focus of this chapter.

91.   a. *And so I think* that wasn't particularly difficult or anything. (Mike
             Dubrovnik, 19)
         b. *Like* there's some stereotypes like. (Caleb Stine, 16)
92.   a. *Yeah oh yeah well you know* you were a little bit at the service. (Daniel
             Peters, 89)
         b. *And like you know* the shower starts ... (Daryn Gadek, 19)

Table 6.3 *Slots and contents*

CONJUNCTION 1	ADVERB 1
and	*then*
because	*now*
but	*actually*
	basically
	then again

Table 6.4 *Sentence starters [SS]*

SLOT 1	SLOT 2 (RARE)
so	*you know*
well	*like*
like	*I dunno*
you know	
I dunno	
anyway(s)	
anyhow	
of course	
see	
you see	
mind you	

By this definition, I will argue that DMs are the words that organize utterances and situate the upcoming sentence in the unfolding discourse. Once we delimit these words and their position, we discover that DMs actually comprise a fairly restricted set, with the vast majority of forms consisting of *so, well, like,* or *you know.* An exhaustive list found in the data is shown in Table 6.4. A second DM can occur, either *you know, like,* or *I dunno,* as in (92). However, this is very rare.

After the DMs, there is a slot for a post-DM conjunction, either *if* or *when,* as in (93).

93. a. *So like if* you need a ride somewhere, everyone knows who you are and where you're going pretty much. (Caleb Stine, 16)
     b. *'Cause like when* I'm dancing like you don't think about anything else. (Betty Mak, 21)

Then, there are three slots for what I will refer to as "Inner Rim" phenomena. In these slots occur subject–verb collocations with a first-person pronoun subject plus a verb, e.g. *I think.* In the discourse-pragmatics literature these constructions are grouped with "modal particles" (Aijmer, 1997). Due to their role in encoding the knowledge or belief the speaker has about the sentence that follows them they are often called "epistemic" (e.g. Thompson and Mulac, 1991). English has several epistemic particles (EP), including *I think, I guess, I believe, I suppose, I know, I suspect,* and *I presume.* They basically tell the hearer what the speaker's views or ideas are about the following statement. Researchers suggest that EPs function as a means to mitigate the force of the utterance (e.g. Brinton, 1996: 232).

When these constructions appear in pre-sentential position (as in those focused on in this study) they often no longer retain their referential meaning, e.g. *I am pondering* for *I think*. Instead, they have lost this meaning and express the speaker's commitment to their utterance. In this way, they make a comment on the sentence that follows. This is why they are sometimes referred to in the literature as "comment clauses" (e.g. Quirk et al., 1985: 977; Thompson, 2002). In the case of *I think*, the construction basically means "I'm not sure," as in (94).

94.   a. [Interviewer] Where did she work as a cook?
        b. *Ah, I think* she worked- . . . *I think* it was a restaurant here. (Kirk Pollock, 18)

Other EPs in the data include *I guess* and *I mean*, as in (95).

95.   a. *I guess* when he was upside down he saw the guy pick it up. (Kirk Pollock, 18)
        b. *I mean*, in Ottawa I can go a-- g-- along the Rideau-Canal or something like that, or I can go kayaking or canoeing in the bush or I can go snowboarding or something like that. So *I mean* I'm never missing home. (Chelsea McMac, 22)

Considerable research has gone into analyzing and explaining EPs. In fact, the same forms can appear in the middle of a sentence or at the end of it, but that is a different story (Denis, 2015; Thompson and Mulac, 1991). Here, I simply want to demonstrate that EPs have a place on the left periphery of the sentence, on the Inner Rim. They are inserted before the sentence begins. To keep these uses in perspective, however, this slot is filled only 1 percent of the time.

It is interesting to discover that adverbs on the left periphery can either go before or after the EPs, as in (96) and (97).

96.   a. *I think now* it's like eight thousand. (Kay Dupuis, 19)
        b. *I think actually* I might have broken my toe. (Simon Van Wilder, 18)

97.   a. *Well actually I think* my grandfather was born in Rouyn Noranda. (Kay Dupuis, 19)
        b. *Actually I think* the person who owned the store called either the school or the police. (Maya Selowsky, 18)

I found no cases of an adverb occurring in both positions in my data. In order to truly establish three separate slots, it was necessary to find cases where all three occur. I searched the largest available corpus, the Corpus of Contemporary American English (COCA). This database is the largest corpus of English in the world comprising 450 million words.[5] A search for strings such as *I think actually* and *actually I think* revealed that the former occurred 164 times while the latter occurred a mere 82 times. Not a single example had the three slots filled. The adverb either comes before or after, but not both. For our purposes, it is sufficient to recognize that the two slots exist.

Table 6.5 *Slots and contents of the Inner Rim*

ADVERB 2	PARENTHETICAL	ADVERB 3
then	*I guess*	*then*
basically	*I mean*	*basically*
now	*I think*	*now*
whatever	*I believe*	*whatever*
actually		*actually*
maybe		*maybe*
		probably
		meanwhile
		currently
		eventually
		finally
		hopefully
		occasionally
		technically
		again
		sure
		you know what

Taken together, the inventory of SSs, comprising Outer Rim forms, DMs, Inner Rim forms, adverbs, conjunctions, and *uhm/uh* shows how rich and intricate the left periphery of the sentence actually is. However, I was amazed to discover that the patterning of words and their positioning was so systematic. Moreover, once the inventory of forms is laid out methodically – as I have done in Table 6.5 – another striking finding emerges. Some words are dated while others transcend generations. Take, for example, the words found in the Outer Rim. Some are decidedly old-fashioned, as in (98), while others are ubiquitous, as in (99).

98. a. *Oh golly*, I forget. Yeah, I don't know. (Elouise Lyntimal, 74)
     f. *Oh geez*, that would be ah in the sixties. (Wendy Carlsberg, 78)
     c. *Oh boy*. Big changes! (Wilbur Carlsberg, 82)

99. a. *Oh my God* my bike got stole. (Alison O'Dwyer, 25)
     b. *Oh my God*. I'm sounding like my parents. (Ryan Dubeau, 61)
     c. *Oh wow* I sweated a lot. (Maxwell Rinkenberger, 22)
     d. *Oh wow*. Well, I knew him and I saw Mae. (Billy Blackwell 60)
     e. *Oh yeah* I took her um and we got some cookies. (Clara Felipe, 18)
     f. *Oh yeah* and we mustn't forget about the assassination. (Jake Ryall, 64)

While the word *oh* is ubiquitous, the words of the second slot of the Outer Rim are – intuitively at least – a more varied lot. Some are circumscribed by age, others are not.

Teenagers may develop new forms for marking the discourse-pragmatic functions typical of sentence initial position, just as *hwæt* changed to *lo* and then to *so* in translations of *Beowulf*. Attention-getters at the beginning of utterances include certain novel forms among teens, as in (100).

100.   If I could go back in time now, I'd tell myself like, "*Yo*, who cares so much about marks right now?" (Daryn Gadek, 19)

Similarly, the EP words of the Inner Rim may be age related as well, as in (101).

101.   a.   That was in September. *And I guess* by Christmas, he proposed. (Ellen Ahlin, 87)
        b.   *I believe* it's less safe. (Lorie Rowoldt, 45)
        c.   *I think* that's something you know to be like really proud of. (Charles Lee, 15)

The DMs, including *so*, *well*, and *you know* do not have an intuitive age interpretation. Only *like*, as in (102), leaves one suspicious of a correlation with teenagers.

102.   a.   *So like if* you see a wolf like, you kind of think there's more around. (Caleb Stine, 16)
        b.   That turned out to be pretty bad. *'Cause like* every time I drink wine I end up puking. (Daryn Gadek, 19)

In the next step of the analysis I will focus on DMs. While all of the other SS types are worthy of study, a comprehensive analysis of all of them is beyond the scope of the analysis presented here. The body of data upon which the following analyses are based comprise all sentences with a DM marker in either column G or H of Table 6.1. As a first step, let us establish the actual number of tokens of each of the main forms, as in Figure 6.1.

In the specific DM slot as defined above there were innumerable forms. However, Figure 6.1 reveals that the vast majority of them are *so*, *well*, *like*, and *you know* in that order of frequency. The next question is how are the main forms in the system distributed by speaker age?

Figure 6.2 displays the frequency of DMs by the date of birth of the speaker. It is evident that the DMs are not all behaving in the same way. There are two distinct trends. Some DMs are not changing at all. The forms *well*, *you know*, and a mixed bag of other forms that occur in the same slot appear at low levels across generations. In contrast, two markers – *so* and *like* – are changing. *So* is decreasing among the oldest speakers but seems to stabilize among the youngest age cohorts. In contrast, *like* increases in a step-wise fashion. It rarely occurs among the speakers born between 1910 and the 1960s. It rises to 20 percent among those born in the 1970s and increases to about 30 percent of all sentence-initial DMs among those born in the 1980s and 1990s. Given this trajectory of

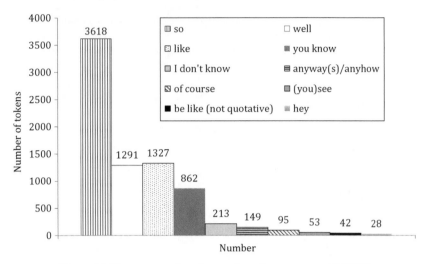

Figure 6.1 Discourse markers by number of occurrences (N=7873)

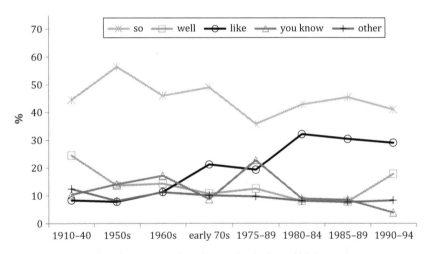

Figure 6.2 Discourse markers by speaker's date of birth

change, let's test for the effect of sex and determine whether women are leading this change as might be expected given Labov's Principles 2–4.

Figure 6.3 divides the main DM forms undergoing change – *so* and *like* – by male vs. female speakers, and shows a period of transition in the DM system across people born in the twentieth century. Where once *so* dominated as the most frequent SS, the DM *like* has incrementally encroached on it.

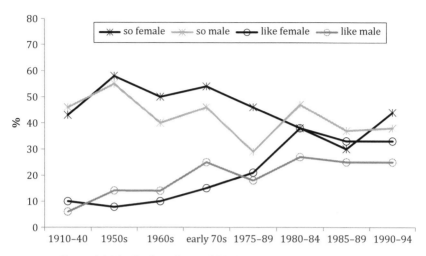

Figure 6.3 Distribution of *so* and *like* by speaker sex and date of birth

Interestingly, the rise of *like* was not originally distinguished by male or female; however, since the speakers born in the 1980s it has taken off among females, and among all the youngest generations there is a widening gap between male and female speakers. As females have eschewed *so*, males among the 1980–1989 cohort are retaining it. However, notice that both females and males have a peak in apparent time in the 1980–1984 group for the incoming DM – *like*. Keep in mind that the conservative frequency levels for the youngest speakers (born 1990–1994) align with their parents' patterns. In sum, the DMs exhibit marked sociolinguistic embedding and all the hallmarks of linguistic change in progress.

The next question is whether or not these social trends are the result of reorganization of the discourse-pragmatic system. In other words, what is changing – the marker(s) or the function(s)? Is *like* taking over *so* or is English developing a new discourse-pragmatic function?

In the next section I will test for what each of these DMs may be doing. Previous research has extensively documented the context of DMs, in particular the nature of the conversational turn, the type of interactional context, and discourse type (e.g. Traugott, 2013). These functions are, of course, overlapping since answers to questions are always new turns and reformulations are a subset of continuous discourse. However, the following set of categorization schemas gives us insight into the behavior of DMs in well-defined discourse situations. You will notice that in some cases the categorization schemas overlap. This is an inevitable characteristic of the diverse roles these forms have in discourse. Their functions are not black and white.

Topic continuity and interaction

Each sentence was coded for topic continuity and type of interaction. New topics can be introduced in the discourse in answer to direct questions, as in (103–105).

103.   a. [Interviewer] Has anything ever happened at one of these where you're just kind of like, "Oh my God, what did I do?"
       b. Uhm *well* there have been occasions where you ah drink more than you should. (Diego Ferreira, 18)

104.   a. [Interviewer] So, what's your medium?
       b. *Well* my main thing before I went to art school was photography. (Anne Muscat, 24)

105.   a. [Interviewer] And all your grandparents as well?
       b. *Ah well* they're originally from Europe. (Richard Gruensten, 26)

New topics can also arise spontaneously from individuals, as in (106).

106.   a. You wouldn't be like, "You're English." And then my mother- *you know what* this is the weirdest thing ... (Annie Muscat, 24)
       b. [Interviewer] He'll have to take up golf or something like that. Yeah, something like that. *Oh* and now, I think his new thing is, he wants to buy a Mercedes. (Betty Mak, 21)

Topic continuity is more often the case. The interviewer may keep the speaker on the same topic as in (107).

107.   a. It was a five pound rainbow trout. [Interviewer] What did you do? [Kay] *Oh* I took a picture of it. (Kay Pollock, 18)
       b. We'd run around in this abandoned mine-shaft. [Interviewer] No way! [Simon] *Well*, not inside it, but on the outside. (Simon Vanwilder, 18)

Individuals may continue topics on their own, shifting from one event to a related one, as in (108).

108.   a. And my sister, she has a baby now. *So* it's the restart of everything else. *So*, it's exciting. He is two months old now. (Mary Belleville, 17)
       b. My mother used to keep the- keep some of the milk and I don't know how. *Anyway* it was in this- she put it in this big metal- it was about that high. A metal churn and it was my job to churn the crank 'til the butter formed. (Kylie Everingham, 91)

The interesting question is: how do the DMs distribute across these discourse-pragmatic contexts? Figure 6.4 displays the distribution of DMs by type of conversational turn and topic.

Figure 6.4 shows that there is a contrast between the distribution of DMs in sentences that represent old and new topics in continuous discourse. Old topics that are contained in ongoing talk by the same speaker are

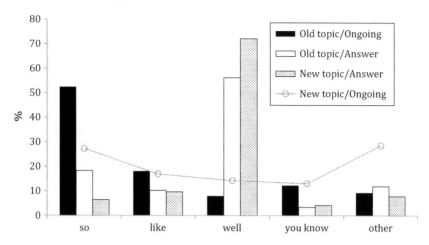

Figure 6.4 Distribution of DMs by type of conversational turn

overwhelmingly marked by *so*. However, new topics that are ongoing (rather than answers to questions) may have any one of the DMs, *like, well, you know*, etc. These sentences – represented by the circle marked line – have a low frequency of DMs in general. In contrast, notice the discourse-pragmatic function for "Answers." Here the DM *well* is by far the preferred form, whether or not the topic is old or new. Interestingly, of all the DMs that have been studied previously, the most regularly cited and well-defined one is *well*. It is reported to be a response marker, a discourse boundary marker, a response utterance initiator, a generalized starter, and an attention-getter. Figure 6.4 confirms this consensus by demonstrating that *well* has the most highly circumscribed function of the bunch. When people answer questions, they are likely to say *well* first. In contrast, when discourse is ongoing and an individual's sentences unfold one after another on the same topic, the preferred marker is *so*.

Discourse type

All the sentences were coded for what the speaker was doing. Is she telling a story, was the sentence part of an ongoing interchange between the speaker and the interviewer, or is the interviewee just talking away?

Storytelling is frequent in the data. In (109a) a host of different DMs are used by the same speaker as he tells a story about an explosion one day in science class. In (109b) a single DM, *like*, does most of the same work in a story about a computer message to a boyfriend.

109.   a. But *ah anyway*, in grade ten, he decided to demonstrate thermodynamics. And *so* what he did is he took a balloon and he partially filled it with gas from the gas jets in the lab, and then blew air into it as well in what he thought was the right mixture. And then he said, "*Okay,* everybody back to the back of the room." "*Boy,* this is gonna be great!" And then he put on his safety goggles and he stood over at the side of the room, lit a bunsen burner, and then from the side of the room, he pushed this balloon full of gas, because it floated. There was about that- that weight that it floated over to the flame. *Well,* he just about blew the windows out of the classroom. It was an incredible bang! You could feel it in your chest, that's how big a bang it was. *Well,* people came running from everywhere. And he looked pretty sheepish. I don't think he'd quite planned for that kind of noise. And *so* he was quite a character … (Ken Smuckers, 53)

        b. *And then* he already set up his webcam *so* I could see his reaction. *So* he's like, "Okay." *So* I sent it to him. And I was like, "But don't turn it up." Because his roommate was already there. *So* I'm like, "Just listen to it on your headphones."*So* then he listened to it. And it was just cute because I could see him smiling. (Clara Felipe, 18)

Other sentences are part of back and forth interaction, as in (110e) and (111f).

110.   a. Head cheese, that's what they make.
        b. [Interviewer] I remember that.
        c. Yeah. Yeah.
        d. [Interviewer] From the old days.
        e. *Yeah yeah yeah. Anyway, so* where were we?
        f. [Interviewer[: You were talking about high school … (Kylie Everingham, 91)

111.   a. [Interviewer] What about your grandpa that you were close to too? What was he like?
        b. *Oh* he was a typical Polish man really.
        c. [Interviewer] Yeah?
        d. Yeah.
        e. [Interviewer] Like what? What do you think that means?
        f. *I don't know* he just like- he was just like a really like relaxed guy you know. (Kirk Pollock, 18)

Many sentences were inside direct quotes, as in (112).

112.   a. I always forget that. I think like, "*Oh* I've put in my time with music." (Carl Balders, 24)
        b. I had to tell them to like, "*Okay,* you have to take that elsewhere." (Calvin Murphy, 20)

Let's now see how the DMs are distributed according to this categorization of function in Figure 6.5.

Figure 6.5 shows that DM *so* is used most often used in storytelling and ongoing discourse, but rarely in quotes and only moderately in interaction. DM

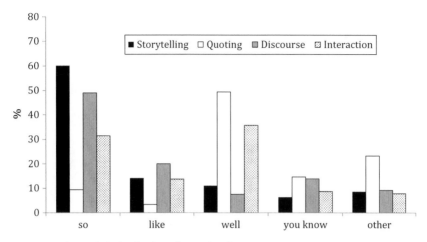

Figure 6.5 Distribution of DMs by discourse type

well is used for quoting and interaction. Notice that *like* and *you know* are relatively rare in any of these categories.

Conversational turn

Each sentence was also coded for the type of conversational turn. In spoken discourse there is extensive reformulation of utterances, as in (113). In addition, I distinguished new turns, as in (114), and ongoing discourse, as in (115).

113. Reformulation
    a. ... And it's a pretty- *like* it's like a five-star. (Tiffany Richter, 51)
    b. I have a lot of school spirit and a lot of- *so* they thought I'd be a good candidate for it. (Mary Belleville, 17)

114. New turn
    a. [Interviewer] Like what sorts of things did you do for work?
    b. *Well*, I was in security at the Embassies. (Daniel Peters, 89)

115. Ongoing discourse
    a. And you had to belong to the Legion to get in to it. *So* I joined it in fifty-six. (Daniel Peters, 89)
    b. Well 'cause the farm was there right *so* we had to rebuild it. (Maya Selowsky, 18)

Figure 6.6 plots the distribution of DMs in these contexts.

Figure 6.6 shows that only two contexts are distinguished by DM. New turns are often marked by *well* while ongoing discourse tends towards *so*. Reformulations may be marked by any one of the DMs, as indicated by the X'd line.

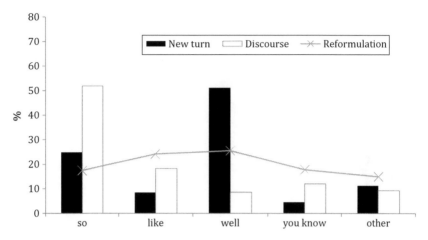

Figure 6.6 Distribution of DMs by conversational turn

In summary, once function is accounted for (even if only cursorily, as I have done here) we discover that some DM forms and functions are stable across the generations. The DM *well* is used for marking inception. This demonstrates that certain forms may endure for a long time. In other cases, "while particular forms may, in fact, be quite transient, the pragmatic functions themselves are preserved" (Brinton, 1996: 278), as in the example from *Beowulf*.

At the same time, these patterns raise a number of questions regarding the function of the rising form *like*. Andersen (2001: 269, 273) suggests it is a discourse link. Instead, I have demonstrated that *like* shows no particular tendency to be a continuity marker (Figure 6.4), a marker of conversational turn (Figure 6.5), or a marker of reformulations (Figure 6.6). However, up to this point *like* has been present for all age groups combined.

To find out how *like* may be changing over time we need to be able to see how people of different ages use it. Figure 6.7 plots the distribution of *like* according to the main patterns uncovered in the data, now distinguishing the different age cohorts in the data.

Figure 6.7 reveals a number of important facts about pre-sentential *like* across the twentieth century. First, there is a steady increase in frequency across functions, most with a peak in apparent time among the 1980–1984 or 1985–1989 cohorts (see also D'Arcy, 2005 and forthcoming). However, notice that although *like* is increasing across all these contexts, one discourse function stands out – the use of *like* for continuous discourse. This context has always been the leading use of *like* from 1910 onwards, but seems to distinguish itself from the other contexts by 1975–1989 and has reached a frequency of nearly 50 percent among the teenagers on the leading edge of change, born

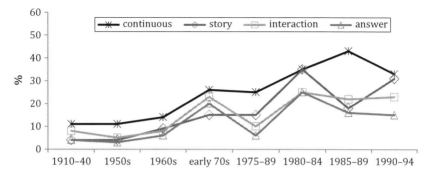

Figure 6.7 Distribution of *like* by function by speaker date of birth

between 1985 and 1989. Thus, instead of spreading uniformly across all discourse-pragmatic uses in pre-sentential position as a "catch all" DM (Pichler and Levey, 2010: 25), DM *like* appears to be specializing. While *like* can be used in many different types of contexts, teenagers appear to be using it as a more orderly marker of discourse continuity.

Despite the pinnacle of usage among teenagers, notice they cannot be responsible for this development. The trend towards *like* has been in progress at least since the individuals born in the early 1900s and has slowly progressed across generations. This means that the parents and grandparents of the teenagers in the early twenty-first century are all part of the story. Those born between 1980 and 1984 in Figure 6.7 show signs of being on the front lines of change. They were in late adolescence – at the height of their incrementation process – when the data were collected. This is visible in the peaks in apparent time in Figure 6.7 and provides a solid indication of an accelerating linguistic change. A methodological note is important. If we only had language data from the adult population – those born between 1910 and 1970 – the interpretation of this trajectory would have been that *like* is a ubiquitous DM. However, with the younger generations in the picture the distinct hallmark of linguistic change in progress emerges: a linear progression in apparent time, rising to a peak among the generation pushing the change forward.

What does this proposed sentential marker look like? The examples in (116) and (117) provide an illustration from two speakers at opposite ends of the age spectrum. Ellen Ahlin, aged 87, is telling the story of how she met her husband. Erin Gadek, aged 16, recounts an incident regarding her sister's clothes. Compare the use of the DMs *so*, *and*, and *like* in each example.

116.   a. *So* I didn't make any comment to that.
        b. *So* we get back to the door
        c. *And* he said "Ah, well, what about Saturday night?"

       d. I said, "Oh, I tell you what. Phone me and if you still want to take me to the show Saturday, we'll make arrangements."

       e. He said, "I don't know your name, I don't know your phone number."

       f. *So* I gave him my name and I gave him my phone number.

       g. He phoned me

       h. *And* we made arrangements to go to a show. (Ellen Ahlin, 87)

117.   a. *Like* my sister came home from Europe

       b. *Like* she brought all her European clothes back

       c. *And* she has so many nice things

       d. *'Cause like* I'll ask her to borrow it

       e. *And* she doesn't want me to

       f. *And* it's like upsetting

       g. *Like* it's really nice

       h. *Like* you don't find this stuff in Canada. (Erin Gadek, 16)

In light of Figure 6.3 which documents a changeover between *so* and *like*, we may now speculate about what is going on. Ellen Ahlin, aged 87, uses *and* and *so* to mark continuity in her story whereas Erin Gadek uses *and* and *like*. Although we know that *like* is increasingly being used in sentence initial position generally, this particular use appears to be breaking away from the rest. It would not be unprecedented for a DM in this position to gradually evolve into a grammatical marker. For example, Sankoff and Brown (1976) documented the development of a relative pronoun from an earlier bracketing device. It is also the case that some languages have markers at the beginning of sentences to link sentences with the same topic. Maybe *like* is becoming one of those.

What's a topic marker?
A topic marker is a grammatical word that introduces the topic of a sentence. It occurs in the same position as a subject and adds emphasis to it. The topic marker is said to function something like English *as for*, *on the topic of*, or *regarding*, e.g. *As for Sali, she likes cats.*

What does the use of sentence starters tell us about teen language?

Sentence starters are part of the grammar of spoken English. The forms and phrases that occur before an utterance begins are not superfluous but enable speakers to navigate conversation. In this analysis, I defined a particular slot between the Outer and Inner Rim as the DM slot. In this position, I discovered that contemporary English has four main markers – *so*, *like*, *you know*, and *well*. Everyone in the community uses these forms from pre-adolescents to octogenarians. Moreover, the discourse-pragmatic functions they mark are stable. A speaker will inevitably use *well* in responses to questions and either *so* or *like* in successive sentences on the same topic depending on their age. A lot of people think that *like* is a teenage thing, but the people who started using *like* as a sentence starter were not the present-day teenagers, but their grandparents or great-grandparents. The use of *like* in this position has been increasing steadily to the point where it may well become a more permanent (and eventually more highly regarded) part of the grammar. Next time someone starts a sentence notice which words comes out first. It will tell you a lot about the meaning of what is about to be said. Like that's the whole reason for a sentence starter in the first place.

Language puzzle

In Chapter 6, I argued that people use many different words and phrases at the beginning of a sentence and this is changing over time. In order to provide a restricted but accountable mini-sample to test this out, I have extracted a relatively frequent subject noun phrase, *my mother*, from the TTC data and the TEC data only from speakers born before 1920. This should provide a contrast for DM use in a restricted, but constant context. The examples are copied below. Use this data set to discover the answers to the questions below. Use proportions rather than raw token numbers so the data can be compared. Remember that conjunctions, e.g. *because*, and adverbs, e.g. *maybe*, are on the Outer Rim. Epistemic markers, *I mean*, *I think*, are on the Inner Rim. DMs are positioned between them. Consult Table 6.1 for guidance.

a. How often do DMs occur overall in this mini sample?
b. Who uses DMs more, the younger or older individuals?
c. Who uses DMs more, male or female individuals?
d. Is there a difference as to which DMs the older and younger speakers use?
e. Who uses a more varied set of DMs?

Answers
a. *12/79, 15.2 percent overall. The majority of sentences have no DM.*
b. *The younger individuals use DMs 16 percent (N=9/55); the older individuals use DMs 12.5 percent (N=3/24).*
c. *Females use DMs 9.8 percent (N=4/41); males use them 21 percent (N=8/38).*
d. *Older speakers use "well." Younger speakers use "so," "I dunno," "like," and "well."*
e. *Younger males use the most varied DMs. Indeed, they use all of them. Young females only use "like."*

Examples of sentences with subject "my mother" in the TTC and individuals born before 1920 in the TEC. Females indicated as "F." Males indicated as "M." Younger indicated as "Y." Older indicated as "O." Total = 79.

FY   because my mother wants to cram all of it into that room

FY   because my mother's family is French

FY   Like literally they kept it a secret until my mother was five months pregnant

FY   not because my mother wouldn't get us different clothes but because

FY   My mother's family all lives in Quebec like in Gaspe

FY   because my mother doesn't do so well with the reading of the maps

FY   My mother has a really big family. She has six brothers

FY   My mother keeps more in touch with her sisters and that's

FY   my mother was putting in like you have to put something

FY   My mother will clean underneath the fridge with a Q-Tip

FY   I don't think that my grandmother cares that much but my mother does

FY   My mother is really worried about what people think

FY   Maybe my mother's more in tune to people's character and stuff I

MY   so my mother and sister decided they want- to come

MY   My mother calls it the Pimp-mobile

MY   'Cause my mother would freak out about that sort of thing

MY   I don't know my mother came back from the Bahamas and bought me a pipe

MY   my mother is I think forty-eight my father's about forty-six

MY   my mother they met my father knew my mother's older brother

MY   My mother buys most of my clothes to be honest

MY   And I don't know my- my mother and I do this thing where occasionally we just

MY   So I don't know my mother and I were doing this one day

MY   Like my mother looked at him and my mother told me afterwards

MY   and my mother told me afterwards she was afraid

MY   but my mother went to the head of the Department

MY   My mother- my mother and I fight over the phone

MY   Like a while ago my mother was trying to get in touch with my father

MY   My mother was in the room she was frantic because she was

FY   because my mother perhaps because she came- she came to Canada

FY   my Mother is some payroll accountant

FY   Like I didn't get a part-time job like my mother was nagging me to do.

FY   my mother and I we went to a priest who had psychic abilities

MY   My mother and father of course but when they're working

MY   my mother we're- we're- we're like best friends basically

MY   but my Mother is just a little more intellectual

MY   my Mother is a supervisor at

MY   my Mother is a supervisor at- at a car seat factory

MY   because I know that my Mother and Father favours the oldest

MY   but my- my mother didn't really have the time to fulfill that sort

MY   Well my mother, she's strict in the sense that ...

MY   but my mother had a very unique trick which I counteracted with

MY   my mother always jokes that she never has to push me to do

MY   but my mother t-- has this tendency just to say things without

FY   My mother doesn't say the same thing

FY   Like my mother has a very ... she's a very surface kind of

FY   and then my mother sprayed me in the face with bear-spray while we

FY   but my mother lets me stay at home and doesn't make me pay rent

FY   and my mother subsequently broke

FY   I think my mother would find your coming out story absolutely hysterical

FY   because my mother was not going to be mean enough to call her kid

FYI   mean my mother happened to have an unfortunate last name but at

FY   I don't have mine because my mother lost it

FY   My mother's only driven with me twice and we crashed both

FY   because my mother wouldn't like let us kneel on the chairs

FY   I think my mother did part of it and then she gave up too

FO   my mother's father was a musician with the Toronto-Symphony

FO   as my mother would say, "Fancy-schmancy types of schools."

FO   and my mother and I lived in a series of flats in the west-end

FO   my mother still lives in the west-end.

FO   and my mother's side they came to Canada from England

FO   well my mother moved to Toronto in- during World-War-Two

FO   but my mother entered me in a beautiful baby contest

FO   and my mother lives within sight of it

FO   my mother and I's circumstance obviously made sense. We were

FO   well if my mother wanted to go shopping, one we'd go to Simpson's

FO   my mother would occasionally go to- my mother- the great

FO   my mother and I lived in one room and we didn't have any

MO   my mother was born in Scotland, so she came to Canada when

MO   my mother's father was a- a sergeant in the O-P-P.

MO   my mother was a single parent.

MO   And my mother worked, my grandmother worked.

MO   I think my mother had a lot of help.

MO   I guess my mother has always been around. My mother is still alive.

MO   My mother is still alive.

MO   my mother remarried. We didn't see much of her really then

MO   my mother used to say that she thought it was candy

MO   and my mother just didn't wanna have any of that.

MO   my mother was quite strict about us taking it.

MO   Well, my mother sent us to dance class and I learnt to do a lot

7   Sentence enders

Finish with a flourish

Now that you are attuned to how people start their sentences, now pay close attention to how they end their sentences. Instead of the nice, neat packages that we see in books, e.g. *Sali is a sociolinguist*, when people talk they inevitably end their sentences with a embellishment of some sort, like a linguistic *TA DAH*, e.g. *Sali is a sociolinguist, you know* or *Sali is a sociolinguist, right?* or *Sali is a sociolinguist or something like that.* Teenagers end their sentences in a lot of different ways, as in (118).

118.   a. I do feel guilty once in awhile *you know*. (Craig Cavalheiro, 19)
        b. I was like eight or nine *right?* (Tina Mancini, 11)
        c. They're like, really quiet and like *whatever*. (Clara Felipe, 16)
        d. Oh all these silly things, well you just- you live with them *so*. (Rachel Patry, 63)
        e. They're going to be just manufacturing DVDs *and all that shit*. (Carl Balders, 24)
        f. Yeah and aren't you like super smart *or something?* (Eleanor Colum, 14)
        g. See, but we wouldn't go into smoking *or anything*. (Catherine Hui, 19)
        h. His sister's like a rebel and has piercings everywhere and goes out *and all that stuff*. (Julie Wang, 14)
        i. They don't really let you do that now, well with the double-cohort and *what not*. (Charles Lee, 15)

The question is, how do the sentence enders (SEs) that teenagers use compare to the rest of the community? Did the individuals in (118) just make up these forms willy-nilly? Is this proliferation of SEs a hallmark of decay in the language? First, let's find out what people actually use.

This study was conducted with my student Derek Denis. We extracted all the SEs from 87 individuals from the TEC/TTC who were strategically selected to provide a balanced sample by age and sex, providing 2,200 tokens (Tagliamonte and Denis, 2010). Figure 7.1 shows the frequency of the main SEs in each age cohort.

Certain SEs are strongly associated with one generation or another. For example, *you know*, as in (119a), is by far the most frequent form among the individuals born between 1910 and 1940. A notable characteristic among those

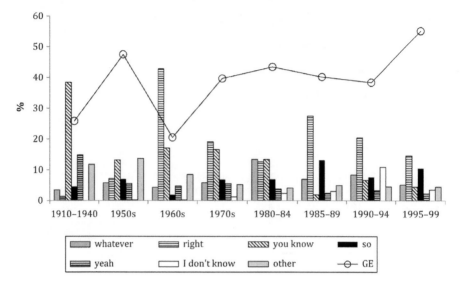

Figure 7.1 Distribution of SEs across generations

born in the 1960s is the use of *right*, as in (119b). Individuals born between 1980 and 1984 use the most *whatever*, as in (119c), and sentences ending with *so* are more frequent among those born between 1985 and 1989 than in any other generation, as in (119d). The use of *yeah* and forms grouped as "other" is more frequent among the oldest generation, as in (119e).

119.   a. There were nice little cottages when we lived here, *you know*. (Ellen Ahlin, 87)
        b. She gets some of the Canadian television, *right*? (Olivia Holtby, 53)
        c. They had to have an up-do *or whatever*. (Vivian Bustamante, 15)
        d. Whenever I need to go a quote-unquote "girl thing" Peter and I go together, *so*. (Jason Levine, 17)
        e. Oh we- we grew up with radio oh *yeah*. (Sherry Brooks, 72)

This shows us that everyone in the community uses the same forms, but to greater or lesser degrees depending on their age. Further, each generation has its favored sentence ender.

Sentence enders that generalize

Among the most prominent SEs are "general extenders," GEs, in Figure 7.1 (the circled line). These are a group of phrases that evoke "some larger set" (Dubois, 1992: 198), as in (120).

120.   a. Planting a garden *or something like that.* (Christopher O'Neil, 11)
         b. Britney Spears or N'Sync or Backstreet Boys *or anything like that.*
             (Amanda Levy, 12)
         c. So we get our student card, and a TTC card *and stuff like that* (Charles
             Lee, 15)
         d. Someone can tell me like a really scary story about ghosts *and things.*
             (Jose-Pinheiro Galvao, 12)
         e. Yeah, lots of towels and sinks *and stuff.* After like, curling irons and *all
             that stuff.* (Quanisha Howard, 11)

GEs generalize from a preceding referent to the larger group of items to which that referent belongs. In each example, the underlined items are the referents and GEs are in italics. For example, (120a) refers to the set of activities one does around the house, (120b) to a set of bands, (120c) to the variety of cards teenagers require, (120d) to items that are scary, and (120e) to things that might be found in a bathroom. The literature contains many names for these kinds of sentence enders, including "set marking tags" (Dines, 1980), "vague category identifiers" (Channell, 1994), "extension particles" (Dubois, 1992), "approximation markers" (Erman, 1995: 136), and "general extenders" (e.g. Cheshire, 2007; Denis, 2011; Dines, 1980; Overstreet, 1999; Pichler and Levey, 2011; Tagliamonte and Denis, 2010; Winter and Norrby, 2000), among others. I will adopt the term general extender or GE here. The notion of extension is found in many of these labels, but there is also common association of GEs with vagueness and approximation (Dines, 1980: 19). Speakers use a GE in order "to suggest the multitude of possible elements of the set" that they are thinking or talking about (Dubois, 1992: 182).

Research shows that GEs are conditioned by social factors such as age, sex, education, and socioeconomic class (Dubois, 1992; Stubbe and Holmes, 1995). Other research suggests they encode various interactional functions (Aijmer, 1985b), marking politeness (Overstreet and Yule, 1997; Winter and Norrby, 2000) or topic shift or change of speaker (Dubois, 1992; Schiffrin, 1982). GEs have also been found to pattern grammatically in terms of their morphosyntactic/semantic features (Aijmer, 1985b; Cheshire, 2007; Dines, 1980; Overstreet and Yule, 1997).

Prototypical GEs have a common function and follow a basic template where a connector is required, a quantifier or a generic is necessary, and the comparative is optional, as in Table 7.1. The first element in the GE is a conjunction, either *and* or *or*, although occasionally GEs occur with no connector, as in (121).

121.   I like a lot of stuff. Classic rock. Pink Floyd, Led Zeppelin, The Who *all that
        stuff.* (Craig Carvalheiro, 19)

The connector is typically followed by a quantifier such as *all*, *every*, or *some*. The third element is a generic noun, such as *thing* or *stuff*. Lastly, an optional

Table 7.1 *Template for prototypical general extenders*

Connector	Quantifier	Generic	Comparative
and	*all*	*thing(s)*	*like that*
or	*every*	*stuff*	*sort of*
	some	*people*	*kind of*
	any	*one*	*type of*
	the odd	*where*	*of that kind*
	the whole	*shit*	*of that sort*
	no	*crap*	*of that type*
		baloney	*around there*
			to that effect

comparative appears either at the end of the construction as in *and stuff like that* or in the middle as in *and that kind of stuff*.

In addition to these typical GE combinations, there are also a group of forms that do not follow the pattern in Table 7.1 but perform a similar extension function. These include *or whatever* (122a), and *and so on* (122b), among others (122c).

122.   a.   Like are you scared of like demon type thingies or you scared of like real life killers *or whatever*? (Katherine Fan, 12)
       b.   And so we just got really close and then we met other guys through them and like the girls' boyfriends and them *and so on*. (Lina Delmonico, 16)
       c.   So, you just kind of have to stop, and go grab another one *and such*. (Craig Thompson, 18)

The sets GEs refer to can be anything from common natural classes such as types of insects, as in (123), to sets that are a bit more tricky to infer, as in (124a). What else would shoes be like having been soaked in soda pop besides sticky? What are the things that go with *winter* in (124b)?

123.   No, I had a tarantula crawl on my arm. In the mall, they had like a whole lot of flies and tarantulas *and stuff*. (Tina Mancini, 11)
124.   a   And there was this one time that we flooded the bees out with pop. Which was not a good idea, because it made our shoes sticky *and stuff*. (Christian Laterman, 19)
       b.   That's cool. Yeah hockey's great. I just think it's such a great sport. 'Cause I really like winter and stuff. (Dana Naskauskaas, 17)

This is the crux of the issue. Are GEs changing in such a way that they started out referring to a readily identifiable set and have evolved to the point where they no longer do and are instead used for any vague generalization?

Simultaneously, it appears that certain GEs are more typical of individuals of one age over another. Is it the case that certain GEs are taking over the system – for example the frequently attested *and stuff*, among teenagers, as in (125)?

125.   a. Lots of towels and sinks *and stuff*. (Quanisha Howard, 11)
        b. I wrote her a letter *and stuff*. (Vivian Bustamante, 16)
        d. 'Cause doesn't Mario like own a house and *stuff*, like. (Katherine Berazzi, 18)
        e. Well, my leg was all twisty and *stuff* and yeah. (Greg Parkinson, 16)
        f. We're going to write songs and *stuff*. (Finnegan Conner, 17)

Before dissecting the speech community, let's first get a broader perspective by considering the historical record.

Historical perspective

A check of the OED reveals that GEs have been present in the English language for many centuries. The earliest forms appear to have been the fixed expression types, such as *and such* and *and so forth*, as in (126).

126.   a. And *swa forþ*. (*c*.1000 Ælfric, *Gram*. (Z.) xxv. 144)
        b. Cures Collicks, Belly-Ach, and such. (1652 *News from Lowe Countreys* 6)
        c. Bark-duste, psidie, balaustie, mumme and sich like. (*c*.1425 tr. *Arderne's Treat. Fistula* 74)

Other early GEs are *and things* in (127a) while *and stuff* is not attested until the late 1600s. Notice that even at earlier times the structures align with the template in Table 7.1. This means that GEs, despite being non-standard, have not only been around for a long time, they have also kept the same structure over centuries.

127.   a. With Ruffes and Cuffes, and Fardingales, *and things*. (1596, William Shakespeare, *The Taming of the Shrew*)
        b. She turned to me and said, "Lewis, I find you pretend to give the Duke notions of the mathematics, *and stuff*." (1697, J. Lewis, *Memoirs of the Duke of Gloucester*)
        c. And as for you, you want a woman..to sit at your feet, and cry "O caro! O bravo!" whilst you read your Shakspeares, and Miltons, *and stuff*. (1852, William Thackeray, *Henry Esmond*, III. iv. 110)

GEs are said to be typical of spoken, but not written language (Cheshire, 2007). They are typically associated with speech and are eschewed in writing, eliciting "disfavorable judgment" (Dubois, 1992: 198). Since the largest source of older varieties of language is the written word, the OED dates for the earliest examples of GEs are conservative at best. Figure 7.2 provides a timeline of several of the GEs found in the Toronto data taken from the OED (Tagliamonte and Denis, 2010: 340, Figure 1).

	Middle English		Early Modern			Modern		
	14	15	16	17	18	19	20	21
and such	(1400–1450) ---							
and so forth			(1574) --					
and things			(1596) --					
et cetera				(1640) ------------------------------------				
and stuff				(1697) ------------------------------				
and that					(1702) ------------------------------			
or something						(1814) ------------------------		
or whatever							(1905) ---------------	
and crap							(1951) ----------	
and shit							(1957) --------	

Figure 7.2 Timeline of earliest attestation of general extenders (OED)

The earliest GEs were *and such* and *and so forth*. It is interesting that *and such* can be found among teenagers, as in (128), while not a single token of *and so forth* is attested in any of the corpora, teenagers or otherwise.

128.   So, you just kind of have to stop and go grab another one *and such*. (Craig Thompson, 18)

GEs with *and* developed first and those with *or* arose somewhat later, in the early 1800s and *or whatever* even later, in the early 1900s (Tagliamonte and Denis, 2010). Considering the time depth of English GEs (see example (126a) from Ælfric 1000), GEs are probably an ancient feature of English, perhaps a foundational component of human language. There are indications that Germanic, Romance, and other language families have their own GEs (see Overstreet, 1999: 8), which suggests that GEs are simply part of the way humans communicate.

Contemporary perspective

GEs are one of the most extensively studied discourse-pragmatic features in the literature. Since Dines' (1980) foundational study of GEs over 25 years ago many research studies have emerged (Aijmer, 1985b, 2002; Cheshire, 2007; Dubois, 1992; Overstreet, 1999; Stubbe and Holmes, 1995; Winter and Norrby, 2000; Youssef, 1993). Each study has attempted in its own way to explain how different factors condition GE usage generally and the individual types specifically.

A common set of forms is reported, including: *or something (like that), and everything (like that), and things (like that), and stuff (like that)*. Some GE types or categories (e.g. those containing *stuff* and *whatever*) are more frequent in large urban centers such as Toronto, Canada (e.g. Tagliamonte and Denis, 2010) or London, England (e.g. Stenström et al., 2002). On the whole, however, there is remarkable consistency in the inventory of main forms across divergent geographic locales, social groups, and registers.

A frequent observation is that GEs are rising in frequency, with a greater usage among younger individuals and in particular, females (Denis, 2011; Stubbe and Holmes, 1995; Tagliamonte and Denis, 2010). Further, in part due to the wide-ranging variety of GE variants, from almost literary (e.g. *and so forth*) to vernacular and non-standard (e.g. *and that, and shit*), different GE variants are often associated with varying levels of formality, register, or style. Certain GE variants are also often associated with class and other socioeconomic indicators. For example, GEs such as *and things* are associated with middle-class individuals while others such as *and that* or *and that lot* (Stenström and Andersen, 1996: 102) are associated with working-class individuals (Cheshire, 2007: 165) and possibly have varietal associations (e.g. British).

The properties of the GE generic (e.g. *stuff, things*) have been shown to influence the choice of GE variant. Grammatically, a form such as *stuff* refers to mass nouns, such as *water*, as in (129a), and a form such as *thing(s)* refers to count nouns, such as *flyers*, as in (129b).

129.   a.   ... the water *and stuff.* (Elizabeth McKinley, 19)
       b.   ... I put up flyers *and things.* (Jason Levine, 17)

Further, inferring the set to which the GE refers is not always straightforward. It is easy to retrieve a set for the referent *running and paddling* in (130a). It is much more difficult to retrieve a set for the referent *a friend of the family* in (130b). What goes in the set of "a friend of the family"? It is difficult to say. You either are a friend or not and what else might be in the set?

130.   a.   I had really good endurance, like when it comes to running and paddling *and stuff.* (Craig Thompson, 18)
       b.   I just kind of went with like a friend of the family *and stuff.* (Craig Thompson, 18)

These examples demonstrate that some GEs do not always function to generalize to a set (Aijmer, 1985b). If not, they may have other functions.

Such changes in GEs may be reflected in other characteristics, for example the nature of the referent or the length of the GE in terms of number of words. Compare *and things like that* to *and things*. Researchers have argued that longer GEs may evolve first and shorter ones arise afterwards due to shortening and expansion.

Researchers have proposed the following trajectory for GEs. First, they generalize from a logical set that is closely tied to the meaning of the generic (mass or count). At a later stage, the tie to a particular set weakens and the GE expands to additional contexts and compresses into a shorter unit.

Social constraints

The most commonly cited factors in GE usage are social. The foremost of these is the correlation of GE use with particular socioeconomic groups. In a comparison of two corpora of Australian English, Dines (1980: 19) links higher overall frequency of GEs to working-class speech, with the form *and that* being one of the most notable (Dines, 1980: 21). In addition, Dines reports on a number of perception experiments confirming that people associate high GE use with working-class speech. This is echoed in Cheshire's (2007) more recent study in England where *and that* is also associated with working-class speech (Cheshire, 2007: 165). Both studies are consistent with the OED entry for *and that*, which has the following comment: "now chiefly in substandard speech or representations of it." Other GEs such as *and stuff* and *and things* occur among middle-class speakers (Dines, 1980: 20). Similar correlations of particular forms to specific social classes are found in other languages. In Montreal French, for example, the working class disproportionately favored the form *affaires de même*, while the professional class preferred *choses comme ça* (Dubois, 1992).

It has also been suggested that GE use is a feature of youth speech (Dubois, 1992; Stubbe and Holmes, 1995). Evidence for this comes from Dubois' (1992) real-time comparison of two corpora of Montreal French, one from 1971 (Sankoff and Sankoff, 1973) and one from 1984 (Thibault and Vincent, 1990). Through multiple regression analysis of the frequency of GEs per person, Dubois found that age was the strongest factor influencing GE use with young people using them the most in both years. This finding led Dubois to conclude that GE usage is an age-graded phenomenon and not a change in progress (Dubois, 1992: 185). In New Zealand, Stubbe and Holmes (1995: 72) found that in the middle class, young people used nearly twice as many GEs as their older counterparts. However, when class and gender were studied together, the users with the highest frequency were the young middle-class females and young working-class males (Stubbe and Holmes, 1995: 77). They provide two explanations for these usage patterns. First, GEs can function to mark in-group affiliation (Stubbe and Holmes, 1995: 83), suggesting that people use them more when they're conversing with friends and associates. Second, GEs are often associated with young middle-class females, suggesting that this social group may be leading a change (Stubbe and Holmes, 1995: 83).

GEs have also been correlated with register. In Stubbe and Holmes' (1995: 79) data, *and so on* and *or so* were used in formal interviews, but never in conversations, suggesting that they are prestige variants. Overstreet and Yule

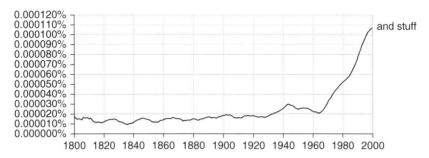

Figure 7.3 Google Ngrams search for "and stuff"

(1997: 252) report a similar finding for American English. They observe that *and so on* and *et cetera* are more frequent in formal discourse, and that *and everything, and stuff, or something, or anything,* and *or whatever* are features of informal speech. This division of forms by register suggests that choice of GE is correlated with formality, style, and other external influences on language behavior (Dines, 1980: 20; Overstreet, 1999: 79).

To put historical and contemporary observations into perspective, Figure 7.3 shows the frequency of the collocation *and stuff* over the last two centuries of written documents using Google Ngrams. You can easily see that *and stuff* has been used at low levels since 1800; however, since 1960 it has swiftly accelerated. (Note that this search will also include all strings that contain the target words, e.g. *and stuff like that.*)

Grammatical change

Recent research on GEs analyzes their distribution in terms of various mechanisms of grammatical change (Aijmer, 2002; Brinton, 1996; Cheshire, 2007; Erman, 1995). Cheshire (2007) specifically tests the hypothesis that GEs are undergoing grammatical development by analyzing GE use among young people aged 14–15 in three English towns – Reading, Milton Keynes, and Hull. Cheshire makes the argument for grammatical change based on a comparison across these towns alongside the patterns observed in several other data sets: (1) a small corpus of six elderly speakers from each town (although these were not systematically compared); (2) the historical record (Channell, 1994: 160); and (3) earlier corpora on English in the UK (e.g. the London Lund Corpus (Aijmer, 2002)) and among adolescents in particular, i.e. the COLT Corpus (Stenström et al., 2002).

Cheshire (2007: 169) argued that the distribution of GEs by syntactic position can be interpreted as decategorization. The assumption is that each of the GE variants was first introduced in contexts where each form matched the features of its referents and was predictable: *stuff* used with generic nouns; *things* used with count nouns. However, through decategorization, GEs no longer match the features of their referent because the form has become bleached of its previous morphosyntactic properties. Indeed, it is expected that the forms on the forefront of grammatical change will be found in positions where their features do *not* match the referents to which they attach. Cheshire's hypothesis is that if grammatical change is in progress, young people should have an extended usage pattern for their GEs. When she tested for this, she found there was a trend towards a more generalized use for every GE (Cheshire, 2007: 171–172).

Reminder:

Decategorization is one of the main mechanisms of grammatical change. It is identified by loss of morphological markers and syntactic patterns that were typical of earlier uses of the same word.

Cheshire, following Aijmer (2002: 227), Erman (1995: 145), and others, argued that the loss of longer GE forms is the result of erosion (morphological clipping), another mechanism of grammatical change (Cheshire, 2007: 167). Further the shorter GEs, e.g. *and stuff*, compared to longer GEs, e.g. *and stuff like that*, and *and things* compared to yet longer GEs, e.g. *and things like that*, exhibit greater extension in usage patterns (Cheshire, 2007: 169). In addition, she provides evidence for semantic change (semantic bleaching) and pragmatic shift. The original function of GEs was to signal that their referents were members of a general set of related elements; however, many researchers have observed that this set is often difficult to reconstruct (e.g. Winter and Norrby, 2000: 4). The short forms are particularly problematic, again supporting an explanation of grammatical change (Cheshire, 2007: 37–38). The GEs observed to be most advanced along the cline of grammatical change were shorter and more extensive in their usage patterns. For example, in the British dialects analyzed by Cheshire, *and that* and *and everything* were claimed to be the most grammaticalized; in the British National Corpus it was *or something* (Erman, 1995: 146). In Overstreet's analysis of American English *and stuff* and *or something* both showed signs of advancing grammaticality, occurring in contexts where "there may not be any discernible 'more' to be understood" (Overstreet, 1999: 146).

In sum, the literature tells us that GEs have certain patterns that expose their status in terms of linguistic change. In some studies they are found to be a stable feature with a common function correlated with social and linguistic factors. In other studies they have also been found to be undergoing grammatical extension and change, specifically in the adolescent population. So, the next step is to conduct a study that can provide some evidence to support one or the other hypothesis.

Method

Every GE was extracted from 87 individuals from the TEC and TTC balanced by age and sex, providing over 2,000 examples. Given the difficulty of attributing to any GE a single discourse-pragmatic function, the set of all GEs is considered a system (Cheshire, 2007; Dubois, 1992). Within this system the distributions of forms can be modeled as a linguistic variable where there are multiple variants that mean more or less the same thing (see Sankoff and Thibault, 1981). I also appeal to the notion of "structural equivalence" to define the variable context, which makes it possible to compare the distribution of a set of forms with the same structure under the envelope of one discourse variable even though individual variants may mean something slightly different, e.g. *and that, and that kind of thing, and all that stuff* (see also Pichler, 2013: 28–32).

Figure 7.4 (adapted from Tagliamonte and Denis, 2010: 349, Figure 2) plots the frequency of GEs per 10,000 words in a number of different studies. The

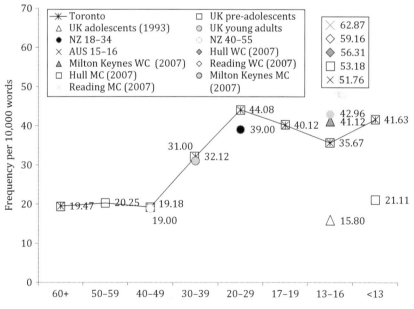

Figure 7.4 Cross-study comparison of GE frequency per 10,000 words

ages of the individuals are shown across the X-axis from oldest to youngest such that adolescents and pre-adolescents are at the far right-hand side. The comparison includes the adolescents in the three English towns studied by Cheshire (2007) – Reading, Milton Keynes, and Hull – separated by working (WC) and middle (MC) class (all from Table 3:163); Winter and Norrby's (2000) study of Melbourne, Australia (AUS 15–16); Stenström et al.'s (2002) study of the COLT corpus (UK Adolescents); Stubbe and Holmes' (1995) analysis of Wellington, New Zealand; and Levey's (2012) examination of pre-adolescents in London (UK pre-adolescents). The starred line indicates the frequency of GEs in the Toronto corpora.

The big comparison in Figure 7.4 shows the actual age of the individuals at the time of the study. The teenagers (aged 13–16) in the different communities have mostly high rates of GEs, greater than the youth in Toronto. Only the early data from COLT (collected in 1996) are lower (15.80). This supports the results observed by Dubois (1992: 185), Stubbe and Holmes (1995), and Cheshire (2007) that GEs are a feature of youth speech. In contrast, older individuals exhibit remarkable correspondence across studies. The data from the earlier studies on 20–29-year-olds, 30–39-year-olds, and 40–49-year-olds match the Toronto speakers nearly identically. This finding lends support to the idea that these features are a stable feature of English, at least in terms of overall frequency. The truly remarkable perspective offered by Figure 7.4 is the contrast between adults and teenagers. While the adults are relatively comparable across studies, the teenagers have a broad range of frequencies. This ranges from 15.80 per 10,000 words in London, England, in 1993 to 62.87 per 10,000 words in middle-class Reading in 2007. The teenagers in Toronto in the early 2000s are more like those in Milton Keynes than those in London, Hull, Reading, or Melbourne in Australia. The question is, are the high rates of GEs among this sector of the population the result of age grading, as Dubois (1992) suggests for the GEs in her Canadian French data from Montreal, or can they be explained by change and development in the GEs themselves, namely grammatical change (Cheshire, 2007)? The first hypothesis, of age grading, predicts that speakers simply use more GEs during their adolescent years and that this use declines as they become adults. The second hypothesis, of grammatical change, predicts a system in which developments among GEs are the result of shifting functions in the language, leading to extension of GEs to other uses and therefore an increase in frequency.

The next section provides highlights of the GEs by grouping them according to their generic element and treating them in terms of their type (*or* vs. *and*). Figure 7.5 plots the frequency of the most common forms with *or* – *or something* and *or whatever* – as a proportion of all GEs.

Figure 7.5 shows the GEs with *or* as a proportion of all GEs. The frequencies of *or something* fluctuate in apparent time while *or whatever* is relatively

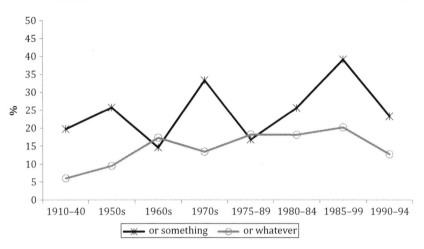

Figure 7.5 Main GEs with *or* by speaker date of birth

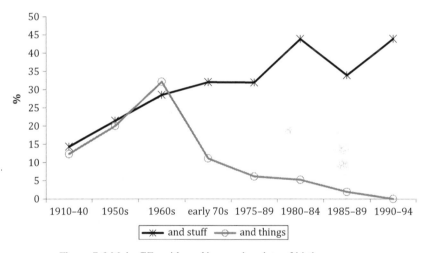

Figure 7.6 Main GEs with *and* by speaker date of birth

stable from the individuals born from the 1960s onwards. *Or something* is consistently often used more than *or whatever* but not among those born in the 1960s or late 1970s. *And stuff* takes off among speakers in the 1970s, but before that *and stuff* and *and things* were used at the same rate.

Figure 7.6 plots the frequency of the most common GE forms with *and* – *and stuff* and *and things* – as a proportion of all GEs.

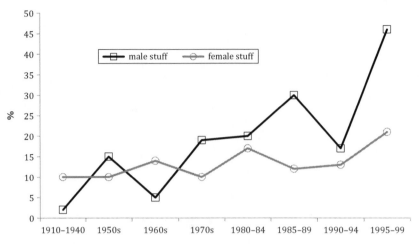

Figure 7.7 Distribution of *stuff* by speaker sex and date of birth

A different trajectory is found for the GEs with *and*. Here the forms with both *things* and *stuff* increase from the 60+ year-olds to those in born in the 1960s. From that point onwards *thing* plummets and *stuff* rises as the speakers get younger.

When a linguistic change is proceeding at this rate, sociolinguistic theory predicts that females will lead the change (Labov's Principles 2–4). We can test this possibility in the data by examining the distribution of *stuff* forms according to the sex of the individual, as in Figure 7.7.

Figure 7.7 exposes an unexpected result. Males, not females, are leading the change towards greater use of *stuff* GEs. In contrast, females across the age spectrum are relatively stable up to the youngest generation. This appears to be a rare instance of a linguistic change from below that is being led by men. In earlier studies male-led changes have been interpreted as signs of solidarity. For example, when male fishermen on Martha's Vineyard in the United States used older pronunciations of certain vowels, Labov (1963) argued that this use symbolized identification with the island and its values, and a rejection of the tourists who go to the island as summer visitors. Notice that in Figure 7.7 not only are young men leading in the use of *and stuff*, but that its use is at its height among young women as well.

Grammatical change?

Finally, let's consider if there is any evidence that teenagers are changing the language. I described earlier observations from researchers that innovations

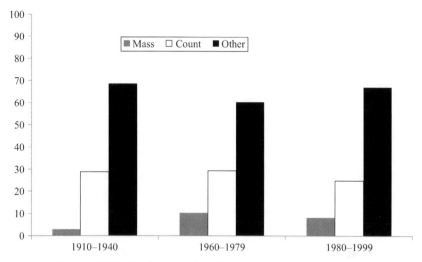

Figure 7.8 Distribution of *and stuff* by character of referent

that are undergoing grammatical change come to be used outside their original
contexts of use (e.g. Heine and Kuteva, 2005: 579). Such a development with
GEs can be gleaned in at least two ways. First, in their basic function, GEs are
thought to have a close relationship with their referent (Cheshire, 2007: 168)
such that mass nouns co-occur with *and stuff* and count nouns co-occur with
and things. However, if *stuff* is extending beyond its original contexts, we
should be able to see that it is used in more contexts than simply mass nouns.
Second, GEs are thought to have developed from longer to shorter constructions, such that forms such as *and stuff like that* gradually evolved to *and stuff*.
Figure 7.8 tests this possibility by showing the distribution of *and stuff* in terms
of the nature of its referent. In either case we may be able to see a development
from oldest to youngest individuals in the corpora if these changes have taken
place over the course of the twentieth century. In the figures that follow, the
data are divided into only three age cohorts to ensure a robust number of
tokens in each group.

Figure 7.8 shows the distribution of *and stuff* according to the character of
its referent. In every age cohort *and stuff* GEs occur in phrases other than mass
nouns more than anywhere else. While this is evidence that *and stuff* does not
simply collocate with mass nouns and has expanded beyond any strong
collocation with mass nouns, it demonstrates that this has not changed across
the time span of the corpora. This development did not take place in the last
century. All three referent types have the same distribution regardless of
generation.

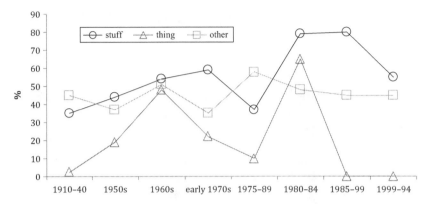

Figure 7.9 Proportion of short GEs out of all variants

Figure 7.9 shows the distribution of the short forms of GEs with *stuff*, *things*, and others according to their length. It also shows that short variants of *stuff* have been the most frequent forms in the system across the twentieth century. There is an apparent upward trajectory towards all short forms from 1910 to the early 1970s. However, after the early 1970s the frequency fluctuates wildly. This is likely due to the favored choices of each cohort (shown earlier in Figure 7.1). Using other statistical measures Tagliamonte and Denis (2010: 352) showed that there was little evidence for change in progress towards shorter GEs. Instead, there is considerable stability in the use of short forms.

Taken together, the evidence reveals that the GE system in North American English is undergoing change. The GEs with *stuff* have surged in frequency among individuals born after 1960, especially those born after 1985 – the individuals who were teenagers in the early twenty-first century. However, this usage is not a change to the GEs overall. Instead, what is happening is that the GEs with *stuff* are taking over as the main form.

What does the use of sentence "enders" tell us about teen language?

This analysis shows how dynamic and robust GEs are. There are a dozen or more different GEs, all of which had been reported before in the literature. Their overall frequency is often similar – when matched by age – to other places where English is spoken among the same age cohorts (Figure 7.4). GEs are more frequent among adolescents in comparison to the adult population. However, there is no solid evidence for grammatical change across the current generation of speakers. The words *and stuff* have been in the grammar since the late 1600s, hundreds of years before our oldest speakers were born (*c*.1920s). Moreover, when we compare the use of GEs from oldest to youngest speakers, we discover that they share the same patterns with respect to the character of their referents. This means that the state of the GE system, at least at this point in time, is stable. Both teenagers and senior citizens end their sentences with a flourish.

Yet there is an independent and relatively dramatic change going on. The GE *and stuff* has become the favored form for youth. Next time you hear someone end their sentence, chances are they will say *and stuff*.

It will be interesting to track GEs into the future and find out if *and stuff* will continue to dominate the system, whether a new GE will develop, and if the same development is happening in smaller communities, rural areas, and other dialects of English. Is the increasing use of *stuff* within the GE system part of a large-scale change sweeping the English language generally? Further comparative study of GEs and other systems will be critical for exploring this and other questions. As we will see in the next chapter, the word *stuff* is involved in a broader change in the generics of English.

Language puzzle

People end their sentences with words and phrases. Which ones? Find out what it is like to try to pin these questions down in real data. I have extracted all the sentences that end with a SE from four individuals in the TTC, two female; two male. Answer the following questions:

a. How many different SEs are there?
b. Which speaker uses the largest number of types?
c. Is there a favored form by age group? What is it?
d. Which SE is only used by women?
e. Name at least two tokens that are unusual.

Answers

a. *There are 11 different types. The following SEs are present: "and stuff," "and stuff like that," "and all that stuff," "and all this," "and everything," "and everything like that," "you know," "yeah," "you know yeah," "and something like that," "that kind of thing," "or anything," "or everything".*
b. *Speaker "C." The elderly woman.*
c. *Both elderly speakers use "you know." Speaker C uses it 6 times and speaker D uses it 4 times. This represents 10/22 or 45 percent of the time. The young people use "and stuff (like that)" 6/10 or 60 percent of the time.*
d. *The ender, "yeah."*
e. *One of the SEs has a "like" in between, e.g. "and like stuff." One of the sentences has two SEs "you know yeah." One of the SEs is unique, "and all this."*

Sentences that end with a SE from four individuals

JULIE WANG, F, 14

We just go do posters *and everything* and sell from last
  year.
his sister's like a rebel and has piercings everywhere and
  goes out *and all that stuff*.
... and tries to find evidence that he was actually the
  killer, and then she starts believing it *yeah*.
Ah, we don't know how she got her license *and everything*.

JAMES MCCREADY, M, 11

he's really picky *and everything*
sometimes it's fun because we do experiments *and stuff*.
she always like gives me time out *and stuff*.
you can make houses out of them *and like stuff*.
there's classes sort-of like Art *and stuff* and Gym.
they have like perms in their hair and they are
  boys *and stuff like that*

JANE CREEKS, F, 80

yes without interruption *you know yeah*.
'Course that's nothing to do with East-York, but
  nevertheless it's something of interest *yeah*.
so we were you know, a really isolated village *yeah*.
Yeah *and something like that*.
she just loved to go into Sunnyside, *you know*?
it was all games of chance *and everything like that*.
they were talking about bullies at school, and having
  guards at lunchtime and- and guards at the entrance *and
  all this*.
I-mean, how many times did you lock your doors *or anything*?
they'd have cookies and tea or lemonade *or whatever*.
there was no windows *or anything*, not that I can remember
  any windows,
I remember it took me a long time to get home *you know*.
We always say lieutenant, *you know*.
I don't feel nervous that anything's gonna happen, *you
  know*
... but I-mean it- it does happen *you know*.

oh I used to think that was wonderful *yeah*.
I used to think that was so wonderful *yeah*.

JEREMY BATTCOCK, M, 74
You know biographies *that kind of stuff*.
Lawyers, judges, *things like that*
but part of the appeal of the books I hoped was Toronto, *you know*.
they're vastly different inside then they once were *you know*.
"We're white-painters," *you know*, *that kind of thing*.
he's one of Canada's great journalists *you know*

8   Generics

Stuffology

[Sali] What did you do at school today? [Shaman] Stuff.

In this chapter I explore a particular use of the word *stuff*. I was first alerted to this type of *stuff* when my children starting answering questions with it, as in the quote above. Then, I found examples such as (131) in the TTC.

131.   [Interviewer] So, what do you do with your friends after school?
        [023] *Stuff*. (Leo McCready, 13)

When I counted the number of occurrences of *stuff* on its own (i.e. not part of a GE) in the TTC, I found that it was used 1,285 times, one of the most frequent words in the corpus. Why would teenagers use the word *stuff* so much?

The word *stuff* is a perfectly good English word, which has been in the language a very long time. The earliest uses of "stuff" come from the seventeenth century and refer to equipment, food, or stock, as in (132a–c). Note the plural marker in (132c).

132.   a. There I found a Carvel of Alfama, that was laden with the horses and
           stuff [Pg. *cavallos e fato*] of a Lord. (1653, H. Cogan, tr. F. M. Pinto,
           Voyages & Adventures I. 2)
        b. Then was the banqueting *Stuff* flung about the roome profusely.
           (*c*.1684, J. Evelyn, *Diary* anno 1667 (1955) III. 480)
        c. O'Ne'r~day *stuffs* we're weel laid in, A sonsy cheese, jist like the
           mune, Wi' crumpy cakes. (1870, J. Nicholson, *Idylls o' Hame* 113)

The OED records many different ways that *stuff* can be used. It can refer to the material an item is made of, whether tangible like "clay" in (133a) or intangible like "dreams," as in (133b).

133.   a. In all the Potters house, is there one vessell made of better *stuffe*
           then clay? (*c*.1631, J. Donne, *Sermons* (1959) IV. 51)
        b. We are such *stuffe* As dreames are made on. (*c*.1616, William
           Shakespeare, *The Tempest* (1623) iv. i. 156)

Later on the meaning of *stuff* came to be used "loosely to denote any collection of things about which one is not able or willing to particularize." These uses begin in the early twentieth century, as in (134).

134.   a. One spring day she had me ascend to the attic and clean up some boxes
            of *stuff* and throw out some *stuff* and put some *stuff* back into its
            imaginary proper place. (1967, R. Brautigan, *Trout Fishing in Amer*)
        b. Once they left we were going to move his *stuff* out and change the
            locks. (1977, J. D. MacDonald *Condominium*, xxxvii. 370)

As language changes people start noticing the change. Because new usages
are not part of the norms (decategorization), they stand out. Inevitably it is the
young people who use these innovations more than the rest of the population
and because the words are found in places that not all members of the
population use with the same frequency or patterning, they are salient and
are noticed. At the same time, when words are used often and in places outside
the prescribed standard, as in (135), they are typically labeled "colloquial
and slang."

135.   a. Yeah, they just sing about scientific *stuff*. (Greg Parkinson, 16)
        b. Weird *stuff* goes on in the background. (Finnegan Conner, 17)
        c. And then you plug in *stuff*, and you get out *stuff* and you weight the
            different networks. (Gordon Combs, 17)

In the remainder of this chapter I will explore what teenagers are doing with
the word *stuff*. Unlike Chapter 7, which focused on GEs, in this chapter
I examine only the use of *stuff* when it is used as a pronoun referring to a
group or set of items.

Method

To begin, remember that it is important that we do not only examine the word
we happen to be interested in. An important diagnostic of linguistic change is
that one form is replacing another, either in time or along some economic,
demographic or geographic dimension (Sankoff and Thibault, 1981: 213). This
kind of trajectory is an indication of the progression of a change in the
grammar. If it is true that *stuff* is increasing then it is likely replacing something
else. Closer examination of the data reveals that *things* may also be used to
refer to an unspecified collection, as in (136–137).

136.   a. [Interviewer] What do you do with your mom when you are with her?
        b. We do *stuff*.
        c. [Interviewer] Like what?
        d. I don't know. Lots of *stuff*, but I can't remember.
        e. [Interviewer] What?
        f. Whole bunch of *things*. (James McCready, 11)
137.   a. Am I rambling on here too much?
        b. [Interviewer] No, this is perfect. This is the kind of *stuff* we love to
            hear. *Things* you don't find in the history books, you know?
            (Jack Mosun, 83)

In addition to my own intuitions, the OED confirms that both *stuff* and *things* can be used to refer to unspecified objects or "an entity of any kind."

Further examination of the data also shows that similar contexts can have a number of variants, as in (138) and (139).

138.   a. So, that's how that *stuff* happens, right (Jim Lear, 51)
        b. I have these dreams. Weird dreams. *Things* happen that . . . it will never happen. (Catherine Hui, 19)
        c. Ah unfortunately, we never bonded. Ah and *shit* happens (Ryan Dubeau, 61)
139.   a. I got to work with a bunch of people and see all the *things* that go on behind the scenes in the making of a play (Jason Levine, 17)
        b. Like because of where my room is I can hear all the *stuff* that happens in that alley (Michael Llewellyn, 18)
        c. And then they flipped out and they tore all the *crap* out of my locker and-stuff-like-that (Brent Kim, 21)

This preliminary investigation confirms that several words can be used for similar meaning in the data, including *stuff*, *things*, *shit*, and *crap*. Although there are other words that have a similar meaning, e.g. *paraphernalia*, this word does not occur in my archive.

Further exploration with Google Ngrams can give us a gross overview of potential changes in this area of grammar. Figure 8.1 shows that the two words – *stuff* and *things* – are gradually shifting across the nineteenth and twentieth centuries. The word *things* has been declining while *stuff* shows the beginning of upward shift from the 1960s onwards.

The next step is to extract all the tokens from the Toronto corpora and find out what is going on at the community level among real individuals talking to each other. Given the large-scale shifts visible in Figure 8.1, the idea that present-day teenagers are the locus of these developments is questionable. Table 8.1 shows the overall distribution of these words when they are used to refer to a group of entities.

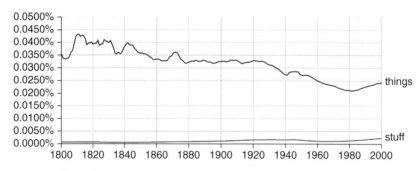

Figure 8.1 Google Ngram of *things* and *stuff*

Table 8.1 *Overall distribution of generic nouns in TEC and TTC combined*

	%	N
things	58.9	1,516
stuff	38.9	1,001
shit	1.4	37
crap	0.6	15
junk	0.1	3
TOTAL		2,572

Table 8.1 shows that *things* is the most frequently used generic word in the data; however, *stuff* is used nearly 40 percent of the time. In order to determine if *stuff* is increasing in usage, we need to assess its frequency according to individuals of different ages, i.e. across apparent time.

Can *stuff* and *things* mean the same thing?

An important question arises: are *stuff* and *things* variants of the same meaning? I have demonstrated that they alternate with each other in the data and that the same speaker in the same stretch of discourse may use one form and then another. However, are they sufficiently similar in meaning to treat as part of the same system in the grammar? According to English grammar *things* refers to items that are count nouns, as in (140a), while *stuff* refers to items that are mass nouns, as in (140b). However, in the data it is often impossible to determine what the characteristics of the referents may be, as in (140c). While we might assume the reference is to the standard of living or to gross national product revenues, intuitively *things* is vague.

140.   a.   The locker rooms were so big, people could put hot plates and different *things* in. (Jack Mosun, 83)
       b.   They gave mother *stuff* she had to put in my eyes. (Bud Combdon, 83)
       c.   So, *things* have changed. The dollar doesn't go as far. (Matt Latimer, 84)

Although speakers sometimes provide a post hoc interpretation of what *stuff* comprises, as in (141), this is rare.

141.   a.   [Interviewer] So, you know, what happens when you step out of line with your parents? Do they ground you or something or?
       b.   [004] Yes, that's their new plan. The old plan was, you know ... smack me on the bum a few times, you know. *Stuff*. And then, I misbehaved again, they were like, so mad, they decided to ground me for a week. No TV, it's like, no bike riding, stay in the house, every time you have free time no reading just do work. That was really tiring. (Alex Chau, 11)

In fact, these words, *things*, *stuff*, *shit*, and *crap* are generic words. They do not refer to specific things but to a consistent, broad group of unspecified objects in the world.

What's a generic?

A *generic* is a word that refers to a large class of items or a group as opposed to specific members of the group.

The philosophy of *stuff*

Philosophers have been debating the relations between various types of entities and the words used to refer to them "at least since Aristotle" (Richard, 1975: 469). I will not go into this debate here other than to point out that conceptualizing what *thing* words and *stuff* words refer to is a complex and intensely studied issue, involving nuanced differences between grains of sand and pieces of cheese (Pelletier, 2010; Wierzbicka, 1988). For the present study, let's simply say roughly that *thing* is a count noun and *stuff* is a mass noun (Miller, 2009: 1). However, a key point is that "portions of stuff are in some sense reducible to things" and that people do not have "particularly finely honed intuitions about stuff" (Miller, 2009: 2). Apparently, neither *things* nor *stuff* may be unequivocally associated with an exclusive set of referents in language. To discover what the use of *things* vs. *stuff* looks like in practice, let's search a single individual's data and take into account each time he uses a single word to refer to a group of entities, as in (142). Finnegan Connor, aged 17, makes use of generic reference 20 times in his interview. Each of the contexts is listed with an interpretation of the possible referent. The referent is the group of entities to which the generic refers.

142.   a.   I found I'd come home all pissed off about *shit* [events?] then I'd just write in it and then it lifts the "pissoffedness" right away.
         b.   Either harm comes to them or they die through different things and weird *stuff* [events?] goes on in the background.
         c.   There's always hidden *stuff*. [events]
         d.   I find it's not worth it to look for the hidden *stuff* [images] because my friend Ben looks for the hidden stuff so he just tells me where it all is.
         e.   I find it's not worth it to look for the hidden stuff because my friend Ben looks for the hidden *stuff* [items] so he just tells me where it all is.
         f.   He like drew *stuff* [items] in and made stuff- made it different.
         g.   He like drew stuff in and made *stuff* - [items] made it different.
         h.   But Strongbad crosses out the *stuff* [items] so that it says, "Some people have Southern accents and those are hot."
         i.   They say *stuff* [words] that comes out harsh.

    j.   My friend Byron is an excellent composer. I love hearing him write *stuff*. [music]

    k.   He and I have practiced so much of that *stuff*. [music]

    l.   Either harm comes to them or they die through different *things* [diseases?] and weird *stuff* goes on in the background.

    m.   And it's not as entertaining as the *things* [images] themselves you know?

    n.   Had anything happened in a different way *things* [circumstances] would be so different.

    o.   Look but you know the ways *things* [events] happen is the way things happen.

    p.   Look but you know the ways things happen is the way *things* [events] happen.

    q.   You know he went back in time and said that he thought these *things* [ideas] up as two different people. (Finnegan Connor, 17)

Assuming that events, circumstances, images, and items are count nouns, Table 8.2 documents the distribution of generic words by the nature of the referent in Finnegan's grammar.

Count nouns represent the vast majority of generic reference contexts in Finnegan's data. However, when we test to determine the effect of the count/mass distinction on the particular word that is chosen, we discover that mass referents are represented by *stuff* but count nouns are more flexible. Although Finnegan uses only two mass nouns, both of them take *stuff*. The majority of the generics he uses refer to count nouns, but of these 47 percent are *stuff*. This means that the generic *stuff* has become available for use with count nouns. In order to find out how this may have happened, we have to consider the older members of the community.

Let's compare two older gentlemen, both born in 1919 in Toronto and 85 years of age at the time of interview. The data from each of them are shown in (143) and (144).

143.   a.   In the old days they used to- Eaton's used to deliver by a horse and wagon, their *stuff* [items] to your house

          b.   I tried to make him not do all the wrong *things* [activities] I did, you know?

          c.   They get rewarded for *things* [activities] . . .

Table 8.2 *Distribution of generics by type of referent by speaker:* Finnegan Conner *(N=20)*

	stuff	*things*	*shit*	Total
Count	47%	35%	6%	18
Mass	100%			2

    d. ... whereas we had to do *things*, [activities] or else we didn't go out to play, you know?

    e. They do *things* [activities] and they get a play toy or something you know to play with you know?

    f. When we grew up there wasn't that kind of money, to buy all the *things* [items] for them you know?

    g. There's so many other *things* [activities] now. Like neither one of our boys was a Cub. (Wesley Patterson, 85)

144.   a. Tom always had a whole bunch of *stuff* in his pocket. He had alleys. He had pen-knives, [alleys = marbles]

    b. He had pen-knives, he had different *stuff*, all kinds of stuff in his pockets. [items]

    c. He had pen-knives, he had different stuff, all kinds of *stuff* in his pockets. [items]

    d. I got a lot of stupid *stuff*. [events]

    e. My mother would take the *stuff* [groceries] out of it, and put it in the hall, and the box.

    f. It was just for delivering the *stuff*. [groceries]

    g. The darn *stuff* would be all- all oil. [peanut butter]

    h. Oh gosh, that was great *stuff*. You'd get a great big jug of it and a- a few little cups. [Honeydew, a type of beer]

    i. He delves back in *stuff* [events in the historical record]

    j. The top on those was a kind of a fabric *stuff* [car roof material] and you used to oil it and that?

    k. Well, what happened, as- as *things* went by [years]

    l. But anyways, all- there's all kinds of *things* [jobs] he used to do with that to make money,

    m. So we'd buy two bottles of Kit-Cola and a bag of *things* [items]

    n. Funny *things*, yeah. [events] (Garry Haslem, 85)

Table 8.3 shows the distribution of generic words for each of the elderly men.

Table 8.3 *Distribution of generics by type of referent by speaker:* Wesley Patterson and Garry Haslem *(N=14)*

	stuff	*things*	Total
	Wesley Patterson		
Count	17% (N=1)	83% (N=6)	7
Mass			
			7
	Garry Haslem		
Count		100% (N=9)	9
Mass	100% (N=5)	0	5
			14

What is immediately apparent is that these data too reveal that generics that refer to mass nouns are much rarer than generics that refer to count nouns. One man uses *stuff* and *thing* for count nouns. The other has a split system – count nouns take *things*; mass nouns take *stuff*. However, the number of tokens is small. We need to look at the whole community.

Stuff across generations

Figure 8.2 shows the complete picture from the TEC and the TTC. It exposes how often people of each age group use *stuff* in contrast to *things*. There is a steady increase in *stuff* for people born in the twentieth century. By the generation born in the 1990s – the teenagers – there is an equal chance of using *stuff* or *things*.

The trajectory of development in Figure 8.2 is stepwise and regular from individuals born in the early twentieth century through to the late 1970s as the word *stuff* steadily replaces the word *things*.[1] At this juncture, however, the two forms stabilize in use. Other variants for generic meaning are present, but at very low levels. This looks very much like a change in progress. As the change nears the 50 percent mark, notice that it levels out.

As previously, sociolinguistic theory says linguistic change is led by women whether the change is a prestigious one that comes from outside the community (Labov's Principle 3) or is a development from within (Labov's Principle 4). Figure 8.3 displays the use of *stuff* by sex of the speaker.

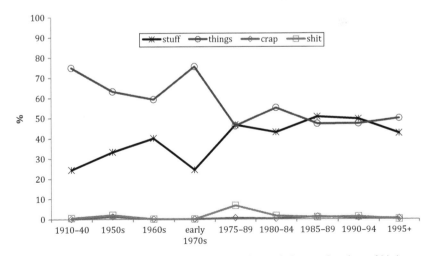

Figure 8.2 Overall distribution of generic words by speaker date of birth

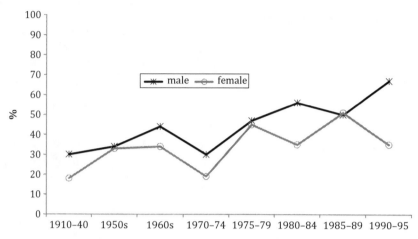

Figure 8.3 Distribution of *stuff* by speaker sex and generation

Figure 8.3 shows that there is little to distinguish men and women from the 1910s through to the late 1970s. The situation is mixed after 1980 – strong partitioning of the sexes among those born in the early 1980s, no difference in the 1985–1989 group and separation among those born in the 1990s. The more interesting observation is that the males are leading the change and there are no well-defined peaks in apparent time for either sex.

While the word *stuff* seems to be undergoing change, the evidence from apparent time and sex differences is equivocal. We need to delve deeper into the grammar to examine the contextual patterns underlying its use.

From the evidence in the OED, we know that the generic meaning of *stuff* began as specific to particular items, equipment for example. However, there-after *stuff* expanded from particular uses to general uses. While both *things* and *stuff* are linguistic devices for marking generic reference, *stuff* is taking over the whole system. If so, it must be doing so by spreading to areas of the grammar that once were the domain of *things*.

In order to prove this, we would have to code the data for the contexts in which *things* as opposed to *stuff* is prescribed and then test for what generic is used in apparent time. Table 8.4 shows the distinction between referents that are count as opposed to those that are mass according to decade of birth.

Table 8.4 reveals a constant pattern such that *stuff* is more frequent with mass nouns than with count nouns in every generation. There is not much change from the oldest individuals (60 percent) to the youngest speakers (63 percent). However, notice the linear increase by generation in use of *stuff* in count nouns from 14 percent among the individuals born in the 1910s to nearly 50 percent among those born in the 1980s and 1990s.

Table 8.4 *Distribution of generic* stuff *by type of referent*

	Count		Mass	
Decade of birth	%	N	%	N
1990s	48	209	63	19
1980s	43	1,220	80	177
1970s	33	202	84	38
1960s	34	125	74	23
1950s	27	211	66	32
1940s	19	108	81	26
1930s	18	73	43	14
1920s	14	106	50	14
1910s	14	43	60	10
TOTALS		1,752		280

Because it now stands in for any generalized groups of entities, use of *stuff* is becoming increasingly broad and therefore frequent and diffused across the population. The next step in this development would be to find *stuff* being used in a context where *things* was once the only option. Sure enough the youngest speakers in the corpora can use *stuff* in contexts such as in (145) and as you will see below, so do some of the older generation!

145. a. [Interviewer] Yeah. And do you go to Club Monaco, or anything?
    b. [013] No. Club Monaco- they used to have kids' Club Monaco, and I had like a couple of *stuff* from there.

What does the use of indefinite *stuff* tell us about teen language?

Taking all the patterns of generic *stuff* into account, it is evident that contemporary teenagers use this form way more than anyone else in the community. But this is not due to an adolescent penchant. The change towards *stuff* as a generic in English started a long time ago. By the early 1900s people were using *stuff* to refer to generic items. In subsequent generations *stuff* has increased in a stepwise linear fashion among both men and women. Further evidence for the development of *stuff* as the predominant generic in English comes from plotting the GEs *and stuff* and generic *stuff* on the same graph, as in Figure 8.4.

In Figure 8.4 observe that the trajectory of *stuff* as a generic is proceeding uniformly whether it occurs within a GE or alone. This suggests that it is the same change. In my earlier research on GEs, Derek Denis and I argued that *and stuff* was not a grammatical development in the GE system,

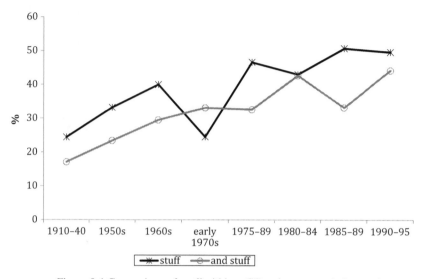

Figure 8.4 Comparison of *stuff* within a GE and as a generic by speaker date of birth

but lexical replacement of the generic item within the GE template. The findings in this chapter corroborate that interpretation. This additional evidence suggests that lexical replacement in the GE system represents only a part of a change in progress in the generic system. Where once *things* and *stuff* divided the system according to the nature of the referent, *stuff* is steadily taking over to become an all-purpose generic.

[Sali] Where are you going? [Duncan] I have to go to Home Depot to get a couple of stuff. (3.9.15)

Language puzzle

Did you ever think people used the word *stuff* so much? Look back through some of the early examples in the book and elsewhere outside of Chapter 8. Check out how *stuff* is used when it is not a GE.

a. Find three examples of *stuff* where it functions as a generic.
b. Find an example followed closely by "crap."
c. Find an example preceded by a colloquial adjective.
d. Find an example that has a mass referent.

Consider the examples in (i–ii) below. These come from some of the most recent data in my archive.

(*cont.*)

(i) I don't want to learn all those *stuff*, I just want to paint. (L. Dennis, UDUT, 2012)

(ii) so i did my own notes. But then those *stuff* weren't on the test (i, SMS, 2010)

e. Why are they unusual?

f. Given what I have discussed in this chapter, how would you explain them?

Answers

a. *You don't find this* stuff *in Canada (clothes); I like a lot of stuff (bands); they're a bit more lackadaisical in how they say* stuff *(words).*

b. *Well, that condo is tiny. Like even now I haven't moved in, I don't know what I'm going to do with my* stuff. *I have so much clothes that he totally underestimates how much* crap *I have.*

c. *Like* you don't find this stuff in Canada. [clothes] (Chapter 6)

d. And you know *wacky stuff* is really amazing out there. [music] (Chapter 10)

e. *They are unusual because they appear with a modifier that is incompatible with a mass noun. According to prescriptive grammar "stuff" refers to a mass noun. The modifier "those" can only be used to describe plural count nouns, e.g. "things."*

f. *"Stuff" is increasing and extending to count nouns. (See Figure 8.2 and Table 8.4.)*

9   Just

Just *what?*

> You can just tell by their body language you know, and their language
> you know, the choice of words, you can just tell how old they are. You
> know, they're just not there yet you know? They're just not there yet.
>
> (Arnie Alletson, 72)

In contrast to words such as *like* and *so*, much less media attention has been
directed at the word *just*. Yet in Chapter 2, I demonstrated that *just* is among
the most frequent words in teen language. In the TTC it occurred nearly 8,000
times! It was also among the top words in both the COLT and MLE corpora as
well.[1] Many uses of *just* appear unremarkable in isolation, as in (146), where
their meaning is *simply* or *only*. This is perhaps why *just* slips by, not attracting
anyone's attention.

146.   a. Well, I dunno, they're *just* kissing. (Clara Felipe, 16)
        b. Some of them are cute, some of them are *just* weird. (Tina Mancini, 11)
        c. You *just* suspect that it's water or like whatever. (Clara Felipe, 16)

The uses in (147), however, show that while the same suite of meanings is
present, the contexts in which *just* is used, particularly in (147b–c) seem to
extend beyond normal limits and the frequency seems exaggerated. This is an
indication that the use of *just* may be changing.

147.   a. So I can just go on the Internet, look up some cheats and then just play.
            (Christopher O'Neil, 11)
        b. I *just* stayed home 'cause someone was taking care of me. And then I was
            just watching TV. And I *just* took a nap. (Christopher O'Neil, 11)
        c. But then the second time he was *just* stupid and *just* not even hot.
            (Clara Felipe, 17)
        d. But it's *just* like flying on the ice. It's *just* amazing. (Elizabeth
            McKinley, 19)

Despite the absence of public outcry, *just* has been the subject of considerable academic research and there are tantalizing hints that something interesting
is going on. However, no definitive conclusion has been reached regarding its
function or present state of development. Most researchers agree that the
meaning of *just* is difficult to establish and to describe (e.g. Aijmer, 2002:

173; Grant, 2013: 176). While it can function as an adjective, e.g. *a just society* (Kishner and Gibbs, 1996: 19) this use is waning in modern English. It is the adverbial use of *just* that is most enigmatic. Most studies present an inventory of examples and interpretations of *just* in one context after another, many of these subtle and nuanced (e.g. Aijmer, 1985a; Erman, 1997; Nevalainen, 1991). In a corpus of North American English, MICASE, a database of academic speech,[2] *just* is said to function most frequently as a hedge or minimizer ("only, simply, merely") (Grant, 2013: 178; Lindemann and Mauranen, 2001: 464). While some researchers suggest that *just* can function as a highlighting or focus device, many resort to calling it a pause filler or a hedge. In fact, many researchers have suggested that *just* is best described as a feature of vagueness or "loose language" (e.g. Andersen, 1996, 1997a, 1997b, 1998, 2001; Miller and Weinert, 1995; Underhill, 1988). Whatever the function, young people are often singled out as the perpetrators of this degeneration of language (Andersen, 2001; Buchstaller, 2013; Erman, 2001; Siegel, 2002). To my knowledge no accountable quantitative study has explored *just* yet. In the analysis in this chapter, I will offer this alternative analytic perspective by conducting a systematic examination of all the instances of *just* in the TEC and TTC. Instead of focusing on the details of the meaning of each example of *just*, I will attempt to determine what semantic types are present in the data and the linguistic contexts in which *just* tends to occur and whether or not the use of *just* is changing over time.

To begin, let's first gain an understanding of the historical and contemporary context. Figure 9.1 shows the frequency of *just* over the last two centuries of written documents using Google Ngrams. It reveals that *just* has been rising in frequency since 1800 and from the 1960s it has extended upwards.[3] Such a steady, long-term trajectory supports the idea that *just* is changing and may be undergoing a spurt of development among youth. How might this be happening?

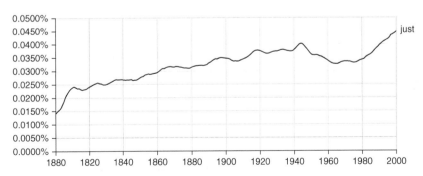

Figure 9.1 Google Ngrams search for "just"

Historical perspective

The word *just* was originally an adjective meaning "righteous, equitable, rightful" but it developed adverbial meanings early on, covering such meanings as "exactly, precisely, actually, closely." Tracking the development of the adverbial functions of *just*, it appears to have expanded to meanings of degree in 1551, time in 1574, amount, number, and quantity by 1583, likeness in 1594, and finally to manner in 1607. The first time *just* was used to modify a verb occurred in the late 1600s, as in (148).

148.   a. The western point where those half-rounding guards *just* met, and closing
               stood in squadron joind'. (1667, John Milton, *Paradise Lost*)
         b. I *Just* did as a bashful Beggar does when he beggs an Alms. (1687,
               A. Lovell, tr. J. de Thévenot, *Travels into the Levant* i. lvi. 84)

According to Erman (1997) the development of the word *just* from adjective to adverb was the first stage of an ongoing expansion of adverbial *just* to a pragmatic particle. The change from content word (adjective) to function word (i.e. pragmatic particle) is the evidence that *just* has undergone grammatical development.

Uh . . .I just- I don't know we just like, "us" as like, the youth of like the world, um. We use like more like abbreviated sentences and not use like full structures and all that stuff. (Nathan Hardwick, 13)

Exactly what function *just* has developed is not clear, especially given the myriad different meanings reported in the literature, e.g. exaggeration, positive politeness, hedging, strengthening, highlighting, etc. (Aijmer, 2002: 160–173). Erman (1997: 87) argues that the pragmatic meaning of *just* is as an emphasizer. Bolinger (1972: 107) suggests that it has become an intensifier. Given the acceleration in the use of *just* since the 1980s these functions may be the underlying explanation for its expansion. However, we have to wonder why there was an increased need for either emphasis or intensification in the language.

Reminder:

A pragmatic marker occurs in sentence initial position; a pragmatic particle occurs within the sentence.

How to study *just*?

When examining the word *just* the language scientist who wants to use accountable methods is faced with a predicament. It is relatively easy to find the instances of *just* and attempt to infer the meanings of one example or another. To get to an accountable analysis, however, the analyst must determine what *just* might alternate with and what the range of potential contexts of alternation might be. Many researchers claim that *just* is frequent (Grant, 2013; Lindemann and Mauranen, 2001) and we have seen that it is among the most frequent words in the Toronto corpora. However, a basic word count does not tell us much about its distribution in the grammar or in the community. It is another step to extract every instance in a given corpus and code the tokens exhaustively for the meaning each form has. This is because many of the potential meanings of *just* are difficult to pinpoint and at least some of them are not mutually exclusive. So the questions: who uses *just*, how often, and under what circumstances are not as simple as they might sound.

In what follows, I present a preliminary analysis of *just* from a representative subset of the TEC/TTC. Every token of *just* was extracted providing 3,419 tokens of *just*. As a first step, let's determine how frequent *just* is when we calculate the number of tokens out of the total number of words per speaker divided by male and female across age group. Table 9.1 shows the result.

Table 9.1 shows that *just* ranges between 0.4 percent and 1.2 percent of the total number of words across generations. There is no reliable difference between male and female speakers. Notice that the young adults – those in their 20s – use slightly more *just* than other age groups and there is a little less use of *just* among the two oldest age groups.

The next step is to consider how *just* is being used. As mentioned earlier, it is often difficult to assign a single function to a token of *just* (Lindemann and Mauranen, 2001: 469). Taking the definitions from the OED and earlier research as a starting point, each token was categorized according to its main function. Table 9.2 shows the distribution of *just* tokens according to these

Table 9.1 *Percentages of* just *out of total number of words*

Age at interview	DOB	Male	Female	Total
< 13	1990–1994	0.74	0.64	0.70
13-16	1985–1989	0.79	0.93	0.86
17-19	1980–1984	1.06	0.96	1.05
20-29	1975–1989	1.07	1.04	1.05
30-39	early 1970s	0.89	0.78	0.82
40-49	1960s	0.71	0.82	0.76
50-59	1950s	0.50	0.56	0.55
60 +	1910–1940	0.39	0.41	0.40
TOTAL		0.78*	0.78	0.78

* *Note:* The totals reflect the average for all females, all males, and everyone. They are not an addition of the averages in each age group.

Table 9.2 *Distribution of* just *by function*

	%	N
simply/merely	66.7	2,193
only	15.7	516
false start	9.4	310
recently	3.2	106
exactly	1.9	61
OTHER	1.2	41
A small amount; short distance	1.1	37
Expression, e.g. just in case	.8	25

categorizations. The older adjectival use of *just*, as in *a just king*, did not occur in the Toronto materials. This is testimony to its obsolescent status in contemporary English (e.g. Erman, 1997). In contrast, adverbial *just* is robust and a wide range of different meanings are present. Many of the meanings documented in the literature, including "equally," "a small amount or short distance," "in order to," "almost," and assorted formulae, e.g. *just in case* are rare. Instead, several main types occur, including "simply," as in (149a), "exactly" (149b), "recently" (149c), and "only" (149d).

149.   a. I'm the one who *just* stays quiet until someone talks to me. (Clara Felipe, 16)
        b. It was *just* like waiting for things to happen. (Michael Llewellyn, 18)
        c. The new swings they *just* put in, those swings feel like they've been lowered two feet. (Christopher O'Neil, 11)
        d. He *just* finished it last week. (Karl Galang, 11)

One frequent context not mentioned in the literature are tokens of *just* in false starts and fragmented syntax, as in (150).

150.   a. It *just*- it *just*- it was like bad karma or something. (Elizabeth McKinley, 19)
        b. But I *just*- I didn't really like it so. It was *just*- it was nice to get a phys-ed course. (Craig Thompson, 18)

Table 9.2 displays the proportion of these main types of *just* out of the total number of instances of *just* in the data and shows that the vast majority of *just* token have the meaning "simply." Every other type occurs at much lower frequencies. We can test whether there is any indication that these functions of *just* are changing by examining the distributions of these functions by speaker age, as in Figure 9.2.

The surprising result in Figure 9.2 is that not only does the meaning of *just* as "simply" represent the bulk of its uses overall, but this is true across

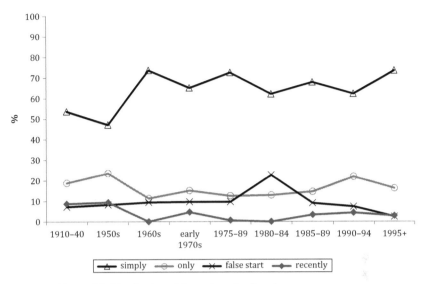

Figure 9.2 Distribution of *just* tokens by function

age groups. If any change has occurred in this time span, its origin is in the generation of speakers born in the 1960s when an abrupt increase in frequency of the "simply" meaning occurs and there is a visible downturn in "only" and "recently" uses. The fact that this timing is marginally at odds with the Google Ngrams data, which records a rise in usage in the 1980s, may be due to the fact that the written language lags somewhat behind the spoken vernacular of these materials. But what would cause an increase in the meaning "simply"?

Research on *just* has demonstrated that the meaning of *just* "can to a large part be determined by knowing what kind of word it modifies," i.e. the following word (Kishner and Gibbs, 1996: 28). Taking the next step towards understanding the meaning of *just*, let's tabulate the words it modifies and assess its frequency across types, as in Figure 9.3.

Figure 9.3 reveals that well over half of the tokens of *just* occur in pre-verbal position (underlined), as in (151).

151.   a.   I *just* need someone to get my ass out the door and to the gym. Basically is what I need. Like if you can get out- if you can get up you can run, you can bike, you can lift weights, whatever. You *just* have to get there and make yourself do it. But I mean, I need someone to push me out the door. So, like- if like- if she and I go together, she goes off to like swim and I do like the bike, that's fine. I *just* need to get there. (Elizabeth McKinley, 19)

       b.   We *just* went and we hit like eighty Swedish meatballs. And for like a year after that every time this kid saw me, "Eighty Swedish meatballs!" So yeah, it *just* went on and on. (Jake Vogel, 19)

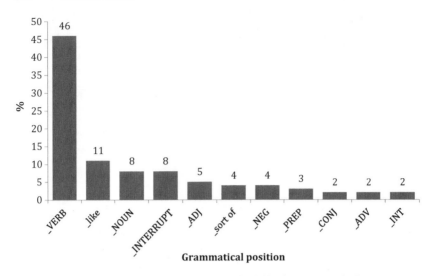

Figure 9.3 Distribution of *just* tokens by following grammatical category (N=3,288)

When I first reported these results (Tagliamonte, 2005: 1905) I suggested that it demonstrated that the word *just* does not occur everywhere. Instead it is even more highly circumscribed than *like*, at least it seemed so. Interestingly, the frequent use of *just* as a so-called "minimizer" in Grant's (2013: 184) corpus-based study of New Zealand lecturers offers the illustrative example in (152). Note that each of these tokens of *just* is pre-verbal.

152.   *just* make sure you name's on your work, *just* collect them all up, *just* leave them until the break, *just* pull that so the blind goes up, so don't *just* copy down what I've done.

The question this provokes is this: is the heightened frequency of *just* preceding verbs due to its use as "simply" or something to do with its collocation with verbs? The results in Figure 9.3 cannot answer this question because we only have half the information required. We have all the tokens of *just* but we do not have all the verbs (or adjectives, nouns, or other words) where *just* could have occurred but did not. Without this information, the high frequency of *just* with verbs may simply be due to the fact that verbs themselves are highly frequent in language (see Altenberg, 1990: 187). Support for this comes from an examination of the wordlists in Chapter 2. Notice that among the most frequent words overall are several common verbs, including forms of "be" (*'s, 'm, is, are*), *know, have, think, go*. These words combined make up a huge proportion of words in any database of the English language and if this underlying tendency is not factored into the analysis, simple co-occurrence counts alone do not assess whether a word is actually associated with its collocate or not. Nevertheless, the very high rate of pre-verbal *just* is suggestive.

Circumscribing *just* to pre-verbal contexts

In order to evaluate whether *just* may have a tendency to occur with verbs what is required is a sample of the verbs in the data. Then, I could assess how often *just* occurs with them and then whether or not this is changing over time.

Fortunately, one of my colleagues conducted a large-scale research project on discourse marker *like* in the TEC/TTC (D'Arcy, 2005 and forthcoming). Her accountable study of *like* required careful circumscription of several syntactically delimited contexts, among them the verb phrase. In D'Arcy's (2005: 167) study, the verbal contexts were defined as any declarative sentence containing a verb and any aspectual or tense markers. The data set comprises 6,528 tokens, which are coded for co-occurring adverbs and other contextual factors relevant to the verb phrase. This strictly delimited data set has the potential to answer the question: How often does *just* occur before verbs?[4]

Table 9.3 documents the distribution of *just* in pre-verbal contexts when all the verbs in the data are in the analysis and this shows that overall *just* occurs 4.3 percent of the time. This rate is starkly different from the proportion of pre-verbal *just* tokens when only instances of *just* are taken into account, 46 percent, as in Figure 9.3! The results in Figure 9.3 lead us astray because the hidden fact is that verbs are far more frequent than any other category. In order to know whether there was a correlation between verbs and *just* we need to have all the verbs in the data in the analysis. This underscores how important it is to use appropriate methods for one's research. If I had I stopped the analysis with the results in Figure 9.3, I would have come to the wrong interpretation. Now, as Table 9.3 shows, even different verb constructions do not have equal propensities for *just*.

Table 9.3 *Overall distribution of* just *by following verb type*

	%	N
aux + V-ing	7.7	797
modal	4.5	737
finite verb	4.1	3,497
aux + V-ed	4.1	193
infinitive	3.7	273
participle	3.6	168
negative	2.3	307
other	2.0	554
TOTAL		6,526

The favored locus of *just* in pre-verbal environments is in preceding aux + V-ing constructions, as in (153).

153.   a. But he's *just* <u>standing</u> there. (James McCready, 11)
    b. I was waiting at the house watching TV and I was *just* <u>waiting</u> for them. (Cheryl Choi, 11)

Finite verbs, as in (154), are extremely frequent (over 50 percent of the verbs in the data). In this context *just* occurs 4 percent of the time.

154.   a. But the fish can die like they *just* <u>float</u> up. (Karl Galang, 11)
    b. Yeah mostly now they *just* <u>laugh</u> at me. (Stephen Hardwick, 15)
    c. I'm the one who *just* <u>stays</u> quiet until someone talks to me. (Clara Felipe, 16)
    d. He *just* <u>threw</u> it like randomly. (James McCready 11)

Is this frequent enough for *just* to have reached the threshold of a grammatical marker? To my knowledge there is no empirical research that evaluates this question. If the evidence from studies of tense/aspect marking in English is any indication, prescribed markers are often absent in the spoken language. The absence of past tense marking via –*t/d* for example can be as high as 33 percent in Standard North American English (Guy, 1991) and higher in ethnic varieties, such as 50 percent in Hispanic English in the USA (Bayley, 1994; Santa Ana, 1996), and in Caribbean varieties much higher, 50–97 percent (Poplack and Tagliamonte, 2001: Table 6.1). Further research on aspect markers and their grammatical trajectories would offer further insight. Then we would be able to establish how often grammatical markers actually occur when they are supposedly "required." As far as pre-verbal *just* is concerned, the fact that it appears alongside only 4.3 percent of the verbs in the data may not be evidence that it is not a grammatical marker.

According to Aijmer (2002), an indicator of grammatical development is collocation with other discourse-pragmatic markers. She suggests that while a word is still ambiguous as to function, speakers have a tendency to use other forms supportive of the evolving meaning. Indeed, in some cases of grammatical change in the history of English, two competing forms have been known to occur simultaneously until one wins out (Nevalainen et al., 2011).[5] Supportive of these lines of inquiry, Cheshire (2007: 185) observed that GEs that were least advanced in terms of grammatical development co-occurred most often with other discourse markers. Extrapolating from this research, I hypothesize that collocation of *just* with other forms would be evidence for an early stage in the evolution towards linguistic denotation. Examination of the contexts where *just* occurs almost immediately reveals an abundance of *like*, and verb particles, e.g. *up*, as in (155).

155.   a. I'll *just* <u>*like*</u> totally go berserk. (Diego Ferreira, 18)
    b. I'm <u>*like*</u> *just* playing around, doing nothing. (Antonio Silvaggio, 16)

c. I *just like* woke <u>up</u>. (Jose Pinheiro-Galvao, 12)
d. Everyone was just sitting there and then Dan *just* like stood <u>up</u>. (Brett Macready, 22)

Let's test for the possibility that co-variation significantly impacts the use of pre-verbal *just*. When particles occur is *just* more likely? Figures 9.4 and 9.5 document the collocation of *like* and verb particles, *up*, *out*, along with *just*.

Figures 9.4 and 9.5 demonstrate that *just* co-occurs with other discourse-pragmatic particles more frequently than alone. Moreover, this is parallel across nearly every age group. It is interesting to note the difference between the use of discourse *like* and *just* in Figure 9.4. While *like* in these contexts evidently sprang into the grammar among speakers born in the 1960s, *just* has been relatively stable across the board.

We are now zeroing in on the linguistic developments of *just* in the verb system. The next question is whether the use of pre-verbal *just* is increasing over the course of the twentieth century. Figure 9.6 plots the distribution of *just* in the two principal verbal constructions – simple verbs and V-*ing* by generation.[6]

Figure 9.6 shows an increase in the use of *just* in both simple and aux-V-ing verbs from the early twentieth century to a highpoint among the speakers born

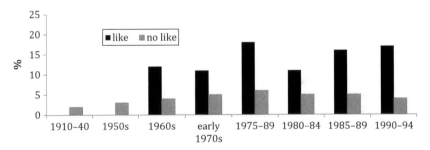

Figure 9.4 Co-variation of *just* with discourse marker *like*

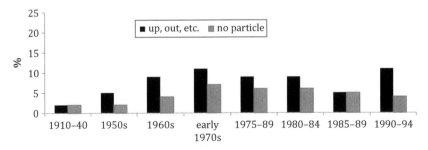

Figure 9.5 Co-variation of *just* with verb particles

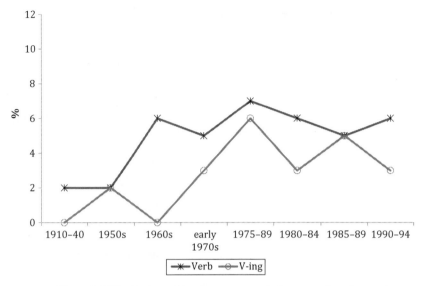

Figure 9.6 Distribution of *just* in two pre-verbal constructions by speaker date of birth

in the late 1970s. Moreover, the rise in usage is statistically significant at the $p < 0.05$ level. The peak in apparent time in late adolescence and early adulthood is a well-known concomitant of linguistic change, which occurs due to incrementation and stabilization in late adolescence (see Figures 1.1–1.2).

This change is incipient at best. The frequency of *just* in pre-verbal contexts is very low among the individuals on the frontlines, only 10 percent of the data. It is possible that the context in which pre-verbal *just* is encroaching needs to be more carefully circumscribed. Consider the Bear Story in (156).

156. Bear Story
    a. We usually get two or three a year [bears].
    b. *Like* yeah, about three weeks ago, I was outside with my best friend
    c. And we're ***just*** sitting on his trailer after we got back from a run
    d. And we're ***just*** sitting there
    e. And we're waiting for like- I don't know what we're waiting for
    f. We're ***just*** chilling out-
    g. And we look
    h. And we can hear like these little claws like on the road
    i. And we like look over
    j. And there's this bear standing there on the road
    k. And we're like in the middle of our lot,
    l. we *just* kind of like crept into the corner of like- our two houses are really close,

m. we crept into the corner of his
n. And it's still looking at us
o. And we *just* jumped the fence, like
p. Yeah we were sitting on the fence
q. And we called our parents and yeah.
r. And then my dad came out
s. And he was *just* watching it for a bit
t. And all the neighbors were *just* watching it
u. And then it *just* ran back into the gully. (Caleb Stine, 16)

In 21 clauses of the Bear Story, Caleb uses *just* eight times; however, this represents 38 percent of the verbs. In future research circumscription of the variable context will be isolated to the use of *just* in storytelling to further narrow down its emerging trajectory of change. This may be the route that a new verbal marker takes as it sneaks into the grammar.

What does the use of *just* tell us about teen language?

The use of *just* is a fabulously versatile feature of contemporary English. However, it too is not a feature of teen language per se. In fact, overall it is not particular to any age or sex. Everyone uses it across the population. While the literature documents a plethora of different functions, many of these are not productive in actual usage. Instead, most of instances of *just* in conversation can be covered with the meaning "simply" and this has been stable across the twentieth century. While other studies have included the tokens of *just* only, in this study I have also examined *just* within the context of the linguistic system. The challenge has been to expose the underlying mechanism that produces *just*. To do so, I tested several methods. This exercise has led to several new understandings. I have discovered that *just* is associated with pre-verbal contexts and this use is increasing among youth. Although *just* can be used for many different nuances, its main purpose in the data is to modify a verb, particularly those in progressive constructions, e.g. *I was just thinking*. This evidence suggests that *just* may be in the initial stages of developing grammatical meaning. The fact that it co-varies significantly with other discourse markers when used in this type of context supports this interpretation.

In sum at the beginning of the twenty-first century, *just* is still polysemous and fluid. I suggest that this is a result of the fact that its (new) functions are still developing. It will be a word to watch over the next 20 years. Wise readers with a penchant for catching language change in action should be keeping an eye on how people use *just*, just in case.

Actually, I think I would never date a poet. Like as good as Eliot is, every time I read him, I'm like, okay that's really beautiful, but I don't like the fact that he's just trying the ugly beautiful, kind of. He's taking the state of society and he's turning it into really beautiful poetry, but at the same time he's not doing anything about it, he's not like proposing a solution to it or anything, he's just whining. (Hilda Tun, 17)[7]

Language puzzle

Consider the following narrative, *Skipping School*, from the Toronto Storytelling Corpus. The story comprises 206 words.

Skipping school
Male, 19
    I think in grade one I skipped school for two weeks
        because there was a day when I didn't do homework
        and I was scared of the teacher.
    So, every day I just took comic books in my backpack
    And I just like walked two blocks away from my house
    And like hid somewhere, like in a corner,
    And read comic books for couple hours.
    And then I'd run back home and check the time,
        because I can see the clock from the door.
    So I just check the time
    And if it was like lunchtime or whatever,
    Because I came back for lunch every day.
    and I'd just check,
        if it was time, I'd just come back in.
        Otherwise, I'd go back and read more.
    And one day when I was like checking the time,
        I came back too early
    And my grandma was there in the room.
    And she saw me, checking the time.
    So she was like, "why aren't you at school, it's too early to be back."
    And then she checked my backpack
    And it was just comic books.
    So I got in trouble for that
    And the next day she dragged me to school
    And I was like crying the whole way.

a. How many tokens of *just* are there?
b. What proportion does this represent of the total number of words, which is 203?
c. What syntactic functions of *just* are represented?
d. How often does *just* occur with another discourse marker?
e. How many verbs are there in the story that "could have" have been modified by *just*? This is a tricky question. If you try to answer it, you'll see how difficult it is to do this kind of work!
f. Find an example of quotative *like*.

(*cont.*)

g. How many times does *like* occur when it is not a quotative or a verb?
h. What proportion does this represent of the total number of words?
i. How many occur before verbs?
j. Can you spot two other discourse-pragmatic features?

Answers
a. *6.*
b. *3 percent 6/206*
c. *5 tokens of "simply"; 1 token of "only," e.g. It was "just" comic books.*
d. *Once, And I just like walked two blocks away from my house.*
e. *Debatable.*
f. *So she was like, "why aren't you at school, it's too early to be back."*
g. *6.*
h. *3 percent 6/2006*
i. *4.*
j. *or whatever, a GE; sentence starter "so," "I think" a potential parenthetical.*

10   Adjectives

The good, bad, and lovely

Weird, very strange. (Jim Lear, 51)
That's our school, different, odd, unusual. (Amanda Levy, 12)

Adjectives describe a range of qualities, including color, dimension, size, time, and human attributes. They offer extra information about the object signified. Adjectives are (1) descriptive; (2) (often) gradable; (3) inflected morphologic-ally; and (4) capable of being used in both attributive and predicative function (Biber et al., 1999: 504–507; Crystal, 1995: 211; Huddleston and Pullum, 2002: 527–535). Adjectives are gradable in the sense that they can denote degrees of whatever quality is being described, e.g. <u>very</u> *blue/big/early/happy.* Adjectives can also show degree comparatively via morphological inflection, e.g. *blue/bluer/bluest.* Finally, adjectives can be categorized according to syntactic position, as attributive, as in (157), predicative, as in (158), and as often the case in spoken data, some of the latter can appear alone, as in (158c).

Attributive

157.   a. Look, okay they have *weird* names for each other, okay (Craig Carvalheiro, 19)
        b. There was that huge gas explosion that was probably the start of our *weird, weird* childhood. (Christian Laterman, 19)
        c. He was like, "No, like almost like it was like poisonous." I was like, "*weird.*" But he didn't say anything (Katherine Berazzi, 18)

Predicative

158.   a. It was just something *weird* that happened (Diego Ferreira, 18)
        b. It's kind of like alternativish ... but it's *weird.* (Andy Eaton, 18)
        c. I think she just didn't just understand. [007] *Weird.* That's true she actually drive me up like four blocks further. (Lauren Welsby, 18)

Attributive adjectives describe attributes of nouns, e.g. *weird names,* while predicative adjectives occur after a verb, e.g. *it's weird.* While not all adjec-tives have all these properties and none of these properties are specific to adjectives (see e.g. Huddleston and Pullum, 2002: 528), they offer a composite picture of adjectival function.

In studies of language, adjectives are most often studied with respect to their preferred left to right order, e.g. *green, soft, nice large cushions* (e.g. Dixon, 1977; Quirk et al., 1972: 924), or their grammatical development from attributive function, *a different place* (meaning a distinct location), to being positioned after determiners and employed in quantifier uses, e.g. *different places* (meaning many locations) (Adamson, 2000; Breban, 2008). Adjectives have rarely, if ever, been studied using dialectological or sociolinguistic methods. Instead, the vast majority of research involving adjectives comes from psychological investigations that rely on adjective choice as a means to study human behavior and change. The well known "Adjective Check List"[1] (Gough and Heilbrun, 1965, 1983) is an assessment tool for identifying psychological states. Individuals check off any number of 300 commonly used adjectives in the check list, e.g. *intelligent, cautious, clear-thinking, determined*, that are salient to how they feel at the time of evaluation. Their choices and how these choices change according to circumstance offer important insights into human nature. Indeed there is a vast literature on this research program (e.g. Formy-Duval et al., 1995; Itzhar-Nabarro et al., 2009; Mayer, 2004) demonstrating that adjectives are a critical window on the human psyche. All these studies suggest that adjectives warrant further study; however, the surprising dearth of research on adjectives means there is little upon which to base a new linguistic investigation.

I think well I think language is ever changing and with like different like groups of people, it's different because you get everyone else's attributes and things like that. (Amanda Burton, 18)

Many adjectives are relatively unremarkable and among the standard repertoire of adjectives in any individual or community, such as *good, bad, first, last, hot, cold, black, white, little, big, wonderful, pretty, funny, nice.* Yet when I started investigating adjective variation further I discovered that it was just as easy to find non-standard, locally situated, and socially marked adjectives such as *cool, shitty, teensy, humungo,* and *sick.* Moreover, contrasts between learned, standard, informal, or vernacular uses abound, e.g. *timorous* vs. *afraid* vs. *scared* vs. *chicken* (in the sense of cowardly, e.g. *he's too chicken to do it*). Some adjectives are regionally delimited such as *gnarly* for older hippy California or *cheeky* for British or *wicked* for New England. Certain words can be associates with communities of practice or social networks such as *epic* for gamers or *foig* (an acronym for "find out in game") for LARPers (live-action role-playing gamers) and there are undoubtedly countless other examples. Many adjectives are typical of older rather than younger individuals, e.g. *wonderful* vs. *sick*; *bad* vs. *bummer*. In sum, adjectives vary tremendously and they have social connotations in abundance.

> **Activity**
> Come up with all the words you can think of in place of mundane adjectives
> in everyday use, for example "good," "bad," "big," "little." Try the same
> experiment with verbs such "throw up," "relax," or "get drunk."

Adjectives have also been the source of prescriptive commentary, particularly with regard to their changing nature and uniqueness, as can be inferred
from the following entry about *weird*, as in (159a–b), from the *Dictionary of
Modern English Usage* by the British schoolmaster, Henry Watson Fowler.

159.   a. *weird*, a word ruined by becoming a "vogue-word." (Fowler, 1927: 703)
         b. vogue-word, Every now and then a word emerges from obscurity . . .
            into sudden popularity . . . they are not part of the normal vocabulary,
            but still repulsive to the old and the well-read. (Fowler, 1927: 697)

The stigma evident in these quotes from the early twentieth century may
have been a herald of things to come, as we shall see. At any given point in
time there will be innumerable vogue words, nouns, adverbs, and intensifiers;
however, adjectives in particular may be well suited for tapping the social
nature of linguistic change. Adjectives vary not only from place to place, from
time to time, and from one social group to another but also according to
internal mental states and processes.

One important characteristic of the adjectives I have just mentioned is that
they are subjective, usually with a fairly strong positive or negative connota-
tion. This attribute may explain their penchant for change. As with intensifiers,
they can easily be bleached of impact by overuse. For example, to say
something is *interesting* may have once meant something highly positive but
nowadays it is so overused that to call something *interesting* is almost
damning. This type of change necessitates the rise of a new word to carry
the full impact of the intended meaning. Since adjectives are more likely to
carry this kind of subjective information, they may be more prone to rapid
linguistic change than nouns and verbs.

Adjectives as a linguistic variable

The problem for the language scientist is to convincingly establish how
adjectives can be studied quantitatively, and in so doing, to determine whether
the choice of adjective is a *bona fide* linguistic variable. First, as I have
demonstrated, variation among (partial) synonyms is much more socially
stratified than might be expected and shifts across generations are evident.
This establishes that semantic fields, like other systems of variation, evidence
longitudinal *layering* (Hopper, 1991: 22–31), the coexistence of newer forms

with an already existing layer of functionally equivalent ones. Second, super tokens – the use of multiple synonymous forms in the same stretch of discourse by the same individual (Tagliamonte, 2006a: 96) – are frequent, as in (160). Even cursory investigation of corpus data makes it apparent that alternation of adjectives for comparable meaning can be found in many semantic fields, including countless alternatives to "good" and "bad" as in (161).

160. a. That's just *dumb*. He really did a *stupid* thing there. (Narissa Wold, 28)
      b. Hey sis! Life is *good*. It's really *great* out here. (Charlie Manetta, 40)
      c. She's really *weird*. She's *odd*. (Kelly Mayewsky, 18)
      d. *Weird*, eh? [Interviewer] That is *strange*. (Jim Lear, 51)
      e. I don't mind him, he's just *weird*, *creepy*. Like, people we work with are *weird*. (Katherine Berazzi, 18)
      f. [041] lol your *sick* [7] im *great* for many reasons. (TOR, MSN, Milen 7 and Terrence Flemwood 041)
      g. Oh she was *strange* – She was *different*. (TOR, Margaret Williams, 49)

161. a. good (great, wonderful, awesome, sick ...)
      b. bad (terrible, awful, lame, shitty ...)

Early work in variationist approaches explored the possibility of using semantic fields as a foundation for circumscribing the variable context for semantic and lexical variables. For example, Sankoff et al. (1978) proposed a model for alternation among partial synonyms using semantic domains. Based on earlier work by Sankoff (1971), they showed that a combination of ethno-semantic methodology and distributional linguistic criteria could work together to substantiate a lexical choice set. In the semantic field they analyzed, Canadian French verbs meaning "to dwell," they discovered that the lexical choices were delimited by social factors: use of *habiter*, "to live" was circum-scribed to highly educated professionals while *rester*, "to stay/remain," was used more often by working-class speakers (Sankoff et al., 1978: 30–31).

Support for this type of analysis within the adjective system comes from historical research on adjectives in the history of English. Breban (2008) conducted a study on the adjectives of difference, i.e. *different*, *distinct*, *divers(e)*, *several*, *sundry*, *various*, and demonstrated that they could be treated as a set of layered forms in the grammar (Hopper, 1991). Taking this cohort as her baseline, Breban's study offered insights into grammatical change inside the noun phrase as these adjectives shifted from attributive functions to determiner and quantifier uses. While Breban's (2008) study focused on grammatical developments that are not the focus of this investigation, the relevant fact is that her starting point was a set of adjectives that expressed the same general meaning. Building on these studies and given the evidence from the information gain analysis introduced in Chapter 2 (see Table 2.15) I decided to target a specific semantic field – strangeness. A methodological point is worth making at this juncture. Figuring out what may be worthy of study, probing the data for verification, and finding supportive evidence in the literature is only the beginning. You also need to extract and code the thousands of tokens in the data. This is where teamwork comes in. The weird tale I'm about to tell was made possible by a course project in my class at the LSA Summer Institute in 2011.[2]

Historical perspective

The word *weird* has been part of the English lexicon for centuries. However, it was not always an adjective. In Old English *weird* was a noun referring to the "principle, power or agency by which events are predetermined," i.e. fate or destiny, as with the Weird Sisters from *Macbeth*. By 1300 it was used as a verb and by 1400 as an adjective, simultaneously developing derivational and inflectional morphology, e.g. *–dom, -ish, -ness, -ed*, etc. Such processes reflect typical mechanisms underlying lexical-semantic change including broadening, semantic extension, etc. (e.g. Forston, 2003: 649). In this study my focus is on variation among synonyms of a set rather than the semantic shifts undergone by a single form.

The first step in the analysis was to find synonyms for *weird*. Using the OED's Thesaurus, I discovered that competition and change within the semantic field of strangeness has been going on in English throughout its recorded history. The adjective *strange*, as in (162a), was first attested in the 1300s and appears to have been the foremost means to convey this meaning for several centuries.[3] Next came *unusual*, as in (162b), *odd*, as in (162c), *peculiar*, as in (162d), and *bizarre*, as in (162e).

162.   a. The kynde of mannes herte is to delyte In thing that *straunge* is.
            (*c.*1374, Geoffrey Chaucer, *Anelida & Arcite* 202)
         b. Some Commet, or *vnusuall* prodigie. (*c.*1616, William Shakespeare,
            The Taming of the Shrew (1623) iii. ii. 96)
         c. So *odde*, and from all fashions, As Beatrice is. (1600, William
            Shakespeare, *Much Ado about Nothing* iii. i. 72)
         d. This Story I mention to you as a very peculiar one, which has
            something of a more vicious Taste in it than I have ever met with.
            (1710, D. Manley, *Memoirs of Europe* I. ii. 175)
         e. The ornament of Writing, which is greater, more various and *bizarre* in
            Poesie than in any other kind. (1668, John Dryden, *Secret-love* Pref.
            sig. a1)

Additional synonyms were added to the semantic field in the eighteenth century, with *eerie*, as in (163a), and a continuing layering of new variants in the nineteenth century, including *funny*, as in (163b), *weird*, as in (163c), and *uncanny*, as in (163d).

163.   a.   Be thou a bogle by the *eerie* side of an auld thorn. (1792, Robert Burns
              Letter to Cunningham, 10 September (1985) II. 145)
         b.   Lady Ellesmere was very *funny* about E. C. Gaskell, wanting very much
              to Know her, and yet quite shy about it. (1855, Lord Houghton, Letter in
              T. W. Reid, *Life of Lord Houghton* (1890) I. xi. 527)
         c.   It is A tale more fit for the *weïrd* winter nights – Than for these garish
              summer days. (*c*.1822, Percy Bysshe Shelley, *Witch of Atlas* lxxviii, in
              Posthumous Poems (1824) 55)
         d.   We walked in and out, and took again and again a fresh look at the
              uncanny stones. (1856, R. W. Emerson, *English Traits* xvi. 278)

The steady, successive documentation of lexical variation across 700 years
or more in real time demonstrates that these adjectives have been engaged in a
progressive reshuffling of words for the same semantic field from one century
to the next, as in (164). The adjectives are ordered by their appearance and
those arising in the same century are placed on the same line. Note that the
1800s were rich in the development of new words for "strange."

164.   a.   Strange – 1300s→
         b.   Unusual/odd – 1500s→
         c.   Peculiar/bizarre – 1600s →
         d.   Eerie – 1796 →
         e.   Funny/weird/creepy/uncanny – 1800s→
         f.   Wacky/freaky 1900s

An issue arises: how far can the net be cast for variants belonging to the
same semantic field, i.e. "meaning the same thing"? One immediately encounters questionable cases, for example *creepy, freaky,* or *wacky,* as in (165).[4]
Should these be included in the variable context or not?[5]

165.   a.   An artistically embroidered coverlet tenanted ... by countless swarms of
              creepy insects. (1889, John Abercromby, *A Trip through the Eastern
              Caucasus* 180)
         b.   Theodora was ... a slippery, *freaky* little creature. (1891 *Blackwood's
              Magazine* 149 107/2)
         c.   They all want to know why he done it, and is he gone clean whacky.
              (1938, "J. Digges," *Bowleg Bill* 28)

The general synonymy of these words (i.e. same semantic field) in addition
to the fact that can all be found in variation in the TEC/TTC, as in (166), is
consistent with the methods outlined in Sankoff et al. (1978).

166.   a.   [007] did your power go all *wacky* too? (Julio McCleary, 16)
         b.   They have like dyed hair or whatever. Their fashion sense is *wack*. (Luke
              Lung, 19)
         c.   And you know *wacky* stuff is really amazing out there. (Richard
              Gruensten, 26)

Casting a wide net, I included all potential synonyms within the same semantic field, but restricted the pool to those that are unambiguous and that can be found in the TEC.

The scenario of variation and historical change in the evolution of these adjectives presents a fruitful area for study from a quantitative variationist perspective. In Chapter 5 I documented the rapid changes going on in intensifying adverbs (e.g. *very*, *really*, *so*). The cycle was suitably telescoped to expose the rolling progression of change. The rise and fall of existing intensifiers was visible in the TEC through the lens of apparent time. What will we find with the adjectives of strangeness?

What type of change?

Variation among words in the same semantic field is by its nature lexical change: (1) the same category and (2) the same meaning. Most studies of semantic change involve the transformations of a single form as it undergoes categorical and meaning shifts (Breban, 2008), and most studies of lexical change involve nouns, e.g. *sneakers*, *pop*, *chesterfield*, etc. (Chambers, 2003a). In this case, the object of investigation is an open class in the grammar – adjectives. How do these facts impact variation and change? The study of intensifying adverbs, another open class category, demonstrated ongoing processes of renewal and recycling. As one form loses its force, e.g. *very*, a new one comes in to take its place, e.g. *really*, *so* (Chapter 5) (Tagliamonte, 2008). Further, social processes appear to be involved in the selection of one form over another. However, older forms in the system do not disappear, but often remain at low frequencies. Further, new and older forms jostle for supremacy over time, sometimes returning to supremacy, sometimes correlated with generation, sex, variety, or geography or some combination of these. Variation and change within a semantic field may well develop and pattern in the same way. Thus, two different processes are relevant. The first is *renewal*, which is when a new form enters the language and comes to be used for the same meaning as an earlier form. This is visible in the historical record of the OED and is suggestive of the information gain results discussed earlier. The second is *recycling*, which is when a set of related forms changes in relative frequency over time such that a dominating form rises and falls in the proportion it represents of the whole. In the analyses that follow I will frame my interpretation according to these processes.

In sum, I have established that adjectives have several key characteristics which make them an ideal choice for the study of linguistic change: (1) versatility and color; (2) capacity for rapid change; (3) renewal of different forms; and (4) recycling of older forms. All of these characteristics suggest constant change as waning forms are replaced with newly coined ones that can more successfully describe qualities. The data exploration tool described in Chapter 2 confirmed that certain adjectives are changing in apparent time in the TEC/TTC and that at least one member of the semantic field of adjectives of strangeness is greatly implicated, i.e. *weird*.

As discussed earlier, in any given variety, at any point in time, the coexistence of different forms may mirror older and newer layers in the process of change. In addition, the adjectives of strangeness have a number of key methodological requirements: they are relatively robust (most individuals use them); they are part of a structured set in the grammar (i.e. the same semantic field); and not unimportantly they fulfill my Principle of Curiosity.

Method

Building on the fact that adjectives meaning "strange/unusual" often alternate, have undergone long-term renewal, and continue to be layered in modern English, *all* synonyms with this range of meanings were extracted from the TEC. Some forms were adverbs, as in (167). These had to be carefully culled from the data.

167.   a. And some of the boys really do dress *weird* to my North American eye.
            (laughs), you know? (Pirkko Runonen, 50)
        b. Like they talk *weird* and they dress *strange* but do you think that reflects?
            (Ellie Shadden, 75)

A trickier problem arose with the adjective *funny*. This lexical item is anomalous because it has two indistinguishable readings: (1) *funny* meaning "strange" and (2) *funny* meaning laughable. The ambiguity of the word *funny* in English is unmistakable in the well-known query "is that funny 'ha ha' or funny 'peculiar?'," as in (168).

168. OED:
        a. *funny-peculiar* adj. colloq. used to distinguish sense A. 2 from sense A. 1
            (= funny-ha-ha adj.), the two antithetic expressions freq. appearing together.
        b. Chris. That's funny. Button. What do you mean, funny? *Funny-
            peculiar*, or *funny ha-ha*? (1938, "I. Hay" Housemaster iii. 78)
        c. John Gubbins leant forward, smiling in a *funny-peculiar* not *funny-ha-ha*
            way. (1959, John Verney, *Friday's Tunnel* xxv. 227)

Although in rare cases it was possible to infer that the meaning of *funny* was "strange," as in (169a–c), in contrast to "laughable," as in (169d), in the vast majority of cases, it is impossible to disambiguate form and function, as in (170a–b).

169.   a. It's so *funny*. It's *weird* (Mindy Chow, 17)
        b. I'm a *weird* 18-year-old girl with *funny* colored hair who hasn't touched a
            boy in public in like at least a year. (Kelly Mayewsky, 18)

      c. My dad- my dad's like a minor author and he's spoken at my school before and they asked him to come in as a speaker. And by coincidence I was chosen as the salutation for my school's graduation. So, my father spoke right after me in my graduation, which was such a *weird* coincidence out of all things to happen. [Interviewer] That is kind of *funny*. (Grant Simkovic, 18)

      d. I thought it was so *funny*, I just stood there laughing and laughing. (June Watson, 49)

170.   a. [010] They smoke a lot of pot there too. [Interviewer] At your job? [010] Yeah, like when we're cleaning up, all the managers are smoking up pot and like- [Interviewer] that's pretty sweet. [010] Yeah, it's pretty *funny*. I kind of like it 'cause it's so different from when I worked at Club Monaco. 'Cause we don't do that there. Let me tell you. (Grant Simkovic, 18)

      b. What's nice about having a big backyard also, um, like we used to set up our badminton net a lot. With that we could play a lot of badminton and stuff, it was pretty fun. Especially when you get my mom and dad playing. That's kind of *funny*. But, ah, it was good fun. (Craig Thompson, 18)

Due to this anomaly, it was infelicitous to include "funny" in the analysis.[6]

Another anomaly presented itself. The interviewers of the TEC produced adjectives of strangeness as ratification markers in their interviewing style, as in (171). These were, of course, excluded from the analysis, which focuses on the individuals in the sample rather than the interviewers. However, they expose an intriguing discourse-pragmatic function worthy of further study.

171.   a. Sean's such a fuck-up. [Interviewer] Really, *that's weird*. Have you called him or? [012] I've hung-out with him. (Kelly Mayewsky, 18)

      b. Her mother taught my cousins in Simcoe which is just- [Interviewer] Oh God *that's weird*. (Brandon Griffo, 44)

      c. [01] I always had to see the team from Ottawa, or Montreal, or Hamilton [Interviewer] *That's strange*, why wouldn't they show Toronto? (Jim Lear, 51)[7]

The limits of the analysis thus defined – unambiguous synonyms in the semantic field of strangeness – provided 1,187 adjectives. The next step is to determine the inventory of strangeness adjectives and how frequently each one is used so that these results can be used as a baseline for other studies. In addition, we will assess the influence and strength of contextual factors, some of which may be implicated in the expansion of one adjective or another into different types and functions. Each adjective was coded for lexical item (i.e. *weird*, *strange*, *freaky*); adjective function (predicative or attributive); the individual and each individual's date of birth, age at the time of interview, sex, and education level.

Distributional analyses

Table 10.1 shows the inventory, frequency, and proportions of adjectives of strangeness in the TEC and TTC.

It is immediately apparent that a single form dominates: 70.3 percent of the adjectives are the lexical item *weird*. The closest contender is *strange*, which represents only 14 percent of the data. All other forms are extremely rare. The extent of homogeneity in this semantic field could not have been anticipated. The next step is to investigate the pattern of change in apparent time. Figure 10.1 shows the distribution of the main adjectives of strangeness in apparent time by age group.[8]

Figure 10.1 shows a (mostly) steady increase in the use of *weird* across the generations in Toronto and the concomitant decline of *strange*. Note that the shift towards *weird* occurred abruptly between the eldest members of the community, over 60 years of age, and the next age group, the 50–59-year-olds. A demarcated point of reversal is evident. The oldest generation has a relatively robust inventory of forms. While *strange* dominates the system, a variety of other forms are part of the mix, including *odd*, *creepy*, *weird*, and others. However, among the 50–59-year-olds the system has notably shifted, with *weird* surging to ascendancy and *strange* in decline along with all the other forms. After this time period, the encroachment of *weird* into this semantic field is abrupt at first and then with each successively younger age group it gains more ground. Among the youngest generation, hardly any other form is used for this semantic sense. *Weird* is supreme.

Table 10.1 *Overall distribution of adjectives of strangeness TEC/TTC, c.2002–2004*

Adjective	N	%
weird	834	70.3
strange	166	14.0
odd	50	4.2
creepy	37	3.1
bizarre	29	2.5
freaky	28	2.4
eerie	10	0.8
unusual	7	0.6
peculiar	7	0.6
wacky	5	0.4
abnormal	2	0.2
TOTAL N	1,187	

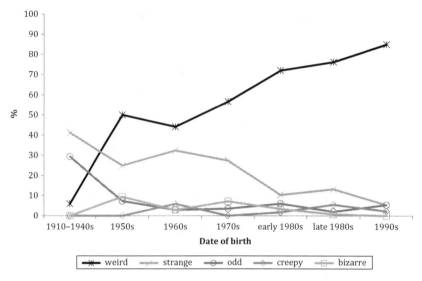

Figure 10.1 Distribution of the main adjectives of strangeness by age group

Sex of the individual

An association of adjectives with women is one of the few results that have been reported in studies on the use of adjectives (e.g. Entwhistle and Garvey, 1969). This fits in with the well-known tenet of sociolinguistics that females lead linguistic change, Principles 3 and 4 (e.g. Labov, 1990). We might hypothesize, therefore, that women would be leading the surge towards *weird*. Figure 10.2 tests this possibility by displaying the distribution of *weird* according to sex by speaker date of birth. The predictions for change are that an incoming form will show a monotonic increase in apparent time and that women will adopt incoming variants at about a generation ahead of men (Labov, 2001: 274).

Figure 10.2 shows the incremental increase in the use of *weird* across generations. The slight male lead visible for the 1950s and 1960s groups is not significant. Therefore both males and females in each age group use *weird* and in each cohort the use of *weird* is increasing. Notice too that there is no peak in apparent time. The evidence from the trajectory of change shows that the form rises to beyond the 50 percent mark (see Figure 1.2) within 30 years. There is a truly spectacular changeover in the adjectives of strangeness over the twentieth century. *Weird* is now the dominant word to describe this quality – used 85 percent of the time among teenagers – ousting nearly all other adjectives in its wake.

It now remains to discover whether there are any linguistic correlates that may underlie adjective use. If so, these would provide further clues about what is going on in the broader linguistic system that is causing this shifting system.

Adjective function

One of the main contrasts among adjectives is the difference between predicative adjectives and attributive adjectives, as in (172). Figure 10.3 tests whether this contrast has an effect on adjective choice.

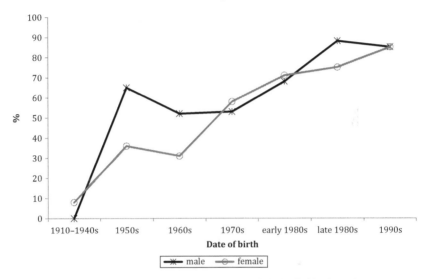

Figure 10.2 Distribution of *weird* by sex of the individual

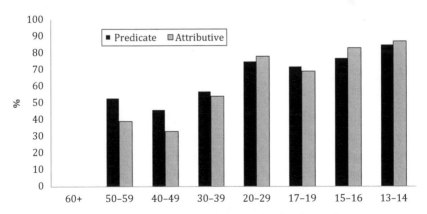

Figure 10.3 Distribution of *weird* by adjective function and age group

172.   I don't know, he's just *weird*. [Interviewer] I think he's just weird to you.
         [010] No he's a *weird* guy. (Christian Laterman, 19)

Figure 10.3 shows that adjective function is not a relevant predictor of adjective use. It may appear to have been a factor in the initial rise of *weird* since the adopting cohorts (the 40–59-year-olds) exhibit a contrast with predicative adjectives having greater use of *weird* than attributive ones. However, a chi square test reveals that neither contrast is significant, p = < 0.53 for the 40-year-olds and p = < 1.00 for the 50-year-olds. Among the 60+ year-olds there are no uses of *weird* at all. Therefore where *weird* exists, the functional contrast between adjective types is stable.

Collocation with intensifiers

Chapter 5 documented the use of intensifying adverbs modifying adjectives. This changeover in choice of adverb might be influenced by the co-occurring adjective. First, the two words naturally collocate in usage, as in (173). Second, it may be the case that using an incoming adjective might lead to the use of an incoming adverb or vice versa. In other words, they may co-vary predictably.

173.   a. That was just *weird* man. (Daniel Friesen, 26)
         b. And we never met each other at all so, it was very *weird*. (Jillian Clarin, 26)
         c. I felt like I was in American high school, like, Saved by the bell kind of high school. Yeah, it was so weird. So weird. (Yve Moise, 21)
         d. [Interviewer] Like how are they weird? [004] Like they just have really *weird* style. (Steve Fraute, 15)

Figure 10.4 tests whether intensifier use impacts adjective use by plotting the use of the main intensifying adverbs that co-occur with *weird* according to age.

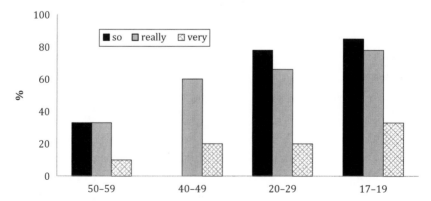

Figure 10.4 Distribution of *weird* when used with an intensifying adverb

The study of intensifiers in Chapter 5 documented the rapid rise of *really* (see Figure 5.4). However, could this simply be due to increasing use of a frequent collocate such as *really weird*? Figure 10.4 shows that the increasing use of *weird* as the favored adjective of strangeness is not patterning independently of this change, but in step with it. There is less use of any intensification among the eldest generation who use *weird*, accelerated use of *really* among the middle generations, and a concomitant increase in use of *so* among the two youngest generations, concurrent with the change in intensifiers from *very* to *really* to *so*. This demonstrates that the two changes are evolving in parallel.

Broader patterns of change

The next step is to put this change into broader context. The most appropriate means at my disposal is to compare the counts of the adjectives of strangeness across other data in my archive, and in other synchronic and diachronic corpora of English that are available.

Table 10.2 displays the raw frequencies of each of the main forms in the semantic field of strangeness in various corpora. SEO is Southeastern Ontario, comprising several small towns in the hinterland near Toronto (Tagliamonte and Denis, 2014). York is a corpus from York, England (Tagliamonte, 1998). North and South are compilations of dialects in the UK from the North and South (Tagliamonte, 2013).[9] Helsinki is the Helsinki Corpus from 730–1710 (1991).[10] In addition, I compare with an overarching check of these same forms from Google.[11] The latter is, of course, a very gross tally of forms and therefore can only cautiously be taken as a gauge of adjective frequency.

Table 10.2 is set up with a prevailing logic to it. The TEC represents the full range of a population from oldest to youngest individuals. The data in the next

Table 10.2 *Counts of adjectives of strangeness across synchronic and diachronic corpora*

Adjective	Toronto	Clara	Friends	SEO	York	North	South	Helsinki	Google 7-10-11
weird	834	66	179	112	51	5	20	20	389,000,000
strange	166	0	13	37	120	36	26	156	436,000,000
odd	50	1	1	60	118	107	88	18	315,000,000
creepy	37	0	10	0	0	0	5	0	89,600,000
bizarre	29	0	2	5	4	1	0	0	166,000,000
eerie	10	0	0	0	1	3	1	0	19,300,000
abnormal	2	0	0	1	0	0	0	0	18,200,000
peculiar	7	0	0	1	6	3	5	10	65,900,000
uncanny	1	0	1	0	0	0	0	0	18,100,000

column come from the Clara Corpus (see Table 2.8). The comparison between Toronto and Clara shows that Clara mirrors the broader community and further, as a member of the youngest generation, she reflects the predominant use of *weird* in the younger generation more generally. This comparison provides a confirmation that the individual reflects the group (see also Guy, 1980). The *Friends* materials provide a comparison to present-day American English among young adults (Tagliamonte and Roberts, 2005). Here too we observe a strong concordant distribution of forms – the Friends data is predominantly *weird*. The next column, SEO, comprises data from Canada, but from several small cities/towns again with a wide range of speaker ages, but it is non-urban (in contrast to the TEC). This offers key sociolinguistic contrasts with Toronto in terms of community size, type of social networks, and nature of the language contact situation (Trudgill, 2011). Notice the qualitative difference between the TEC and the Southeastern Ontario materials (SEO). The adjective *odd*, which we observed to be in decline in Toronto, is more frequent in the outlying areas of Canada. This is to be expected given the urban–rural contrast in the data and the expectation that rural areas will be more conservative than urban ones. The next column shifts the perspective to the British Isles. Here, we observe that *odd* is also more frequent in Britain generally, in York and in the North and South, consistent with the idea that British English is more conservative than American English. As with the Southeastern Ontario materials, this supports the idea that the data represent an older stage in the trajectory of forms in which *odd* was a more popular form. The data in York come from a relatively standard variety of northern British English with an age span of 19–92. In this data, notice that *strange* holds the most frequent slot with *odd* as a close second, and *weird* is rare. This suggests that *strange* and *odd* are old-fashioned forms in the Toronto system. This interpretation is supported, if we take another (metaphorical) step back in time by looking at the next columns over, the North and South. In this case the data labeled "North" come from small villages in Southwest Scotland, Northwest England, and Northern Ireland, far distant from any large cities and representing the oldest members of the community in each case. The data labeled "South" come from several small villages in Devon, Somerset, and Sussex in the South of England, again from the oldest generation. This means that the data in both these categories represent not only traditional areas but also the most conventional individuals in those areas. In all these locales, *odd* is the dominant form. *Strange* and *weird* are present, but less frequent than either of these. We are able to take one more step backwards in time with a comparison to the Helsinki Corpus (*c*.730–1700) where we see that *strange* dominates the system and *odd*, *weird*, and *peculiar* are infrequent, although is important to note that these historical data come from written sources only. Orientating back to the present-day perspective, Google offers a contributory viewpoint. Given the nature of this universal data repository, the fact that the same main adjectives of strangeness occupy the top spots (i.e. *strange, weird, odd*) is an overarching confirmation that the whole is not discordant with the corpus-based "parts" in the rest of the comparison. If we interpret the array of corpora in Table 10.2 as a proxy for diachronic development, we now have an arresting picture of adjectival change in English.

To further substantiate these trends, I probed Google Ngrams for each of the main adjectives in our analysis: *peculiar, strange, weird, odd, eerie*, and added *funny*. The results for American English are shown in Figure 10.5 and for British English in Figure 10.6.[12]

Together, Figures 10.5 and 10.6 show remarkably similar profiles suggesting broad processes underlying the developments. The adjective *peculiar* dominated these two major varieties of English until the mid-seventeenth

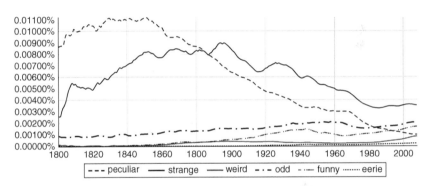

Figure 10.5 Google Ngrams search for adjectives of strangeness – American English[13]

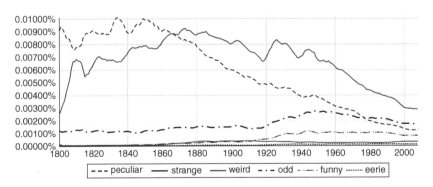

Figure 10.6 Google Ngrams search for adjectives of strangeness – British English

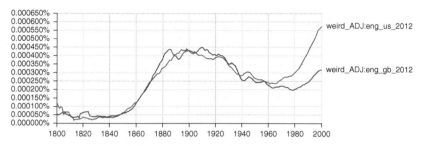

Figure 10.7 Google Ngrams search for adjective "weird" in American and British English

century; then *strange* took over. *Funny* increased in frequency in the early twenty-first century and *odd* increased sometime later. *Weird* shows a distinct rise in American English in the late 1800s, heralding the results we have presented here from the TEC. In sum, the corpus data as well as the Google searches are consistent with both the TEC results and the cross-corpora comparison in Table 10.2.[14]

In order to focus on the evolution of *weird*, Figure 10.7 presents another Google Ngrams search, this time with only the frequency of *weird* plotted for viewing and a comparison between American English and British English.

Figure 10.7 reveals two notable accelerations in the frequency of *weird:* one in the late nineteenth century with peaks in 1885 and 1910 in Great Britain and 1890 for the US, and a second upswing at the end of the twentieth century beginning with American English and British English in the 1980s.

The change towards *weird* is part of a broadly diffused tide of change across North American and British varieties of English. However, a further revelation is the particular points of acceleration in the use of *weird*. Although lexical change is not deeply embedded in the linguistic system, it evidently happens at a very particular time and place.

Discussion

The use of adjectives of strangeness is undergoing dramatic lexical change in North America – *weird* is becoming the dominant form. A notable finding is that the use of *weird* increases in parallel among both males and females. Several pieces of corroborating evidence suggest that this was not the result of internal semantic developments. First, *weird* was not a new adjective for strangeness in the late 1950s and 1960s when the people in the TEC started using this form, but one that had been around since the 1400s according to the OED and remarked upon as frequent in the early nineteenth century (1817). We know that by the early twentieth century in Britain (1927) it was subject to overt commentary, but judged transitory. Yet 50–59-year-olds in Toronto appropriated this form rather abruptly (high frequency) and thereafter it gains momentum and increases by age to the point where young people hardly use any other form. The age group who started this shift was born between 1944 and 1953. Given the overt commentary against *weird* from commentators (1927), it is conceivable that it was actually the parents or grandparents of these individuals who started to use the word *weird* frequently enough for it to become noted. If so, it must have taken another generation for this variant to begin incrementation and diffuse further into the population. However, this transition was not the result of typical processes of linguistic change such as analogical extension, pragmatic strengthening, and the like. Nor was it the result of internal linguistic conditioning. When we examined plausible internal factors influencing the choice of *weird* we found little to trace it to a mechanistic process such as extension from one type of adjective function to another. Even the proportion of attributive vs. predicative uses of *weird* was stable across the population. Moreover, the incoming adjective patterned in synch with a changeover in the use of intensifying adverbs. All the evidence points to the fact that the fluctuating inventory of adjectives is the result of lexical change rather than any underlying grammatical development. It was, and is, just what Fowler decreed, a word "in vogue."

Why *weird*?

What would have caused the adjective *weird* to become the favored form in the semantic field of strangeness in the late eighteenth century and then to accelerate again in the late nineteenth century? Some cursory sleuthing uncovered a series of suggestive correspondences. Interestingly, in the late eighteenth century, a new genre of fiction developed. It was called *Weird Fiction*. *Weird Fiction* is a subgenre of speculative fiction embracing all things strange and macabre that blends the supernatural, mythical, and scientific. Many popular writers of the time used the term *Weird Fiction* to describe their work (Joshi, 1990). The major authors of this genre span a range of American and British nationalities. H. P. Lovecraft and Clark Ashton Smith were American. William Hope Hodgson, Arthur Machen, and M. R. James were English. Lord Dunsany was Irish. This makes the development a transatlantic phenomenon. The early development of *Weird Fiction* occurs precisely when the word *weird* shows an upswing in the Google Ngrams search in Figure 10.7. Moreover, when the same genre undergoes a revival in the 1980s, *The New Weird*, there is another upswing in use of *weird* visible in the figure. Given that the data source of Google Ngrams is books, i.e. fiction and other published materials, it is not surprising to discover these correspondences. However, the links between the word *weird* and the time and place are germane to the question of how this change was actuated. The next question then becomes, can it be linked to vernacular usage? The use of the word *weird* and the rise of *Weird Fiction* and all its attendant uses of the adjective "weird" in the Google Ngrams searches do not automatically explain the abrupt rise of this word in the Toronto speech community among the individuals born after 1944. However, there is another influential cultural trend that may have reinforced and supported the rise of *weird* as a popular word for this semantic field. Beginning in the 1950s, a long line of comic book series became popular with repeating titles such as *Weird Fantasy* (1950), *Weird Adventures* (1951), *Weird Horrors* (1953), *Weird Chills* (1954), among many others. These early series were rekindled in the 1970s, also with titles such as *Weird War Stories* (1971–1983), *Weird Western Tales* (1972–1980), *Weird Mystery Tales* (1972–1975), etc. In fact, the sheer number of adjectival uses of *weird* in comic book titles is astounding (e.g. Overstreet and Carter, 2000: 773–775).[15] The individuals in the Toronto corpus would have been the same generations exposed to and possibly reading *Weird Fiction* and *Weird* comic books. Unfortunately, neither Jim Lear, examples (160d, 171c), nor any of the other individuals in the TEC was asked about their pastimes or reading habits. So, the degree of influence that these may have had on their language use is purely speculative; nevertheless, the timing and data from the world of popular literature are noteworthy. Further exploration of such cultural and other social influences on the choice of these or other adjectives in spoken or written language is beyond the scope of the present investigation, though they offer tantalizing observations for future exploration and study.

What does the use of adjectives tell us about teen language?

The study of adjectives has unveiled a new arena for the study of teen language since it offers fresh insights into linguistic developments and lexical choices. First, it appears that changes in the use of certain adjectives begin relatively abruptly; this is visible in both the TEC and in the Google Ngrams pattern for *weird*. Second, the nature of this process is not linguistically mechanistic according to any documented process. Instead, while synonyms may be plentiful within semantic fields, particularly the adjectives of strangeness, people do not make copious use of all the different words that are possible. Instead, semantic fields appear to be dominated by one form and then another over the long term. As Figures 10.5 and 10.6 suggest, this happens in waves of change across time: as one form rises, another takes its place and the former dwindles in frequency. Third, the selection process for which form dominates at any given point in time may not be entirely local, at least insofar as the contrast among Canada, the US, and Great Britain is concerned. Instead, it appears that the choice operates unconsciously, in tandem across localities, subtly influenced by broader cultural trends. Such changes are not without precedent. A parallel phenomenon is evident in the selection of children's names reported in Labov (2002), referencing research by Liebersen (2001) in which it is demonstrated that individuals select their children's names thinking this is their conscious personal choice, unaware that there are higher-level forces that determine these selections. Indeed, Labov suggests that:

> While most language forms are stable and customary, a few rapidly changing variables may be closely compared to fashions. Change and diffusion of fashions – in clothing, cosmetics – appears to be closer to linguistic change and diffusion than any other form of behavior. (Labov, 2002)[16]

If clothing and cosmetics can influence language change, why can't comics?

Whether the adjectives denoting strangeness are exceptional in this way or whether semantic fields behave like this more generally remains an important question. Many of these results entice curiosity, with respect to other adjectives, a wider range of stylistic repertoires and registers, and a more fine-grained social analysis. Given the host of semantic differences among the adjectives, we might predict that shifts within and across semantic fields will vary according to social, cultural, and economic trends. Yet linguistic change may be guided by even more all-embracing forces. New mega corpora of language (e.g. COCA), and the virtually endless new computer-mediated forms of written language offer an unprecedented range of real-time, online language data and so open up the opportunity to document a change in adjectives while it is happening. This may be the way forward to grasping the actuation problem of linguistic change.

The Actuation Problem refers to the cause of linguistic change: "Why do changes in a structural feature take place in a particular language at a given time, but not in other languages with the same features, or in the same language at other times?" (Weinreich et al., 1968: 102)

Language puzzle

WORDLISTS compiled from corpora are a great place to find the adjectives in a corpus. For this puzzle consult the WORDLISTS for the TEC and the TTC that can be found on the CUP website. Search for these six adjectives: *awesome*, *brilliant*, *fantastic*, *great*, *lovely*, *terrific*. Leaving aside, for the moment, that these adjectives may well have varying meanings, conduct a preliminary analysis as follows:

a. Find the adjective in the WORDLIST. How often does it occur in the TTC? How often does it occur in the TEC?

(cont.)

b. Find an additional adjective that means more or less the same thing.
c. Are these numbers of the adjectives a little or a lot? Compute the proportion out of the total number of each adjective in each corpus. Then multiply by 1,000. Put them into a table.
d. Which differences between TEC and TTC are significant; which are not? Conduct a chi-square test for each adjective. Add these to the table.
e. Peruse the results in Table 10A. What does this comparison of the TTC and TEC suggest?
f. Which results stand out as unusual?
g. What could be the explanation? Conduct another analysis, this time comparing the number of *awesome* tokens in the WORDLIST for the 20-year-olds and those for the 40+. Calculate the chi-square. What is the result?
h. What is the problem with this type of analysis?
i. Look for these adjectives (or others like them) that I have used in this book. What do they tell you about me?
j. What type of data would be ideal for studying adjectives?

Answers
a. *See Table 10A.*
b. *Some good possibilities are: "excellent," "amazing," "fabulous."*
c. *See Table 10A.*
d. *Four out of six adjectives differentiate teenagers (TIC) from the rest of the population (TEC). Some adjectives do not, e.g. "awesome." Some are less differentiated than others, e.g. "brilliant." This result suggests that other semantic fields within the adjective cohort are changing over time.*
e. *The result for "awesome" is unusual because the expectation is that the two corpora would be distinct. "Awesome" is a young person's word. But these results show no statistical difference between the two corpora.*
f. *Recall that the TTC is only teenagers. The TEC comprises individuals aged between 20 and 92. When the 20–29-year-olds are separated, we discover that they are heavy users of "awesome": 126/384,036 compared to 12/678,842*

Table 10A *Differences in adjectival use between TIC and TEC*

Adjective	Count	Prop	Count	Prop	P value	Sig
awesome	74	0.12	141	0.11	0.725	NS
brilliant	7	0.011	14	0.011	0.997	NS
fantastic	2	0.003	24	0.019	0.005	< 0.01
great	167	0.289	855	0.687	0	< 0.01
lovely	2	0.011	78	0.062	0	< 0.01
terrific	0	0	10	0.008	0.025	< 0.01

(*cont.*)

> *among the 40+ year-olds. This result is statistically significant at the $p < 0.01$ level.*
> g. *The problem is that the WORDLISTS are simply counts of form. There is no way to tell if these adjectives are being used to mean "very good." That would require further investigation.*
> h. *This question is open-ended and encourages readers to speculate based on known parameters. It perhaps goes without saying that adjectives may not be welcome in a relatively academic book; however, I used "great" as an adjective once, "great insights."*
> i. *Possible sources: Want ads. Evaluations. Fiction. Women's magazines.*

11   Other funky teenage features

You know what? I dunno. Whatever!

> Like every generation has its weird slang that doesn't make any sense
> except to them.
>
> (Kevin Chamis, 16)

Many people notice that teenagers use words and expressions that no one else
in the community uses. When I started building the TTC I identified a group of
words and phrases that occurred frequently and with intriguing uses in the data
in order to tap into teen language and uncover some of the changes going on in
contemporary English. I called them the "funky features." Among these
features were a group of unusual expressions not well studied or widely
discussed: *you know what?*, *I don't know*, and *whatever*. What are these
phrases doing in teen language and how did they get there? In this chapter
I offer some preliminary observations.

You know what (I mean)

A frequent expression used by teenagers is *you know what (I mean)?* It
occurred 400 times in the TTC. A substantial number of these uses are normal
questions, as in (174).

174.   a. Do *you know what* your sister said to me? (Elizabeth McKinley, 19)
      b. *You know what* freaks me out though actually? (Annie Muscat, 22)
      c. *You know what* Duke said to me once? (Clara Felipe, 18)

In (174a) the standard question formation is used including *do*-support. In
(174b–c), however, notice that although the questioning nature of the expression is maintained, the *do* is not present.

There are a large number of uses of *you know what* that co-occur with
I mean. These comprise one of a varied group of GEs, as in (175) (see
Chapter 7).

175.   a. I think cause and effect is like chicken and egg *you know what I mean*?
        (Finnegan Connor, 17)
      b. They're supposed to be tight against your leg, *do you know what I mean*?
        (Emma Griffo, 17)

    c. And they are kind of sad, *you know what I mean*? (Emma Griffo, 17)

    d. It just felt more like a pinch *you know what I mean*? (Diego Ferreira, 18))

There is another use of this phrase in the data. Often it functions to ask a question to the listener but no answer is wanted. The speaker just keeps on with the story. The phrase is acting as rhetorical question, as in (176).

176.   a. It's the kid who looks like Harry Potter and *you know what* I'm older than him. (Finnegan Connor, 17)

        b. *You know what* those black seats are better. (Karl Galang, 11)

        c. If I talk to someone, *You know what I mean*? Like what do I do?
          (Elizabeth McKinley, 19)

The OED documents these phrases as colloquial forms that express "a hope that one has been understood." The earliest date of attestation is remarkably from 1575, as in (177a), although most examples come from the mid-1800s and onwards, as in (177b–c).

177.   a. For feare of Hobgobling, *you wot wel what I meane*, As long as it is sence, I feare me yet ye be scarce cleane. (1575, William Stevenson, *Gammer Gurtons Nedle* v. ii. sig. Eiii)

        b. There would be a want of reverence in it, if *you understand what I mean*. (1846, G. E. Jewsbury, *Select Letters to J. W. Carlyle* (1892) 203)

        c. A couple of my old mates let someone down, and they just got beaten up and darked, know what I mean? (1995, *Smash Hits*, 29 March, 14/4)

To put historical and contemporary observations into perspective, Figure 11.1 shows the frequency of various collocations of this expression using Google Ngrams.

Figure 11.1 documents a remarkable difference among this set of forms. The group that includes *you know what I mean*, *you know what*, and *if you know what* are a very small subset of the collocation *you know what*, which shoots up above them. This suggests that the collocation *you know what* – rather than the others – is the one undergoing development. The use of *you know what I mean*, *do you know what*, and *if you know what* are highly infrequent in

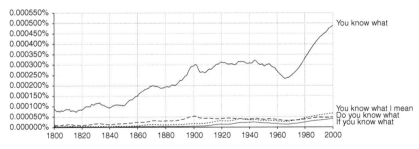

Figure 11.1 Google Ngrams search for collocation "you know what I mean"

comparison. Further there is a distinct pattern in time. It was used at very low levels in the early nineteenth century, but started increasing by the end of that century and was stable across the early twentieth century. Notice that the early 1960s are the launching point.

Further examination of early uses of *you know what* reveals that its referential meaning is present, as in (178a). However, by the end of the 1990s examples such as in (178b) are the norm.

178.   a. "I see *you know what* that unmixed happiness is," replied she. (1876, Grace Kennedy, *Dunallan*, 300)
        b. So, I began thinking about why I had asked that particular question in my initial encounter. And *you know what?* I ended up discovering the very answer I'd been looking for. (1998, Timothy Shurr, *What To Do When You Don't Know What To Do*, 15)

How do teenagers use these expressions? Table 11.1 displays the distribution of the 400 tokens according to the different uses.

The novel function of this form as a rhetorical question to the listener in the running discourse of the speaker represents 36 percent of the data. Typical uses are shown in (179).

179.   a. But then eventually I'm like, "*You know what?* I don't know what jazz is. But *you know what?* It's really fun. I really like it." (Ned Lui, 18)
        b. It was like, "*You know what?* I'm just going to let the fish go." So yeah. (Kerry Hong, 18)
        c. *You know what?* He's not my cup of tea. (Alyssa Sailner, 29)

These uses are correlated with the position of the phrase in the discourse, as in Table 11.2 which shows most of the phrases occur when individuals make comments on their own utterances (shaded). However, one particular use of *you know what* is localized to the DM slot in pre-sentential position, as in (180–181).

180.   a. [Interviewer] But painful afterwards?
        b. [073] Actually *you know what*, no it wasn't. It wasn't that bad at all. (Alicia Karan, 24)

Table 11.1 *Distribution of* you know what (I mean)

	%	N
Literal question	42	168
General extender	22	87
Rhetorical question	36	145
TOTAL		400

Table 11.2 *Distribution of* you know what (I mean)

POSITION IN DISCOURSE	TAG *You know what I mean?*	QUESTION literal	RHETORICAL QUESTION *You know what*	TOTALS
Final	63% (17)	33% (9)	4% (1)	27
Medial	49% (148)	20% (61)	31% (93)	302
Initial	4% (3)	24% (17)	72% (51)	71
TOTAL	168	87	145	400

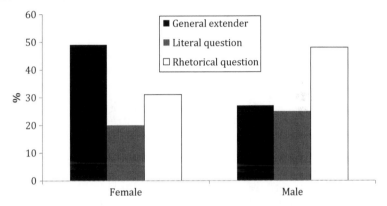

Figure 11.2 Distribution of types of *you know what (I mean)* by sex

181. a. So I went and had dinner by candlelight. But *you know what?* Glad
          I did it. (Joseph Tayles, 26)
      b. It's a nice box anyways. *You know what?* Why don't you just take it off?
          (Janice Hu, 9)

Taken together, this evidence suggests that where once these constructions
were full-fledged questions, they have become DMs. Figure 11.2 displays the
distribution of types by sex.

Figure 11.2 shows that there is no difference between male and female with
regard to the literal (standard) use of this phrase. However, there is a contrast
with respect to the other uses. Females use more of the GE, as in (182a), and
males use more of the rhetorical question, as in (182b).

182. a. I think she's really ... bitchy like in a weird way, but she's nice, *do you
          know what I mean?* (Katherine Berazzi, 18)
      b. But then *you know what?* I'm like, "Screw you. If you don't like me
          around and you're not gonna care that I'm not gonna be here I might as
          well leave since I like choir a lot more." (Ned Lui, 18)

The fact that males are using much more of the DM and females are using more of the GE offers some preliminary evidence that males are leading the development of DM *you know what*. If so, it would be a case of males leading a discourse-pragmatic change.

Where did this rhetorical function come from? In earlier research, Alexandra D'Arcy and I argued that storytelling styles have changed over the twentieth century (Tagliamonte and D'Arcy, 2007a). This comes to the fore when storytellers perform their stories with quoted speech. In tracking the development of *be like* across the twentieth century (in apparent time) we documented the development of a particular narrative style, individuals telling stories by regaling their audience with a running stream of their own inner thought processes, as in (183).

183.   a.   I'm like, "Oh my God!"
        b.   I'm like, "He's going to get wet. I give it ten seconds."
        c.   ... sure enough, Ø "Boom!"
        d.   I was just like, "Oh man, you guys are so predictable."
        e.   I'm like, "Shit, my parents are going to wake up 'cause of that."
        f.   I'm like, "Oh shit."
        g.   I'm like, "Okay, I gotta pretend like something happened. Think
             something; think something," right? (Daniella Loca, 17)

This type of storytelling is in fact a recent phenomenon and has increased across the present generations of speakers. It may be the case that rhetorical questions to the listener such as *you know what?* are part of this kind of self performance and may be developing in tandem. Figure 11.3 plots the overall proportion of quotations in narratives of personal experience that represent inner dialogue as in (183) (based on Tagliamonte and D'Arcy, 2007a: Figure 4) compared to the frequency of this type in the data.

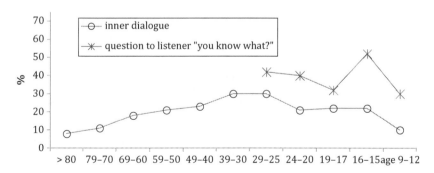

Figure 11.3 Frequency of inner dialogue in storytelling by speaker date of birth

Figure 11.3 shows that the proportion of inner monologue increases steadily in apparent time to the young adult population. Among the younger age groups the shift from 9–12-year-olds, who are still developing their oratory abilities, to higher rates of inner dialogue in adolescence and early adulthood likely represents incrementation. If so, this is a change that peaks later in the life cycle (late twenties) than any change reported thus far. The proportion of use of the rhetorical question *you know what* is plotted in the starred line. Given that this use is rising in frequency among youth (and taking the spike among the 15–16-year-olds as an anomaly of small numbers) it may well be the case that this form is a device that permits storytellers to perform dialogue in their own discourse, one of a suite of features including the quotative *like* that grandstand the storyteller as a participant in her own story (see also discussion in Tagliamonte and D'Arcy, 2007a: 210–211).

[077] "Eh." "Like" and "eh." [Interviewer] "Eh," yeah. [077] "Yeah" too. "Yeah." Those three words are terrible. (June Watson, 49)

I don't know

Teenagers seem to *not know* quite a lot these days. I started noticing this several years ago. Ask a teenager a question and they will inevitably say *I don't know*. In fact, they may not pronounce the words. Instead, they will just hum the sounds of the words. But it is still recognizable, enunciated something like *da-da-dum* with the stress on the first *da* and represented in writing as *iono* (see example 202o). Is it really the case that teenagers know so little?

I found over 3,000 examples of *I don't know* in the Toronto materials. Some of these examples mean what you would expect them to mean, i.e. that the individual does not know something, as in (184). These are what I will refer to as the referential meaning.

184.   a. And then they were talking about like, this tea. *I don't know* what it was for. (Clara Felipe, 16)
       b. Like, Mario, was he- what did he do? Like *I don't know*, do you know? (Katherine Berazzi, 18)
       c. *I don't know* where my sister's going at all. (Luke Lung, 19)

However, when teenagers say *I don't know*, they often don't mean anything of the sort. In fact, each instance of *I don't know* is followed by an explicit statement of something the speaker clearly *does* know. As I have discussed before, words that were once meaningful do not have their original meanings anymore; it is a sign of change. Consider the examples in (185).

185.   a. [Interviewer] What is so special about dogs? [007] *I don't know.* I just
            want one. (Karl Galang, 11)
        b. *I don't know.* He's so weird like that. (Clara Felipe, 16)
        c. So, *I don't know.* I think it's going to be like a weird trip. (Clara
            Felipe, 16)
        d. I was just like, *I don't know*, it felt- it felt kind of out of place. (Chris
            Ming, 21)

Historical perspective

Does the use of *I don't know* have a history in the English language? The OED
documents a "colloquial form" *I dunno* (and several orthographic variants)
from the mid-1800s, as in (186).

186.   a. There I vlounder'd like a zow, An' ramm'l'd out *I dun-no* how. (1842,
            G. P. R. Pulman, *Rustic Sketches*, 34)
        b. *I dunno* as it's ushle to print Poscrips (1848, J. R. Lowell, *Biglow Papers*,
            1st Ser. vii. 87)
        c. Now indeed I *dunna* what to do. (1867, P. Kennedy, *Banks of Boro*, xxiii)

By the early 1900s the usage patterns shift from the Standard English
referential meaning of "I don't know" to meanings that seem in line with
contemporary teenage usage, as in (187).

187.   a. If you had asked her why, she would have replied, "*Dunno.* It's a bother
            speaking to people when you're out." (1926, R. Macaulay, *Crewe Train*
            i. ii. 10)
        b. He'll begin to say to himself: "Well, I *dunno.* P'raps I'm wrong."
            (1938. C. L. Morgan, *Flashing Stream* ii. ii. 1860)

To obtain a further historical perspective, Figure 11.4 shows the frequency
of the expression *I don't know* using Google Ngrams. It reveals that *I don't
know* is an expression that has increased since 1800. Like many of the words
we have been exploring, it surges upwards in the 1980s.

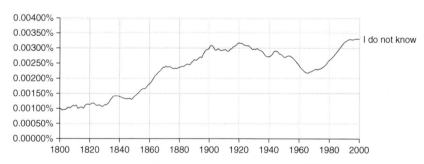

Figure 11.4 Google Ngrams search for collocation of "I do not know"

Figure 11.5 Google Ngrams search for collocation of "I dunno"

Now let's shift the perspective and consider the form *I dunno* which is the orthographic rendering of the sing-song version of "I don't know" that is often heard among teenagers. Figure 11.5 shows a Google Ngrams search of the collocation "I dunno."

A striking portrait emerges from Figure 11.5. The collocation *I dunno* emerges after 1840, precisely from the period documented in the OED examples. It surges upwards to a pinnacle in the 1920s, plummets into the early 1960s, and then begins a steep rise into the 2000s. What could account for the apex in the 1920s? Cursory examination of some typical examples reveals that most of them are contained in direct quotes as in (188).

188.   a. "*I dunno, sah; I dunno,*" said Arabella, all uninterested. (1920, George
            Kibbe Turner, *Hagar's Hoard*)
        b. "*I dunno. Dunno* much about it." (1922, *Life Magazine*, volume 80)
        c. "I DUNNO." "*I Dunno,*" a new hand, came on one night. (1921, *Pulp and
            Paper Magazine of Canada*, 1004)
        d. *I dunno* but it 'mounts to jest about as much as sendin' money to
            missionaries. (1919, Mary Eleanor Wilkins Freeman, *A New England Nun
            and Other Stories*, 172)

Why this use should surge upwards at this temporal juncture is beyond the scope of this analysis; however, it would be interesting to try to find out. Meanwhile, notice how much its use in quoted speech in the 1920s is like that of the teenagers, especially (188d), which shows an initial *I don't know* followed by a firm declarative. All this demonstrates that *I don't know* is not a recent phenomenon, nor the invention of contemporary youth (see also Pichler, 2013: 199).

Synchronic perspective

The use of *I don't know* has not gone unnoticed in the discourse-pragmatic variation literature. Several studies have been conducted on American English

(Bybee and Scheibman, 1999; Scheibman, 2000). Pichler (2007, 2009, 2013) studied this form in a dialect of British English. She grounded her analyses of this form in the examples provided by the OED and also observed the development between 1832 and 1938. In her corpus *I don't know* has many different pronunciations, including *I dunno, duno,* and a local Middlesbrough variant *I divn't knaa.* She discovered that among the 300 or so tokens of *I don't know* variants, the reduced forms *dunno* or *dono* correlated with younger speakers and the pragmatic function of the form. In contrast, the full form *I don't know,* correlated with referential meaning and older speakers. Similar results had earlier been documented by Bybee and Scheibman (1999) and Scheibman (2000). While *I don't know* conveyed the meaning of lack of knowledge, the reduced forms such as *I dunno* performed interpersonal and textual functions. As forms develop pragmatic meaning, they become reduced, one of the signs of grammatical change. Therefore it appears that *I don't know* has taken on the function of a pragmatic marker in contemporary Middlesbrough English.

Method

TEC and TTC provided over 3,000 tokens of *I don't know.* An important methodological point is necessary here. All the corpora in my archives have been made machine-readable using standard orthographic conventions. The reason for this is practical. When a research team is transcribing hundreds of thousands of words, to stop and figure out what the pronunciation of each one is and then render it consistently becomes overly complicated and burdensome and importantly, unreliable (see Tagliamonte, 2007). The analyst must return to the original audio files in order to hear pronunciation. In other words the data have been transcribed such that all varied enunciations of "I don't know" were rendered orthographically in the same way, i.e. "I don't know." This means that the difference between full pronunciations and reduced pronunciations, as has been the focus of most other studies of *I don't know* (e.g. Pichler, 2007, 2009; Scheibman, 2000), is not accessible for the TEC/ TTC corpora without re-listening to the (hundreds of) interviews. Therefore, in this study I focus on the distributional patterns by social and linguistic factors. The data were coded for age, sex, meaning (referential or not), and interactional status.

To begin, let's consider to what extent there are meaning differences in the data. Table 11.3 documents the distribution of variants by age of the individual according to whether the form had its referential meaning of not knowing something as in (189), or some other meaning, as in (190). Both meanings are used by the same individuals, i.e. layering.

Table 11.3 *Distribution of referential meanings of* I don't
know *by age*

	Referential meaning	
9–12	50.6	328
13–14	57.7	208
15–16	29.0	518
17–19	32.8	1,247
20–24	33.0	455
25–29	31.3	396
TOTAL		3,152

189. a. *I don't know* what the hell it was. It was just something weird. (Diego
         Ferreira, 18)
      b. *I don't know* if it's mimicking what they see on TV. (Krista Faherty, 24)

190. a. *I don't know*, I guess you learn from your mistakes. (Diego Ferreira, 18)
      b. *I don't know*. I get really like flabbergasted. (Krista Faherty, 24)

Table 11.3 provides a startling discovery: the use of *I don't know* to mean
"I don't know" is greatest among the pre-adolescents and youngest teenagers.
This provides a good example of children mirroring their caretakers. By mid-
adolescence (15–16 years old) the referential use has plummeted, and it stays
at the same rate into adulthood. The adolescents and young adults use the
pragmatic function of *I don't know* more. Is this linguistic change in progress?

Figure 11.6 shows the distribution of the referential meaning tokens by
speaker age and sex. It shows that younger individuals use referential *I don't
know* more than older individuals and the change across age cohorts is
statistically significant at the $p < 0.05$ level. Notice that among the oldest
individuals a sex difference is evident – females show a resurgence of the
referential meaning while males continue to use more of the other functions.

Next, each token was coded for its interactional status: turn-initial vs.
standing by itself, as in (191a), or turn-initial and the beginning of new
discourse as in (191b). Did it occur at the end of a turn, as in (191c) or the
middle of a turn, as in (191d)?

191. a. [Interviewer] What makes her so pretty? [004] *I don't know.*
         [Interviewer] Why's she pretty? (Steve Fraute, 16)
      b. *I don't know*. I don't know what I'll do with a turkey. (Sandy Griffo, 15)
      c. So he's a little upset at me for that but *I don't know*. [Interviewer] Was
         it a big decision choosing science? (Dana Naskauskaas, 17)
      d. But even when my parents were home, *I don't know*, I just wasn't
         really sleeping well. (Julio McClearly, 16)

Table 11.4 *Distribution of* I don't know *by position in discourse*

Position	%	N
End of a turn	5.3	166
Turn initial, continuing	15.4	486
Turn initial	3.2	102
Middle of sentence/utterance	76.1	2,396
TOTAL		3,150

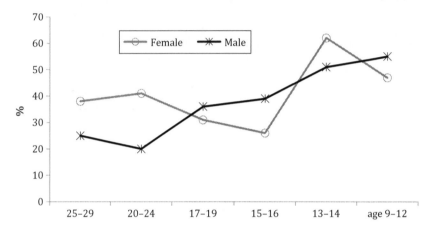

Figure 11.6 Distribution of referential *I don't know* by speaker age and sex

Table 11.4 shows the distribution of *I don't know* according to its inter-actional position in the discourse and demonstrates a notable trend: *I don't know* occurs inside a sentence far more than anywhere else in the discourse. This means that it is employed by the individual not as a conversational organizer between interlocutors but as a way to introduce one's own upcoming talk. What kind of introduction? Pichler (2007: 179) suggests that *I don't know* signals either that the following discourse "loosely communicates speakers' thoughts and/or that speakers are unsure of their choice of wording." Tsui (1991) suggested a "softening" or "mitigation" function which serves to lessen the impact of upcoming disagreement. The fact that individuals follow *I don't know* with explicit statements of their own (strong) opinions, as in (192), makes me think that Tsui might be right.

192.   a.   That's pretty like *I don't know* kind of ugly, wouldn't it be? (Craig
                Thompson, 18)

   b. *I don't know.* I have a problem with that Siblings store. (Vivian
      Bustamante, 16)
   c. *I don't know.* I hate that place. (Katherine Berazzi, 18)

The rhetorical use of *I don't know* as meta-commentary on one's own
discourse is reminiscent of the use of *you know what.* It seems that *I don't
know* may be another one of multiple developing pragmatic particles that
enable individuals to perform their own stories.

[Interviewer] So what do you think the word "whatever" means? [003] I don't know.
[Interviewer] Well everyone says it all the time. [003] Whatever. Nothing. [Interviewer]
It means nothing? So why do you think everyone says it? [003] Because they want to.
(Tony Griffo, 13)

Whatever

The word *whatever* started out as a pronoun, but it is also used colloquially to
mean "whatever may be the case." Its use with this meaning is relatively
recent, apparently as late as 1870, as in (193). The other attestations in the
OED appear in the twentieth century (194).

193.   I cuddent leave t'pleass *whativver* wi'out seein' her. (1870, Roger
        Piketah, *Forness Folk*, 15)

194.   She's got a tidy pair of ankles, *whatever.* (1900, "A. Raine," *Garthowen*, 93)

In order to gain an overview of *whatever*, I searched for two collocations
that might provide the best match for "whatever" as a pronoun, i.e. "whatever
is," and "whatever" as an adverb, "or whatever." The result is shown in
Figure 11.7.
Figure 11.7 shows a linear decline in the use of *whatever is*, a pronoun, from
1800 until 1960. Then this use levels out. Notice that the collocation *or*

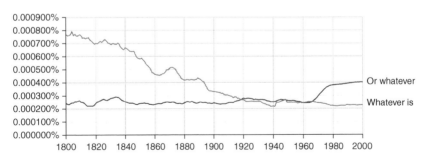

Figure 11.7 Google Ngrams search for collocation "whatever is" and "or
whatever"

whatever is a low frequency collocation until the mid 1960s. Then it shoots up. No wonder there has been a perceptible increase in use of *whatever* among teenagers.

When we take a closer look at the early uses of *whatever* we find, as predicted, copious use of the pronoun, as in (195).

195.   a. To conclude: *whatever* substance begins to exist, it must, during its existence necessarily be the same: *whatever* composition of substances begin to exist … (1824, John Locke, *An Essay concerning Human Understanding*, 276)
        b. *Whatever* is loose must be shaken, *whatever* is corrupted must be lopt away; *whatever* is not built on the broad basis of public utility must be thrown to the ground. (1825, Anna Letitia, *The Words of Anna Letitita*, 372)

In contrast, uses in the 1990s include the examples in (196). Something has evidently changed because some of these are clearly GEs.

196.   a. But during the day they're open for selling shoes *or whatever*. (1997, Hearings on Reform, US GPO, 350)
        b. I mean just to be thorough *or whatever*, right? (1999, Bonnie Bryant, *Conformation Faults*, 166)

Method

Building on this background, all tokens of *whatever* were extracted from a sub-sample of the TEC and TTC producing 859 examples. Some are unremarkable. Anyone in the community might use *whatever* like this, as in (197).

197.   a. She says she could watch *whatever* she wanted. (Christopher O'Neil, 11)
        b. Oh, I don't care, *whatever* it takes. (Jamal Namji, 16)
        c. Oh, cool, I can do *whatever* I want. (Stephen Hardwick, 15)

However, many uses of *whatever* appear after *or* or *and*. Like the word *stuff*, they are often used as part of a GE (see Chapter 5), as in (198).

198.   a. And then I was supposed to be a bee or *whatever* attacking her. (Tina Mancini, 11)
        b. There's no like lights and *whatever*, but there's this big loud explosion. (Leo McCready, 13)
        c. Do you go to church, or *whatever*? (Quanisha Howard, 11)
        d. Like I don't mean to be rude to God or *whatever* but that was so boring. (Leo McCready, 13)
        e. So um whenever I cried or *whatever* like I would just be like quiet. (Jane Wong, 14)

In (198a) the speaker is talking about acting in a scene in which she was supposed to act like a bee would act, or some animal behavior reminiscent of a bee. Similarly, in (198b), the speaker is talking about setting off Roman Candles, fireworks that make a loud noise rather than lights, colors, flashes, and other features typical of other fireworks. The important thing is that the *and/or whatever* makes reference to other similar objects, as a GE.

Let's try to understand what teenagers are doing with the word *whatever*. First, there are instances where *whatever* appears after other linking words such as *but*, *so*, and *like*, as in (199).

199.   a. Like if you want to take my credit like *whatever*. Like take it. Like I don't
           really mind. (Luke Lung, 19)
        b. Actually my parents like, they are- they want what's best for me so
           whatever- if I'm having fun then they'll like definitely cheer me on and
           stuff like that. (Janet McDonald, 19)
        c. Like there's so many things that go wrong but *whatever* there's more than
           enough things that go right. (Grant Simkovic, 18)

Second, there are instances where *whatever* stands alone, as in (200).

200.   a. Okay never mind. *Whatever.* Oh who cares. (Ricky Tang, 16)
        b. You know like puking doesn't count, *whatever.* (Michael Llewellyn, 18)
        c. You're just kind of like, "Oh yeah, *whatever* mom." (Ernest Wong, 17)

To begin, let's consider the function of *whatever* among the individuals in the TTC, as in Table 11.5.

Table 11.5 shows that the use of *whatever* as a GE with the form *or/and/-but/like whatever* dominates in the grammar of these young people. However it is the stand-alone version that is the innovation.

The next step is to consider to what extent this use is changing across the current generations. Figure 11.8 displays the distribution of this type of *whatever* by age of the individual now separated by sex. The proportion here is based on the total instances of *whatever* as a stand-alone form in each age group.

The differences between males and females in Figure 11.8 is not statistically significant in any age group; however, the overall trajectory in apparent time, with a height among the adolescents is ($p = < 0.05$).

Why are teenagers using *whatever* so much and what do they mean? Kleiner (1998: 609–610) suggests individuals use *whatever* "to suspend argumentation when resolution or agreement is deemed unlikely" (Kleiner, 1998: 610).

Table 11.5 *Distribution of* whatever *by function*

Function of *whatever*	%	N
Pronoun	16.4	184
General extender	51.2	1,125
Stand-alone	32.4	365

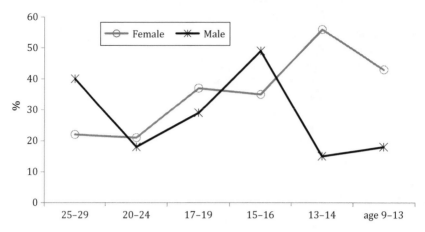

Figure 11.8 Distribution of stand-alone *whatever* by speaker age and sex

However, the data in the TTC suggest that for these youth, it is simply a linguistic means of shrugging one's shoulders, i.e. "I don't care." In a series of utterances in (201a–n), Cynthia Fernandes explains:

201.   a.   Yeah like discipline means you're going to be more like nice and things like that.
        b.   But if you aren't disciplined you're going to be like, "*Whatever. Whatever. Whatever.* Yeah, yeah, yeah. *Whatever.*"
        c.   I don't like mean like strict but maybe like in between.
        d.   Sometimes you're like, "Yeah yeah. I know. I know. I know."
        e.   But sometimes you're like, "Yeah *whatever.*"
        f.   Like me. Like sometimes I don't care about things and sometimes I do.
        g.   So like being too disciplined is not good and not being disciplined isn't good so in the middle is good.
        h.   Like with your friends you're like, "*Whatever. Whatever.*"
        i.   With the teacher you're like, "oh yeah yeah. Yeah. I understand," and things like that.
        j.   So if you're not you're going to be like, "Yeah *whatever*" to teacher.
        k.   And then if you're strict like disciplined you're going to be to teacher, "Oh yes. Oh yes."
        l.   And to your friends, "Oh I totally agree!"
        m.   But in your head, "*Whatever.*"
        n.   So it's like that, yeah. (Cynthia Fernandes, 11)

What does the use of these *funky* features tell us about teen language?

Young people at the turn of the twenty-first century use a ton of thought-provoking expressions. Among the most frequent phrases are the ones I have

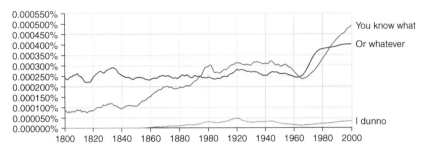

Figure 11.9 Google Ngrams search for funky collocations in Chapter 11

examined in this chapter, the rhetorical question *you know what*, the leading comment *I don't know*, and the use of *whatever* as a GE or lackluster aside. Figure 11.9 uses Google Ngrams to plot each form on the same graph.

Once again the early 1960s are the launch point for these forms and they accelerate from that time onwards. The trajectories tell us that the use of all these forms increases in written documents at the same time as the frequencies are emerging in pre-adolescents and teens.

It will be interesting to see what happens to these forms in the next generation. Will they develop other functions or fade away? At this point in time and with only these preliminary distributions as evidence and the relative infrequency of the forms, it is difficult to say. What is interesting is that young males have a high frequency of these features, in some cases more than the females in their age group, e.g. *you know what*. If males participate in linguistic change, why is it that these particular forms are the ones they push forward? This is a question to jumpstart further investigation.

A convergence of forces is engendering a new attitude toward both speech and writing. We might dub this attitude "linguistic whateverism." Its primary manifestation is a marked indifference to the need for consistency in linguistic usage. (Baron, 2008: 169)

Language puzzle

Play the "what should I study?" game with me. Pretend you've just collected and transcribed a corpus of language data. You run a WORDLIST and you decide you'll look for "funky features" in the data. You do this because (1) by identifying such features you will inevitably tap into linguistic variation and change in your data and (2) by finding interesting features you will be fulfilling the Principle of Curiosity so that while you are slogging it out in the research trenches you will be amused. Carefully read through the WORDLIST for the TTC. In order to direct

(*cont.*)

your attention, I provide some provocative questions below, but if you wish to simply notice what draws your attention, that is okay too.

a. Find the most frequent word that starts with "q."
b. Find a spelling mistake. (A corpus is never finished!)
c. Find a rock band, a place name, a super hero, a mental illness, and an actress.
d. Find three entries whose meaning you have no inkling of.
e. Find two frequent words that mean the same thing (one of them > 900) that I did not study in this book.
f. Find three words that are (relatively) frequent and potentially undergoing change these days.

Answers
a. *Quite N=100.*
b. *TTC, "actaully," "juxtopposing." There are many more!*
c. *Fleetwood Mac, Huntsville, Spider Man, Split Personality Disorder, Julia Roberts. Perhaps there are others!*
d. *I can't provide an answer for this one. The question pertains to fish and fishbowls as follows: You only tend to notice things you don't understand. But it's a good tendency to exploit for research purposes. If you want to notice something, but you are in your own fishbowl, ask someone who is outside of it to look at the data.*
e. *The downtoners "kind of," "sort of."*
f. *Aside from the features I have studied in this book, you will be able to spot several more in the WORDLISTS. In fact, there are innumerable others worthy of study in contemporary varieties of English anywhere in the world. I leave that choice and adventure up to you!*

12   Internet language

Everyone's online

Language is at the heart of the Internet.

(Crystal, 2006: 271)

Many people who were born in the 1970s onwards grew up with the World Wide Web. Each generation thereafter has increasingly caught on to new means of communication, beginning with Instant Messaging, which was rapidly followed by Facebook, then Twitter, then Instagram, Tumblr, Pinterest, Snapchat, Tinder, and beyond. The generations of the 1980s and 1990s are digital natives.

Teen language and the Internet

Language is always being criticized in one way or another; however, teenage language in particular has come under intense condemnation in the last half of the twentieth century. Since the advent and expansion of the Internet there has been a veritable uproar of scorn. Thurlow (2006) presents a list of 101 popular news articles about the language of CMC and young people. The headlines surveyed suggest a threat to literacy, the destruction of language, and widespread use of abbreviations and truncated language. Teenagers are implicated in most of the articles which draw a direct correlation between Internet usage and bad grammar. Countless popular news sources suggest that the language of CMC and SMS and IM in particular is not only leading to grammatical ruin, but also impeding children's ability to write properly, as this oft-cited quote from the American Teachers' Association suggests:[1]

Text and instant messaging are negatively affecting students' writing quality on a daily basis, as they bring their abbreviated language into the classroom. As a result of their electronic chatting, kids are making countless syntax, subject–verb agreement and spelling mistakes in writing assignments.

Kiesler et al. (1984: 1126) suggest that CMC is littered with examples of profane language – later termed "flaming" (Baron, 2003a: 21), a lack of standard salutations and structure, and reduced self-regulation. Davies (2005: 103–4) describes the language of text messages as follows:

writers of text messages quickly become adept at reducing every word to its minimum comprehensible length, usually omitting vowels wherever possible, as in *Wknd* for *Weekend*, *Msg* for *Message*, or deliberately using shorter misspellings such as *Wot* for *What*.

Not only is language reported to be adversely affected, so is sleep ("Text messaging is spoiling teenagers' sleep") (Dobson, 2003), intelligence ("Infomania worse than marijuana," *Daily Mail*, 2005),[2] and social skills ("Teen texting soars; will social skills suffer?" NPR News).[3] Teenagers have a bad reputation for many aspects of behavior, but most especially the breakdown and degradation of language.

Given these serious criticisms, one would think that the evidence brought to bear would be substantive. However, virtually all the discussion about teenage language on the Internet is based on anecdote, hearsay, and self-reports. There are very few empirical studies of authentic usage, which leads to the important question: what are teenagers *actually* doing? Further, as most linguists know, linguistic innovation among youth is not solely the result of the Internet. Language is in fact always changing. A more informed question is whether or not the Internet is making any difference to the otherwise normal processes of language change.

Research on language use on the Internet is by now an industry complete with themes, factions, and fields of study (e.g. Androutsopolous, 2014). However, essentially all of this research is based on what is publicly available on the Internet. What remains hidden is how people are interacting with each other *inside* the Internet where one-on-one discourses are transpiring in a worldwide beehive of communication. What type of language do people use when they communicate with each other using device-based mediation, a phenomenon referred to as "Computer Mediated Communication" (Kiesler et al., 1984)? This question seems simple, but it soon becomes apparent that neither scientists, nor journalists nor teachers are actually privy to the day-to-day online interactions between people as they tap away at their computers and phones. What type of language do they use? Most compelling, what type of language do the digital natives use?

Yeah like . . . like everybody now the way they talk is like . . . like text messaging talk. Like that's how they talk. (Abdul Aarak, 21)

In this chapter, I take you on a discovery mission to a place where adults rarely go, and show you what Internet language is like among the sector of the population that uses it the most – teenagers. The first study is based on the TIMC collected between 2004 and 2006 and the second is based on the TIC collected between 2009 and 2010.

Computer Mediated Communication

The term Computer Mediated Communication (CMC) was first used by Kiesler et al. (1984: 1123) whose goal was to analyze the social-psychological implications of the rise and spread of the Internet and network-based communication. At the time, CMC users were a rarefied sector of the general population, primarily the participants of ARPANET, a system created by the United States Department of Defense and GTE Telenet:

> Because electronic communication was developed and has been used by a distinctive subculture of computing professionals, its norms are infused with that culture's specific language ... they use language appropriate for boardrooms and ballfields interchangeably. (Kiesler et al., 1984: 1126)

Thirty years later, Internet language is no longer relegated to computing professionals. It has spread to the point where virtually everyone in Western society uses the Internet on a daily basis: business people, baseball players, and everyone in between.

In the early 2000s David Crystal coined the term *Netspeak* to refer to the language that was developing on the Internet, defining it as "a type of language displaying features that are unique to the Internet ... arising out of its character as a medium which is electronic, global, and interactive" (Crystal, 2006: 20). However, it soon became apparent that these features of Netspeak were not unique to the Internet. Variants of laughter, including the infamous *lol* emerged as a feature of CMC; however, two of the most common variants, *haha* and *hehe*, have existed in written language since as early as 1000 AD (OED) and the supposed Internet acronym *omg* was apparently used in a letter written by Admiral John Fisher to Winston Churchill in 1917.[4] Moreover, many researchers note that even "the abbreviations and non-standard spellings typical of ... [CMC] ... are not really new. They carry on earlier practices from chat; going back further still ... much like [how] teens of earlier generations passed notes 'encrypted' in special alphabets or writing permutations" (Herring, 2004: 32–33). Therefore, not only have specific forms common in CMC existed for centuries, the use of acronyms, non-standard spellings, initialisms, and other short forms have long-term precedents as well.

An "acronym" is an abbreviation formed from the first letter of the words in a phrase and pronounced as a word, e.g. *NATO*. An "initialism" is pronounced saying the individual letters, e.g. *ttyl*. Notice that *lol* can be both. An abbreviation, or short form, is a reduced form of a word, e.g. *tmr*, *2morro*, "tomorrow," *sry*, "sorry," *tho*, "though." A non-standard spelling is anything else, e.g. "pwn" for *own* meaning "defeat."

By the early twenty-first century CMC had become a diverse range of different registers rather than any monolithic variety. The only commonality is that the communication happens by way of an electronic device and is typed (i.e. written rather than spoken). While early definitions restricted CMC to computers, i.e. "any natural language messaging that is transmitted and/or received via a computer connection" (Baron, 2003a: 10), more recent definitions extend the scope to mobile phones, e.g. "predominantly text-based human–human interaction mediated by networked computers or mobile telephony" (Herring, 2007: 1). This circumscribes CMC to written communications through technology. Because technology is so varied, so too is CMC. Because what people talk about is even more varied, CMC is a window on the world.

The Instant Messaging era

> My sister and I were going through MSN withdrawal. We were actually in Scotland at this time. So my parents were like, "Okay. God! We're gonna just go to an Internet Cafe and you can go on for a couple of hours." And we were fine after that.
>
> (Karen Paul, 19)

What is Instant Messaging, IM? Technically speaking it is "one-to-one synchronous ... computer-mediated communication" (Baron, 2004: 13), "internet-based synchronous text chat, with point-to-point communication between users" (Grinter and Palen, 2002: 1). IM is "direct, immediate, casual online contact" (Schiano et al., 2002), "interactive written discourse" (Ferrara et al., 1991: 8). Both participants communicate at the same time, regardless of where they happen to be in the world – down the hall or across the planet. In the early 2000s, it looked something like Figure 12.1, which is a screen shot from my computer from 2007.

In Figure 12.1 you see a photo from my computer and in Figure 12.2 from my daughter Freya's computer. There are technical reasons for these differences, including different operating systems and software versions. However, the contrasts I want to highlight are those related to the personalized layout, which was customized to the individual's pleasure. You can see immediately that our preferences are quite distinct. Mine is basic. Freya, then age 13, had set hers up to be a pond with fish swimming through and lily pads.

In this type of communication not only can teenagers have different individual conversations going on with several of their friends at the same time but they could also be doing other activities as well. The typical teenager at the computer can be listening to music, watching television, surfing the Internet, having a phone or face-to-face conversation, and ostensibly doing homework (Baron, 2004: 339; Schiano et al., 2002). This type of multi-media potpourri

Figure 12.1 Screen shot of Instant Messaging set up on computer, *c*.2007, Sali, 47

often takes adults by surprise. When I walk into my daughter's bedroom and find her with the TV on, her iPod in her ear, her school books on her lap, in the midst of composing her latest English essay, and at the same time talking to several (or more?) of her friends via IM, I wonder how she can possibly be doing it all at the same time!

When did IM first come into the picture? Crystal (2006) calls it an innovation of the twenty-first century. By the early 2000s, 80 percent of Canadian teens and 74 percent of American teens had used an IM program (Lenhart

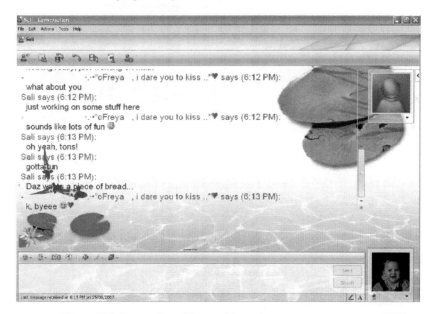

Figure 12.2 Screen shot of Instant Messaging set up on computer, *c*.2007, Freya, 13

et al., 2001: 3; Randall, 2002: 21). By August 2007, 91 percent of UK teens said they used IM at least once per week, while more than 50 percent use it every day.[5] IM's skyrocketing popularity among teenagers raised the concern of parents, teachers, psychologists, and grammarians. Internet language is "a distinctive genre of worry" (Crystal, 2006: 1).

Innumerable articles in the popular press have targeted IM. They suggest that it is leading to a "breakdown in the English language," "the bastardization of language,"[6] even "the linguistic ruin of [the] generation" (Axtman, 2002). In contrast, linguists argue that discourse on the Internet is a "new species of communication," complete with its own lexicon, font styles, grammar, and usage conditions (Crystal, 2001: 48). Teachers often pinpoint CMC as the root of students' lax attitude towards spelling and grammar. However, Baron (2003b: 88) suggests that language use on the Internet is part of a growing tendency for all writing to become more informal, less edited, and more personal – lending a speech-like character to much contemporary writing. In other words, IM may be a bellwether of future trends in the evolution of English writing and perhaps the language more generally. For a sociolinguist like myself, this possibility is exciting. What are the kids doing in IM? This was the burning question on my mind in the mid 2000s as I listened to the constant dinging of the computer in my living room.

I set myself up with a Hotmail email account and downloaded MSN Messenger, the IM program that my children were using. Then, I put my kids into my "buddy list." Instantaneously, I could see they were all "online" and, the best part was that they would (sometimes) "talk" to me. A whole new world opened. Here is a conversation with my youngest daughter, Freya. In this excerpt, she was 13.

202. a. Freya says: hey!
      b. Sali says: morning honey
      c. Sali says: how are things there?
      d. Freya says: gd and there?
      e. Sali says: watching Pirates of the Caribbean
      f. Freya says: when i come back courtney is coming she was on msn last night
      g. Sali says: oh good
      h. Freya says: youp
      i   Sali says: you guys will have fun
      j. Freya says: yuppers
      k. Freya says: so whos coming?
      l. Sali says: count . . . I think there will be 17 of us
      m. Freya says: lol ok
      n. Sali says: what's for dessert?
      o. Freya says: iono
      p. Sali says: okay, so we'll just do ice cream and chocolate
      q. Sali says: sound good?
      r. Freya says: yup
      s. Sali says: check
      t. Freya says: uhhuh
      u. Freya says: g2g
      v. Freya says: bye
      w. Sali says: c u soon . . . xxx

This is an intensely in-group conversation. Without knowing the situation it is difficult to make sense of it all. If I tell you that I was writing from our family home where I was with my youngest son, Daz(zian), aged 3, and Freya was elsewhere along with her two older siblings (Tara and Shaman) you can begin to understand the situation. Later, the whole family and some friends were coming back to the house for supper. Freya has also contacted one of her best friends (Courtney) who will also join us. You may also have noticed that I have attempted to get Freya to make dessert, something she is very good at, but she deflects with a classic *iono*.

Once the situation is clarified, it now becomes instructive to consider the nature of the language we both use. Freya tends to use short forms and short turns. IM acronyms are visible, including *lol, gd "good," gtg "got to go,"* etc. She also uses an unusual number of spellings for "yes," such as *youp*, *yup*, *yuppers*, and some very abbreviated forms, such as *iono* "I don't know" (see Chapter 11). She doesn't capitalize "I" and she doesn't use apostrophes. In contrast, notice that I do not use nearly as many short forms, my turns are longer, and I use apostrophes. At the same time, I have "learned the lingo." I do not use capitals at the beginning of sentences and there is an occasional short form, e.g. *c u soon*. Of course, this may just be me attempting to be "cool." IM is well known to be a stylistically playful register (Crystal, 2001: 71). Nevertheless, I know from discussion with my children that they consider it odd to talk to adults in IM. According to them, we just talk differently than they do. The truth is that adults do not fully engage with the appropriate IM conventions and in so doing mark themselves as outsiders.

It became obvious to me at the time that in order to study the way teenagers really use language in IM, I needed to be able to study their conversations with each other. Unfortunately, no matter how hard I have tried to cajole my children into giving me the records of their communications with their friends, they would not do it – not even for money. I am not the only linguist faced with this problem. One of the foremost linguists writing about the language of the Internet claims only to have had access to a single exchange of IM among teenagers (Crystal, 2006: 255). How could I find out what teenagers are doing in IM when they do not let anyone outside their social networks see what they are saying? The only way to do it was to collaborate with teenagers themselves, which led to the TIMC corpus described in Chapter 2. It comprises thousands of words of teens and young adults chatting with each other, with no adult or outsider of any kind present.

Characteristics of IM

Crystal (2006: 247–256) highlights the following characteristics of IM language:

- Interlocutors know each other well and have a background of shared knowledge.
- There is minimal small talk, "often no more than a simple 'Hi Jim' . . . before people get down to business" (Crystal, 2006: 250)
- Short messages in which individuals break up their sentences into small bits, i.e. "chunking," are the norm.
- First-person and second-person pronouns, i.e. *I* and *you*, make up the majority of subjects, and they are often omitted, e.g. *I have to go* → *have to go*.

Crystal (2006: 254–255) goes on to identify a series of linguistic phenomena, including:

- abbreviations;
- uncorrected typing errors;
- absence of punctuation;
- typographical idiosyncrasy;
- high level of informality;
- stylistic variation.

Now that there are computers I see the kids writing different. Like the short form letter eight. It's the lazy language. The less effort taken to get from point A to point B is their language now. (Julie Ho, 38)

In the mid 2000s, no large-scale study of actual IM language had ever been done on teenagers to substantiate the validity of these assertions. The TIMC provides an opportunity to find out. The examples in (203–207) were randomly selected from the corpus to illustrate the typical IM conversation.

203.   a. [044] hey cassandra, sorry to bother you, i have a question
        b. [5] fire away
        c. [044] ok, i forgot to bring home my homework folder, which has
            the physics questions we did last class. i'm just wondering -waht
            question did we get up to on monday? cuase i;m gonna finish
            that now
        d. [044] i just can't remember were we got up to
        e. [5] kk, one sec
        f. [044] thank you so much! sorry . . .
        g. [5] kk, the last question we did was 321 on pg. 86 . . .
        h. [5] (sry, #21)
        i. [5] we still have pg 87 #1–8 and pg 92 #1–4
        j. [044] so now we just have pg 87 # 1–4?
        k. [044] ohh ya thats whay i menat
        l. [044] thank you SO MUCH I OWE YOU1
        m. [5] you're welcome, heck considering how much I pester you in class,
            you don't have to worry
        n. [044] no, are you kidding, i pester you!!!
        o. [044] –
        p. [5] mutual "pestering"
        q. [044] haha okay, im gonna go finish tehse questions: ttyl xo
        r. [5] good luck

204.   a. [8] hey
        b. [038] hi
        c. [8] can you download the Mission Impossible theme for me? and send?
            plz?

      d. [038] tsk … FINE
      e. [8] thank you!
      f. [038] sends Theme – Mission Impossible Theme.mp3
      g. [8] Coolness, thanks.
      h. [038] you need to get your limewire in order
      i. [8] yeah, I do...
      j. [8] I tried to get Ares, but it wouldn't d/l anything.
      k. [038] hmm
      l. [8] I'm re-d/ling the Limewire
      m. [038] ok

205.   a. [040] what do we have to include in our chem rapport?
      b. [8] I don't know.
      c. [8] I have to go though, sorry.
      d. [8] Is it due tomorrow?
      e. [040] yes
      f. [8] 'kay
      g. [8] bye!
      h. [040] bye

206.   a. [029] who's gonna do jumping jacks tmr?
      b. [3] ill do them sorry iw as away err … did we have to change
      c. the lab because now we're doing it over 2 dsays??
      d. [029] hmmm
      e. [029] i guesss
      f. [029] i'll read over it tonight and change the wording
      g. [029] its only a little
      h. [029] its the same process
      i. [029] just add water
      j. [029] and add an extra day
      k. [3] yeah well we have to add to the process water and thats it
      l. [3] yepp
      m. [029] so i'll do that
      n. [029] and u bring ur gym clothes tmr?
      o. [3] yepp no problem
      p. [029] do you have a ruler?
      q. [029] mines only 20cm
      r. [3] i have a 30cm ne
      s. [3] *one
      t. [029] lol
      u. [029] okay
      v. [029] good. bring that one
      w. [029] study time now
      x. [029] i'll show u my new haircut tmr!!
      y. [029] and dont worry bout the prelab … its in my hands ^^P
      z. [3] me too haha okie see u tomorrow then~
     aa. [029] nites

207.   a. [1] boo
         b. [020] hey there
         c. [1] just finished a book in one sitting.
         d. [1] i feel good :)
         e. [020] wow
         f. [1] i used to do it all the time.
         g. [1] but i don't really have time anymore.
         h. [020] man . . .
         i. [020] ur brain's going to explode
         j. [1] . . .
         k. [1] why!?
         l. [020] too much knowldge
         m. [1] it was a novel! ; p
         n. [1] at least i wasn't reading a textbook . . .

The participants in these conversations obviously know each other very well and have a wealth of shared knowledge. They are in the same school, often in the same class. You can observe that the IM environment provides them with a place to discuss homework, download music, and engage in various activities in addition to having a conversation. Contrary to prediction, many of the teenagers' IM exchanges were hundreds of turns long. When reports suggest that teenagers spend several hours per day on IM, I can believe it! You can observe that the teenagers tend to be direct in identifying reasons for initiating an exchange: note the first three exchanges in excerpt (203). Nevertheless, there appears to be a substantial amount of conversation for its own sake – proverbial chitchat.

Short turns are the norm across all these conversations. Crystal (2006: 252) identifies two types: (1) *single-theme chunking* breaks up a long utterance making a single semantic point; and (2) *multi-theme chunking* separates a series of different points, often as a response to different utterances in the same conversation. You can observe single-theme chunking, as in (208–210), as well as multi-theme chunking, as in (210).

208. Single theme chunking
         a. [ma2] yea but
         b. [ma2] thats
         c. [ma2] in 2009
         d. [ma2] I don't have anything to do right noe
         e. [ma2] except study (a, IM, 2009)

209.   a. [l] don't worry
         b. [1] cuz
         c. [l] I am depressed (l, IM, 2010)

210.   a. [8] I don't know.
         b. [8] I have to go though, sorry.
         c. [8] Is it due tomorrow? (MSN, 2006)

Note too, the very frequent use of first- and second-person pronouns *I*/*we* and *you*. Although I selected these excerpts at random there is not a single instance of a third-person personal pronoun in any of them!

Most linguistic characteristics are readily visible: there are a number of abbreviations, e.g. *sec*, *kk*, *sry*. There is lack of punctuation, use of lower case, use of upper case for emphasis. The interlocutors are patently unruffled by the innumerable typos. Informal features proliferate the discourse. You may also notice freshly coined words are used, such as *coolness*, *novel* as a predicative adjective, and *nites* as a closing comment. Although some of the abbreviations seem recent and unusual, a number are rather mundane and have been in use for some time, e.g. *sec* for "second," *chem* for "chemistry." There are undoubtedly adults who might even use these abbreviations in their own speech, e.g. *wait a sec*. Stylistic variation is rampant. Notice, however, that although individual [029] abbreviates "tomorrow" as *tmr*, her interlocutor [3], uses the standard orthography, *tomorrow*. Similarly, individual [044] spells *sorry* standardly, but her interlocutor [5] uses a short form *sry*. Consider the word "okay." It is spelled in many different ways, sometimes varying within the same individual, e.g. [044] uses *ok* and *okay*; but more often each individual seems to have her own use: [5] uses *kk*, [8] uses *kay*, [029] uses *okay*, [3] uses *okie*. Similarly, punctuation is absent in some cases, yet appears in standard usage elsewhere. Sometimes sentences begin with a capital letter, sometimes not. Sometimes questions have a question mark; sometimes they have two. Sometimes, an individual uses uppercase "I"; sometimes an individual uses lower case "i." The point I want to emphasize is that IM is not categorically one thing or another. It is an amalgam. Until we have a way to study this type of language more scientifically, it is impossible to evaluate what it is like and what it is not like. We need to look at the total behavior of the teenagers in our corpus across a range of conversations, not just the instances where they do something outside the normal range of standard language use. People have a tendency to see the things that are unusual but they miss the ordinary.

In my research on IM, I took a different approach. I tried to identify and characterize the norms of practice among the group of teenagers I was studying. I did not look at one example or even a dozen; I looked at thousands. In fact, I tabulated every single time every one of the 71 teenagers used the forms under investigation. Let's see what I found out.

Vocabulary

One of the most common claims about IM is that teenagers are using short forms due to the speed of interaction and the desire to keep messages brief.

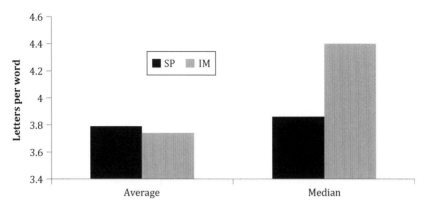

Figure 12.3 Comparison of word length in spoken conversations and IM

The two corpora in my study provided an efficient way to test these hypotheses. To begin with, I simply counted the words in each of the two corpora – IM and spoken interactions – and then counted up which corpus had the longest words. You will be surprised by the results.

Figure 12.3 shows you the average and median word length for the spoken conversations (SP) and the IM conversations (IM). Contrary to expectation, the IM conversations actually contain words of greater length than the spoken conversations.

IM forms

Given the media hype about IM, one is led to assume that it is riddled with non-standard features. Leaving aside typos, an inevitable product of fast typing and already well-established short forms, such as *cuz* and emoticons, which we were unable to study systematically, the features that stand out in IM are acronyms and abbreviations, as in (211–217). In addition, we counted all the forms that stand in for emotional responses such as laughter and other sounds, as in (211b) and (216d).[7]

211.   a. [1] WHATEVER, MEANIE.
        b. [1] hrmph
        c. [021] ... *wtf*?
        d. [1] you're so unsupportive

212.   a. [1] watch we end up knocking on some random guy's door.
        b. [1] anyway *brb*, shower.

213.   a. [009] I love sunchips
        b. [2] me too
        c. [2] *brb*

    d. [009] yo done digesting?
    e. [2] yes
    f. [009] *omg* I'm so tired
    g. [009] yes ... me too

214.   a. [013] *nvm*
       b. [013] i figured it out

215.   a. [2] gotta go
       b. [2] yes
       c. [2] *ttyl*
       d. [2] have fun

216.   a. [013] reg made me try on this PINK dress today
       b. [01] *hahaha*
       c. [02] i know
       d. [013] *ugh*
       e. [3] yep yep anyway im so bored I don't want to ztudy
       f. [008] ok! Lets talk about .... prom!
       g. [3] ..... okay, what about??
       h. [008] *err* ... are we going?
       i. [3] *uhh* ... I don't know yet lol robably it realy is a once in a lifetime thing
       j. [008] ok ... then *err* ... where are we going for after party?
       k. [3] *uhhh* I dunno *lol* its likke all the way in may

217.   [007] *haha* thatz basically it ... o well let her live in her bubble *argh* screw this waterloo app I'll do it 2morroe

The first question I asked was: how often do teenagers actually use such features when they are talking to each other in IM? Table 12.1 taken from Tagliamonte and Denis (2010: 12, Table 3) shows the most numerous forms used by the teenagers and their proportion of use in the data.[8]

Notice that laughter variants, shaded, are the most frequently used abbreviations.[9] The most heavily used acronym (and also the one stereotypically associated with IM) is *lol*, which at least at its origins stood for "laugh out loud."[10] Notice, however, that the proportion of use of this form is well below the more traditional *haha* at just over 4,500 times. Next is *hehe*, another laughter variant but with connotations of giggling (N=1,783).[11] Then comes *omg*, the IM acronym for "oh my God" and then *hmm*, a fairly mundane form expressing contemplation. Thereafter the numbers decrease markedly and this is where we find many of the famed IM forms, such as *brb*, "be right back," *ttyl*, "talk to you later," and *wtf*, "what the fuck." The others are sparse.

The sheer infrequency of the so-called "characteristic IM forms" is impressive when we look at the results by considering how often the forms are used out of the total number of other words. All the forms combined represent only 2.44 percent of the corpus. This is a minuscule proportion of the words the teenagers use. In fact, the vast majority of words are regular nouns, verbs, etc.

Table 12.1 *Frequency of top CMC forms in the TIMC, c.2006–2007*

Feature	Total N	Percentage of Total N
haha *laughing*	16,183	1.47
lol *laugh out loud*	4,506	0.41
hehe *laughing*	2,050	0.19
omg *oh my God*	1,261	0.11
hmm *thinking*	1,038	0.09
brb *be right back*	390	0.04
ttyl *talk to you later*	298	0.03
btw *by the way*	249	0.02
wtf *what the fuck*	218	0.02
argh *frustration*	197	0.02
hwk *homework*	99	0.01
nvm *never mind*	78	0.01
gtg *got to go*	68	0.01
np *no problem*	65	0.01
lmao *laughing my ass off*	63	0.01
nm *not much*	32	0.00
TOTAL	26,795	2.44

This might seem incredible, but it is actually parallel with the few other studies that have been done on IM (e.g. Baron and Ling, 2003). This initial result shows that the teenage generation in Canada between 2004 and 2006 use acronyms, short forms, and symbolic uses in IM, but they are much rarer than the media has led us to believe.

lol

Take for example, the most eminent IM form, which originates in the acronym "laugh out loud." The frequency of use of this feature, 4,506 instances, provides an opportunity to examine the social distribution of different laughter variants within this teenage speech community. Because the corpus is comprised of writers with a range of ages, it is possible to test for whether teenagers of different ages use this form differently. Figure 12.4 shows the distribution of the IM laughter variants, *lol*, *haha*, and *hehe* according to age of the individuals.

There is a marked difference across age. The younger individuals use a lot more *lol* than the older ones. In contrast, the form *haha* is the favorite among the older group. It seems likely that as the teenagers get older (and more experienced in the IM register) they turn to more "standard" forms. When I asked my oldest daughter *Tara* at age 16 about her use of *lol* she retorted, "I used to use *lol* when I was a kid."

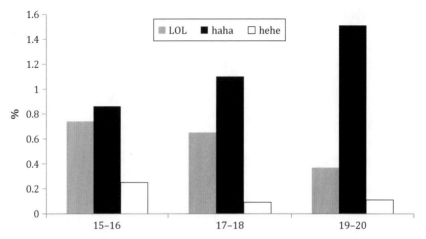

Figure 12.4 Distribution of laughter variants in IM by age of the individual

So far, it looks like the way teenagers use language in IM is a lot more ordinary than the popular press has suggested. Nevertheless, the hundreds of individual instances of innovative acronyms and short forms tell us that there is something new going on. The question is what?

It was at this point that I decided to look deeper into the grammar represented in data. I selected features that I knew a lot about from earlier studies. Conducting dependable analyses as to how teenagers use these features in IM compared to speech can give us insights into how their grammar is influenced by the different registers in which they operate.

In order to tap the underlying grammar of these registers, two linguistic features were selected for investigation. The first is a linguistic change that took place among teenagers in the early 2000s: the use of intensifier *so* (see Chapter 5). The second is a change that has been going on for centuries, but is nearing the end of its development, at least in Canadian English. This is the use of *have to* for expressing necessity or obligation, an area of grammar called *deontic modality*.

What's deontic modality?

Modality in language expresses information about the action or the attitude of the speaker. Deontic modality, in particular, expresses a duty or commitment imposed on the interlocutor. When children are told, "You *must* do your homework," or "You *have to* do your homework," or even "You *gotta* do your homework," the speaker is using forms of language that express deontic modality.

By studying these two different sub-systems of language undergoing change, but which diverge in terms of time-depth in the language (one new and one old) we can establish where IM is positioned with respect to the spoken language. If IM is like speech, it should contain forms and patterns similar to speech. If IM is more advanced than speech (in terms of linguistic change), newer forms should occur in greater proportions than they do in speech.[12] On the other hand, perhaps IM, as a written register, actually patterns like written language after all. Let's find out.

Intensifiers

[T]he use of intensifiers is typically associated with colloquial usage and nonstandard varieties.

(Tagliamonte and Denis 2008: 18)

Intensifiers maximize or boost the meaning of the adjectives they modify (e.g. *very, really, so,* etc.) (see also Chapter 5). They are of interest in the speech of adolescents because they change very rapidly (Stoffel, 1901: 2). Not only do they vary from place to place, from time to time, and from one social group to another but also according to internal mental states and processes. In a series of previous studies, I discovered that the locus of much of the change going on in the intensifier system was the adolescent population. This raises the compelling question of what teenagers are doing with intensifiers in IM. Intensifiers change continuously, in part due to the fact that they say something about the person who uses them. They can portray the individual as original, highlighting his or her verbal acumen, and function to "capture the attention of their audience" (Peters, 1994: 271). This presents us with an ideal feature to target for investigating adolescent language in IM and to begin to test the hypothesis that this new register is on the leading edge of linguistic innovation (Schiano et al., 2002: 1). Here are some examples of intensifiers from the IM data, as in (218).

218.   a. [008] got your emails ... *very* informative.
       b. [008] they were *very* good emails.
       c. [4] I'm *really* sorry – I set my clock and everything! But I guess I was *really* tired
       d. [024] I'm *so* mad
       e. [028] hez *soo* witty ha ha [028] aww I feel *soo* bad now ... like he thinks I hate him I wish I was nicer now
       f. [1] also, it's *super* 80s and *super* wacky

In earlier research on spoken language corpora, including contemporary British English, the television series *Friends*, and Canadian English, I discovered that *very* – the standard variant – is most frequent among older individuals (Ito and Tagliamonte, 2003: 257). This form has long been cited as the most frequent intensifier in English (e.g. Bäcklund, 1973: 290; Fries, 1940: 201).

In contrast, *really*, a newer variant is increasing among the younger generation. In Toronto English, the same variety spoken by the teenagers in this study, the younger a person is, the more likely they are to use *really* (see Figure 5.4). Between 1995 and 2008, a new intensifier was on the horizon. There was an acceleration of intensifier *so* among adolescents (Tagliamonte, 2008).

In order to study teenage use of intensifiers in IM, I extracted 16,320 adjectives from the TIMC, keeping track of whether the adjectives were intensified or not. Take a favorite adjective of the adolescent population such as *random*. In (219a) it is not intensified, but it can be intensified by *really*, *very*, or *so* as in (219b–d).

219.   a. [1] i can buy *random* stuff
        b. [003] i think it's *really random*
        c. that seemed *so random*
        d. [018] its *very random* you see

The questions I wanted to answer were: What intensifiers are used in IM and how frequently are they used? As a baseline, the IM conversations were compared to spoken conversations (SP) with the same individuals. Where will IM be positioned vis-à-vis speech?

Figure 12.5 shows the distribution of the main intensifiers as a proportion of all the adjectives in the data.

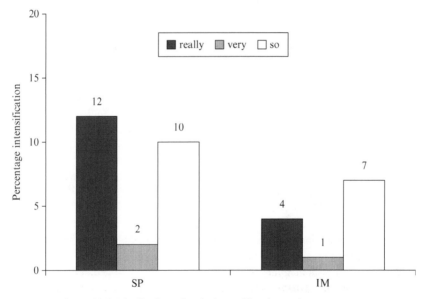

Figure 12.5 Distribution of main intensifiers by register

The most frequent forms in these data, both SP and IM, parallel those found in spoken data in earlier research – *really*, *so*, and *very*. Consistent with earlier research, *very* is rare among adolescents. However, it is the relative proportion of use of *really* and *so* that is informative. In SP *really* and *so* are used to the same degree: 12 percent *really*; 10 percent *so*. In contrast, in IM the teenagers are much less likely to use intensifiers but when they do use them, *so* is the most common word. Because intensifiers are associated with colloquial usage and non-standard varieties (e.g. Fries, 1940; Stoffel, 1901), this result suggests, first of all, that IM is a more formal register than speech. Also we discover that the same individuals use far less intensification in IM than in SP. Yet they use more *so* in IM than in SP. This is the first indication that IM cannot simply be labeled a speech-like register. It has an overarching conservative nature, but at the same time exhibits innovative trends.

Modals of necessity

Another feature that is undergoing change in Toronto is the area of grammar that expresses obligation and necessity. In IM, just as in the spoken language, a number of different variants alternate, as in (220).

220.   a. [026] i'll resort to that if I *must*
         b. [027] that's not that bad, just *gotta* recognize it
         c. ive *gotta* go study some more
         d. so I *have to* see u this weekend

In earlier research on Toronto English I discovered that teenagers almost always use *have to* (Tagliamonte and D'Arcy, 2007b). The other variants of deontic modality appear infrequently and are mostly restricted to the older individuals. The question is what are teenagers in the IM media doing with this change? Is the variation in deontic modality uniform across IM and speech? Unlike intensifiers, this system has been changing incrementally across the entire population. Figure 12.6 shows the distribution of variants in SP and IM.

Figure 12.6 reveals that consistent with the earlier research, these teenagers use *have to* the most often regardless of whether they are speaking or typing. However, there is a notable difference in their use of forms between SP and IM. In SP *have to* dominates at 83 percent compared to 54 percent in IM. The SP data has barely any *must* or *have got to* or *gotta* – only a few tokens apiece. In contrast, in IM the teenagers use the full complement of the variants present in this system in the language – formal (i.e. *must*), standard (i.e. *have got to*), and colloquial (i.e. *got to*). IM once again presents as a more conservative register. Further, where SP is categorical, IM has variety.

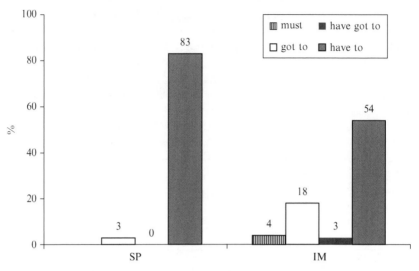

Figure 12.6 Distribution of variants of deontic modality by register

What do these results tell us about teen language in IM?

In a million and half words of IM among 71 teenagers talking to their peers (c.2007–2008) the use of short forms, acronyms, and emotional language is low – less than 3 percent of the data. The proportion of use is almost identical to the rates found for the same features among 20-year-olds (Baron, 2004). These results challenge the perception of IM as a register filled with non-standard features. Consistent with Baron's (2004) suggestion that young people outgrow stylized IM forms (Baron quoted in Ghenu, 2005: 8), the teenagers in this study are already conservative. If the results are indicative, adolescents appear to abandon the truly defamed IM features at a very young age, suggesting that such forms are a product of age grading. Nevertheless, I have tapped a vivacious new register of communication with its own distinctive style (see also Crystal, 2001; Ferrara et al., 1991; Herring, 2003, 2004). Language use in IM is part of a much broader modern trend towards more informal language generally (e.g. Biber, 1988, 1999; Hundt and Mair, 1999). Given these findings, where should IM be placed in relation to other registers?

First, the language of IM follows the model of the language that is used in the community in which the teenagers live. The way teenagers use intensifiers and deontic modals in IM reflects the same patterns and variation that are present in the ambient community. Yet IM has characteristics "that never existed before" (Ferrara et al., 1991: 26). The consensus in the literature is that IM is a hybrid. The findings I have shown you here permit me to identify what kind of species it is. For every linguistic variable, IM exhibits a characteristic fusion of variants. Simultaneously, it makes use of formal variants such as *must*, informal variants such as *have to*, and highly colloquial variants such as *gotta*. It also contains heightened use of incoming forms such as the intensifier *so*, providing evidence to confirm that IM is a truly innovative register on the forefront of change.

This blend of features is easily visible in all of the examples in this chapter. The examples in (221–223) underscore this eclecticism:

221.　a.　[008] how was workk
　　　b.　[3] quiet and unexciting haha
　　　c.　[3] im very alive now which is good, because i must stay up tonight
　　　d.　[3] lol

222.　a.　[2] anyways, must go
　　　b.　[2] ttyl!!!

223.　a.　[2] i dunno what u're talkinga bout man
　　　b.　[013] ok ...
　　　c.　[013] nvm
　　　d.　[013] my desk lamp doesnt work
　　　e.　[013] im very depressed
　　　f.　[013] i shall go get some alcohol ... brb

In excerpt (221c) a formal intensifier, *very*, appears alongside *haha* and *lol*. In (222a) deontic *must* occurs alongside *ttyl*. In (223e) *very* and the ultra-formal *shall* appear along with informal items such as *dunno*, lower case "i" and *u* for "you" as well as numerous IM forms, including *nvm* and in the same line *brb*.

Why do teenagers engage in this type of mixing? I think it is because IM offers them a register where they are free to utilize all the forms of expression they are capable of. In formal written language, colloquial variants are not acceptable: teachers are attempting to teach and enforce the use of standard language practice. In teenage conversations, formal variants are equally undesirable. Forms of written language sound stuffy and inappropriate in conversation. But IM is a venue in which anything goes. Teenagers in IM are picking and choosing from all the available variants that their linguistic systems have to offer. They draw from the entire stylistic repertoire of the language that exists at the extant point in time. In fact, it seems to me that this is what characterizes IM language most: the juxtaposition of written and spoken forms. In so doing, teenagers demonstrate just how lucid their linguistic abilities are. In fact, they give themselves away in these data, demonstrating beyond a shadow of a doubt that they have fluid mastery of the sociolinguistic and linguistic resources of their grammar. If anything, IM provides a training ground for experimentation and creativity in language use.

Computer mediated communication can be thought of as a kind of linguistic centaur, incorporating features from both traditional writing and face-to-face discourse but ending up being more than a simple amalgam of the two. (Baron, 2003a: 23)

When I first started presenting the research findings from the TIMC contrasting IM and spoken conversation, people said, "But why didn't you get a sample from their formal written language too?" Guess what I decided to do in my next study?

Cross-register comparison

By 2009 texting on phones had become rampant. Where once there was a family phone (a landline), by that point every member of the family had their own phone and it was just at their side or in their hand. It is not surprising that in some places (e.g. Germany) a mobile phone is called a "handy." The same daughter who used to type relentlessly on the family computer now chiefly uses texting on her phone, SMS, to communicate. Teenagers rarely use email anymore. Email is old fashioned. Voice calls are rare, restricted to serious conversations.

In the next analysis, I present an analysis of the TIC (see details in Chapter 2). The data come from private communications among young Canadians aged 17–21 at the time of the interviews between 2009 and 2010. They come from a range of different CMC registers: Instant Messaging (IM) on computers, email (EM), and text messaging on phones (SMS).

The one thing that I've noticed though over the years is that I think the language has actually shrunk. [Interviewer] Really? [056] And I think a lot of that has to do with computers. (Marinella Travis, 54)

Norms of language use in CMC have been in the process of conventionalization over the past 20–30 years. Thus, in the midst of technological and cultural developments, there is a tremendous opportunity to tap how language is changing across new emerging registers of written language.

As a framework for comparison, I make use of Baron's (2003a: 56) continuum of CMC registers, which is based on situational parameters of register variation (Biber and Finnegan, 1994: 40–41, table 2.1). Four factors distinguish the CMC registers represented in our study: *participants*, *platform*, *time*, and *editing*. Participants refers to whether the communication is monologic (i.e. no immediate feedback) or dialogic (incorporating feedback). Formal writing is generally monologic, whereas speech is generally dialogic. Platform refers to the physical characteristics of the register. Formal writing is found in print. In this study the written component comprises a written document submitted for assessment in education, i.e. an essay. EM and IM are used on a computer but on different platforms. SMS is used on a mobile phone. The factor of time refers to whether the register is time-independent and durable or time-dependent and

Table 12.2 *Comparison of CMC registers*

	Writing	CMC register		
Criterion	Essay	Email	SMS	IM
		Situational Factors		
Participants	Monologue	Dialogue	Dialogue	Dialogue
Platform	Print	Computer	Mobile phone	Computer
Architecture	Longest turns	Long turns	Short turns	Shortest turns
Time-dependency	Longest time to prepare	Long time to prepare	Short time to prepare	Shortest time to prepare
Durability	Most	Durable unless deleted from server	Durable until automatically deleted from mobile device	Durable depending on chat client
Editing	Considerable	Some	Little	Least

ephemeral. Writing is generally time-independent. Writers may take time to edit and structure their texts in order to create a permanent document. Speech is time-dependent and ephemeral. Speech requires an almost immediate response and is typically not permanent. CMC registers are positioned between. Finally, there is the factor of editing. Writing typically allows for proofreading whereas speech does not. These criteria offer the categorization schema shown in Table 12.2 based on Baron (2003a: 56).

The goal of this study is to compare and contrast language use across registers of CMC using evidence from the frequency and patterning of linguistic features. It is an attempt to answer, on a practical level, the question of what characteristics of language use make CMC a "linguistic centaur" (Baron and Ling, 2003 23).

Three analyses were conducted for the purpose of maximally triangulating across linguistic variables from different levels of grammar and among features representing different types of change. First, following in the footsteps of earlier research (e.g. Ling, 2005: 294; Tagliamonte and Denis, 2008a: 12), I assess claims regarding the frequency of the short forms, acronyms, and initialisms that often serve as shibboleths of CMC communication (see Romaine, 1994 on register-makers in sports announcing). As a cover term, I will use the term "CMC forms." Beginning with a straightforward inventory of the 20 most common CMC forms in the data, I compare their frequency across registers. Previous research suggests that these forms are characteristic of all types of CMC (Ferrara et al., 1991; Tagliamonte and Denis, 2008a; Thurlow, 2003); however, SMS may have a greater frequency of shortened forms because texters try to convey as much information in as little text as possible (Davies, 2005: 103–104). To date no comparison across registers has been reported, let alone an investigation of how the same speakers might shift from one register to another.

Second, I delve deeper into linguistic patterns by targeting not simply the surface forms, but also their alternation with like forms. The variants of laughter, including *lol* and *haha* are an ideal choice due to their frequency and diffusion across the individuals in the corpus. Laughter can be regarded a litmus test for the speech-like nature of a register since it is endemic to spoken discourse. Third, I consider the variants of orthographic "you" and "are," as "u" and "r," features which are ubiquitous in media reports on CMC language. Finally, I examine two areas of English grammar that are presently undergoing change. Research has demonstrated that teenagers push forward innovating forms (e.g. Eckert, 1988; Tagliamonte, 2008). CMC registers can be expected to offer insights into their diffusion. It could be that speech-like CMC registers will pattern along with the spoken language in taking up innovative forms sooner than written language. It may even be the case that changes in CMC antedate changes in the spoken language, that is, if CMC is truly on the vanguard of innovation in language. Further, by probing linguistic systems that have been recently studied in contemporary English, it will be possible to examine CMC patterns in comparison to the extant language of the speech community in which the CMC is situated – in this case an urban centre in North America. By studying the use of intensifier *so*, as in (224–225) we can establish whether CMC registers use more of this incoming form. This variant has not yet penetrated written language and remains a colloquial feature.

224.   a. [l] its *so* true!
        b. [ml13] x)
        c. [l] for girls, its *so* true . . . (l, IM)

225.   it was *so* stupid most of those people are plastic teeny bobbers! it made me *so* mad (m, EM)

The second targets a linguistic system that has been evolving for several hundred years in the history of English – the future temporal reference system. This is an ongoing linguistic development in which the verb "go" has come to be used in places where *will/'ll* is the standard (prescribed) variant, as in (226).

226.   a. I'm *going* to be home . . . like . . . ten ten (q, SMS)
        b. the stress of Grade 12 *is going to* shock her so much. (M, EM)
        c. i like this pen, i think *im gonna* steal it (z, EM)

While "going to" is not non-standard, it continues to be regarded as an informal feature and its frequency as a grammatical marker ranges from 50 percent in urban Toronto (Tagliamonte and D'Arcy, 2009) down to barely 10 percent of the system in conservative British dialects (Tagliamonte et al., 2014b). More speech-like registers can therefore be hypothesized to pattern along with the spoken language and be advancing this change. Written-like registers can be expected to lag behind and retain conservative variants, perhaps even more than peripheral dialects. Nuances of register may also come to light in the comparison of linguistic variables from different levels of grammar. Changes may also proceed differently depending on their social evaluation (i.e. prestigious vs. stigmatized). For example, intensifier *so* and future marker *going to* are both incoming forms but they have different social evaluation: while both are informal, *so* is trendy but *going to* is only informal. The results from the four different phenomena (CMC forms, orthographic variants, intensifiers, and tense markers) also provide coverage across the grammar in order to give insight into the linguistic nature of CMC.

Rules for good writing (*c*.1946): Never use a metaphor, simile, or other figure of speech which you are used to seeing in print; Never use a long word where a short one will do; If it is possible to cut a word out, always cut it out; Never use the passive where you can use the active; Never use a foreign phrase, a scientific word, or a jargon word if you can think of an everyday English equivalent. (Orwell, 1946)

The CMC registers in the TIC are defined as follows: Instant Messaging (IM) is simultaneous, one-to-one messaging via a computer. Messages tend to be brief and sentences can carry across several transmissions due to the immediacy of the interaction (Baron, 2003a: 13). A typical example is shown in (227) where two individuals are discussing the Disney/Pixar movie *Up* and the typical student conversation in (228).

227. Instant Messaging
    a. [f] sorry I was watching the movie up! ...
    b. [f] everyone says it's so good
    c. [friend] its really
    d. [friend] good
    e. [friend] but its still sad!
    f. [f] this movie is so weird!!
    g. [f] as if the house floats away
    h. [friend] :((f, IM)

228. Instant Messaging
    a. [s] Heyyy, still in bed? Or did u come for tut?
    b. [friend] I came haha! Where r u?
    c. [friend] My class dismissed
    d. [s] Ohh ... My class is almost finish too ... Do u mind meeting on the second floor just beside the stairs?
    e. [friend] Sure (s, SMS)

The brief interactions in (227) and (228) illustrate several well-documented conventions of IM, in particular the nature of the turns, which are represented here by line breaks as they were in the original discourse. According to Baron

(2004) turns are a single transmission, i.e. when concluded a person hits the "send" key. This is distinct from an utterance, which can extend over several turns. IM turns tend to be short, approximately five words per transmission. Jones and Schieffelin (2009: 84) report an average of 5.7–5.8 words and Baron (2004: 409) reports 5.4 words per transmission. A single clause can be spread across transmissions. This is the so-called characteristic of *utterance chunking* (Baron, 2004: 408), as represented in (229).

229. Utterance chunking in IM
       a. [friend] they went out partying?
       b. [l] and drinking
       c. [f] lmao
       d. [l] hahah
       e. [l] LOL
       f. [l] i know
       g. [l] i was like
       h. [l] damn
       i. [l] alchaholic
       j. [l] S
       k. [friend] lol (l, IM)

The participant [l] uses a total of six turns, as in (229e–j), to express a single conversational turn. Notice too that the segmentation of chunks can be as small as a morpheme. This is visible in (229j) where the plural suffix, *S*, appears on a separate line. Similarly, in (229g), participant [l] inserts a paragraph return after the quotative *I was like*, effectively segmenting the structure of the sentence into matrix clause and direct quote. In addition, there are several features which are commonly thought of as CMC markers more generally such as the lack of apostrophe in *its* (Squires, 2007), the use of the emoticon, :(, in the last turn of (227h) (Baron, 2003a: 20), and the lack of capitalization in the first turn of (227a) and (229a) (Ferrara et al., 1991: 26–29).

Email (EM) is one of the oldest forms of CMC, having been developed for personal use in the early 1970s (Baron, 1998: 141). Since then, EM has become one of the most common forms of communicating across the Internet. EM is defined here as asynchronous and computer-to-computer (Baron, 2003a: 12). As mentioned above, at the time of this study, there was no demarcation between EM and IM in terms of the device used for transmission. Both EM and IM were used exclusively with a computer. Even so, EM usage was even at that point in time becoming a circumscribed register for the young people. It had become restricted to communication with professors, parents, and other established members of society. For this reason a criterion was imposed for data collection of email in this study so that only EM communications that were: (1) one-to-one and (2) with a friend of similar age were viable for the course project, as in (230).

230.　　a.　How were exams? Can't wait to hear about everything else!! oh
　　　　　　yeah–please sign my yearbook! hahha … and pass it on (F, EM)
　　　　b.　Can I call you one night this week on your cell? Is your number [xxx]?
　　　　　　Exams were soooo hard! Oyyyyy! Where's your yearbook? I would
　　　　　　looooove to sign it! (e, EM)

There are a number of notable differences between the EM interaction in (230) and the IM interactions in (229). First of all, in EM each turn has several sentences; this differs from the extensive utterance chunking found in IM. More conventional use of capital letters at the beginnings of sentences is evident. At the same time, the EM interaction is similar to IM in terms of the presence of stereotypical CMC features, including the use of two exclamation marks in (230a) and segment duplication as in (230b). Both features are argued to convey emotion or emphasis that may not otherwise be attainable in the text-based nature of CMC (Baron, 2003a: 20).

Written messages on phones, originally 'Short Messaging Service' (SMS), has become better known as 'texting'. SMS is asynchronous and usually one-to-one communication. By the early 2000s SMS was cited as the most frequently used form of CMC. Ling (2005: 335) reports an estimated average of 280,000 text messages sent every hour in Norway. Thurlow (2003: 2) cites the Mobile Data Association statistic which says that 1.7 billion text messages were sent in Britain in May 2003.

It is important to highlight details of the state of technology at the time of this study of CMC. An early defining characteristic of SMS was the 160-character limit assigned per transmission due to the restricted bandwidth required for sending an SMS message. By 2009–2010 longer SMS messages were possible, but the system would automatically parse the message into 160-character chunks that the interlocutor would receive as separate transmissions. Popular news sources at this time often cite this character limitation as a reason for the reported over-abundance of acronyms and short forms. In fact, research on SMS length discovered that overall, messages are often much shorter. A study of Norwegian youth reported an average of 32 characters and between 5.5 and 7.0 words per transmission (Ling, 2005: 342). Thurlow (2003) reports longer messages for British university students, who averaged 65 characters per transmission, though there was much variation (1 SD = 45). By using a word-count feature in a word processor, Thurlow found an average of 14 words per transmission. Both studies found that the average text length was well below the 160-character limit.

Another critical dimension to these CMC data is that mobile phones in the 2000s typically only had a 12-digit number pad (numbers 0–9, #, and *). In order to compose a message, the sender would press the appropriate button for the letter that they wanted, the requisite number of times for each character that they wanted. This will seem quaint to the digital natives of the 2010s and beyond. For example, the number 4 on a standard telephone keypad was used for the letters G, H, and I. If texters wanted to type the letter "i," they would have to hit the number key three times. This was quickly rectified with T9 predictive texting, which allowed a user to only hit the appropriate numbers once for each character they wanted and the software would predict what word the user wanted based on the input and words stored in the device's memory. By the end of the first decade of the twenty-first century, smartphone technology had developed mobile devices with QWERTY keyboards. QWERTY phones offered an automated spell-check or predictive text feature similar to T9, which gave users the option of correct spelling and punctuation for mistyped sequences. These developments came *after* the present study. When the TIC was compiled smartphones were not available and only some of the students had phones with keyboards. This changed almost immediately afterwards.

Demographic data on individuals using the different registers of CMC during the same time span as this study can be found from market research statistics. Internet World Statistics (IWS, 2010) reported approximately 1.8 billion Internet users worldwide, with most of these subscriptions coming from Asia (764.4 million), Europe (425.7 million), and North America (259.6 million). Relative to the populations of different parts of the world, North America shows the highest penetration of the Internet at 76.2 percent of the population, followed by Oceania/Australia at 60.8 percent, Europe at 53 percent, and Latin America/the Caribbean at 31.9 percent of the population. Despite having the largest gross number of Internet subscriptions, Asia only shows a population penetration of 21.5 percent.

A marketing study conducted by the Pew Internet and American Life Project (Pew, 2010) surveyed 800 youth between the ages of 12 and 18 in four US cities via telephone interview about what communication methods they used when talking to their friends. Researchers asked the subjects "What methods of communication do you use to contact your friends daily?" They found that teens preferred using SMS to other methods such as talking on the phone, sending email, or using IM. Of all the teens interviewed, 72 percent said that they texted their friends and 54 percent of these individuals reported doing so regularly all through each day. This is a sharp increase from the 51 percent of texters in 2006 to the 72 percent reported in 2009. Thirty-three percent of teens reported talking to their friends face-to-face, which was the third most popular choice, behind texting and talking on a cell phone. Instant Messaging and social networking sites (such as Facebook) had reported daily usages of 25 percent and 24 percent respectively, followed by email at only 11 percent. The Pew researchers suggested that email, "appears to have become a passé 'legacy' technology among the under-18 population."

While the subjects in this study are somewhat older than the teens in the Pew (2010) research, they shared the same sentiments. In 2010, a demographic survey was distributed to the students regarding their interlocutors and Internet usage preferences. When asked what CMC register they preferred, 12 of the 20 students chose Facebook over conventional EM. Further evidence of the sense that EM is outdated comes from class discussions. The 2010 class explained that EM communication is for "older people." The declining use of EM among young people and the restricted context of use indicate a level of formality and (social) conventionalization (Ferguson, 1994).

This summarizes the state of CMC at the time of the study. The TIC is unique in terms of vernacularity, speaker sample, and size (Tables 2.3 and 2.4). Further, and most critically, it comprises representation from the same speakers across the extant CMC registers of 2009–2010. To my knowledge no other corpus permits such a comparison.

CMC forms

CMC forms, including abbreviations, initialisms, and short forms, are the most often cited characteristics of CMC, undoubtedly because they are the most striking (e.g. Thurlow, 2006, Appendix), as in (231–232).

231.   a. [q, IM] *OMGGGGGGGGGGG*! that's the kind we have!!!
       b. it's sooooo good!!!!! i had the hazelnut a few days ago, it was delicious!!!!!!!!!
       c. [friend] OMG! are you serious!

232.   a. [friend] *r u* going to psych?
       b. [o, SMS] yup! sure! y not?
       c. [friend] Okay ... tell me when *ur* leaving then
       d. [o, SMS] *k,* i'll call *u* later
       e. [friend] Hey do *u* know *wat* our tutorial code is?
       f. [o, SMS] WB3
       g. [friend] Thx! *gl* on exam
       h. [o, SMS] no *prob, U* 2 (SMS, 2010, o)

The reported frequency of these CMC forms varies from study to study. This is due to divergent methods of analysis and varying decisions about what to include in the assemblage. British teenagers are reported to use 18.75 percent abbreviations in SMS (as a proportion of number of words) and approximately three per message (Thurlow, 2003: 7). This count includes all non-standard orthographic forms, e.g. *uni* for "university," misspellings such as *excelent* for "excellent," common acronyms (*DI* for "Detective Inspector"), abbreviations (*bud* "buddy"), g-dropping as in *huntin* "hunting," non-conventional spellings like *rite* "right," and accent stylization such as *wivout* "without." Other studies

Table 12.3 *Frequency of the top CMC forms in the TIC, 2009–2010*

CMC Form	Gloss	N	%
lol	"laugh out loud"	829	40
haha*	laughter	490	24
lm(f)ao	"laugh my (fucking) ass off"	100	0.05
om(f)g*	"oh my (fucking) God"	90	0.04
kk*	"okay"	77	0.04
cuz/becuz/bcuz	"because"	70	0.04
tmr*	"tomorrow"	55	0.03
ppl*	"people"	43	0.02
btw	"by the way"	42	0.02
ttyl	"talk to you later"	37	0.02
hehe*	laughter	36	0.02
tho	"though"	31	0.02
hmm*	thinking	29	0.01
ic/i c	"I see"	23	0.01
thx	"thanks"	23	0.01
wtf	"what the fuck"	21	0.01
sry*	"sorry"	19	0.009
msg*	"message"	16	0.009
np	"no problem"	13	0.006
brb	"be right back"	12	0.007
TOTAL		2,056	1.7

* These categories comprise a variety of different combinations of the same characters.

have taken a more circumscribed approach to what is deemed a CMC variant, including only acronyms, short forms, and abbreviations. These studies report far lower frequencies. Baron (2004: 412) reported 1.03 percent CMC-specific forms. Tagliamonte and Denis (2008a: 12) reported 2.44 percent. Taking this approach in our own study, Table 12.3 shows the frequency of the 20 most common acronyms, short forms, and abbreviations found in the TIC. Variants of laughter are shaded.

Table 12.3 shows that these CMC forms represent over 2,000 items, but as a proportion of the total number of words in the TIC, they represent a mere 1.7 percent. This proportion is remarkably parallel to earlier reports (Baron, 2004; Tagliamonte and Denis, 2008a) (see Table 12.1), offering a certain degree of confidence in the new findings. There was not a single instance of any of these CMC forms in the 58,222 words of formal written language from the same individuals. This provides a first indication that young people are sensitive to register. Let's now determine whether there is any difference in their usage of the same CMC forms across EM, IM, and SMS. Note too that most of these items are initialisms, not acronyms.

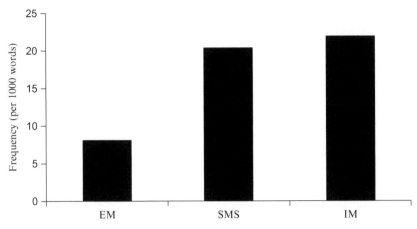

Figure 12.7 Frequency of CMC forms by register

Figure 12.7 shows the frequency per 1,000 words of the CMC forms as a group across the three registers and reveals that EM has the lowest frequency of CMC forms at 8.1 tokens per thousand words. IM and SMS have much higher rates of CMC forms at 21.99 and 20.38 per thousand words, respectively. The difference between SMS and IM is not statistically significant. The fact that EM has a significantly lower frequency of CMC forms supports the hypothesis that it is the most formal register of CMC, while the comparable frequencies in SMS and IM point to similarities between them. This is an interesting result because researchers have argued that in SMS, texters are inclined to use short forms by "reducing every word to its minimum comprehensible length" (Davies, 2005: 103–104). These results suggest that despite space limitations, IM (on computers) and SMS (on phones) are not distinguished, at least not with regard to the frequency of these CMC forms. In IM and SMS the students use these CMC forms at the same frequency despite the 160-character limit.

The next analysis focuses on linguistic systems in order to further probe the nature of CMC language in the TIC.

Variants of laughter

One of the notable results in Table 12.3 is the sheer number of forms comprising variants of laughter, including *haha*, *hehe*, *lol*, all shaded. These variants can often be found interspersed throughout a CMC conversation as in the examples in (233–234).

233.   a. [friend] watd u do last night?
        b. [t] oh i had to work, it was so boring but not terrible lol. then i went out
            with friends ... u?
        c. [friend] oh sweet, i went out, very interesting things happened lol
        d. [t] no wayyyy!!! like what???
        e. [friend] umm we never actually made it newhere til we ditched and went
            to a bar
        f. [friend] this girl jst passed out like 7 timed
        g. [t] lmao.
        h. [friend] fell out of elevators, cars, so on
        i. [t] omg! no way! ahahaha
        j. [t] was he ok?
        k. [t] *she
        l. [friend] nope. took him home with a puke bag
        m. [t] lol ... her
        n. [friend] ya ... her ...
        o. [t] wow thats intense tho. hhaha aw poor grl
        p. [friend] it was her bday too! shes not gonna member a thing
        q. [t] hahah your not suppose to! lol
        r. [friend] you wanna member ur bday! its the day after to forget (t, IM)

234.   a. Yo i have another question.
        b. K. so youre giong to baking party? Cause if you are and im with you -
            i assume that means im going too? lol.
        c. Also, as yuo know laura is in tdot again. SOO she was mentioning getting
            together befoer baking thing. Did she discuss that with you also?
        d. One more thing. Sunday. I'm either going to go with you to dancing or go
            home early via train. What do you think? lol.
        e. k so that wasnt one question rather a bundle of questions. haha
        f. also as you know im a little short on cash flow. Which means i might be a
            cheapy this weekend. :S
        g. i'll try and figure something out. (n, EM)

As a reasonably coherent set, the variants of laughter can be systematically
studied using the notion of the linguistic variable (Labov, 1972a: 127). My
previous quantitative study of laughter variants (Tagliamonte and Denis,
2008a: 13) offers the possibility of a reliable comparison. At the time of this
earlier study (with data collected in the early 2000s), the variant *haha* was the
most prevalent of the short forms, comprising 1.47 percent of the entire data
set: it was also the most frequent laughter variant. While *lol* was also frequent,
the study documented a systematic retreat from *lol* in apparent time such that
15–16-year-olds had the highest rates of *lol* and 19–20-year-olds the lowest
rate, with a corresponding increase in use of the variant *haha*. The results for
the TIC in Table 12.3 show that by 2009–2010, the most frequent of the CMC
forms is *lol* at 0.69 percent, much higher than *haha*, at 0.40 percent. Assuming
that the overall inventory of CMC has stayed stable, this suggests an increasing

use of *lol* from 2008 to 2009–2010. Examination of the two time points, 2009 and 2010, separately reveals that *lol* represents a larger proportion of all laughter variants in 2010 than in 2009 (55.4 > 47.8%). The question is: are the differences significant and do they indicate a change in progress?

Even by the early 2000s researchers had noticed that *lol* did not always mean "laugh out loud" or actual laughter. For example, Baron (2004: 416) described *lol* as "a phatic filler, roughly comparable to *OK*, *really*, or *yeah* in spoken discourse," and Tagliamonte and Denis (2008a: 11) suggested that *lol* was used "in the flow of conversation as a signal of interlocutor involvement. This function of *lol* is corroborated by online commentary: for example comedian Billy Reid says: *'I'm typing LOL! I'm typing, but I'm not laughing'*."[13]

How are the major laughter variants used across the TIC registers? The answer to this question will not only shed light on variation among the laughter variants, but will also help to place the three registers on the written-to-spoken spectrum. Figure 12.8 shows the distributional results.

Figure 12.8 comes from an exhaustive count of all the laughter variants, a total of 766. Distributional differences across the three registers are apparent. As expected from the overall distribution in Table 12.3, *lol* and *haha* are the most common laughter variants across the board. However, while *lol* vies with *haha* in EM, *lol* is the dominating form in IM and SMS. The variant *lmao* is infrequent generally, but is most frequently used in SMS. These distributions support the hypothesis that EM is a more conservative register than either SMS or IM and that IM is a hotbed of iconic CMC forms, e.g. *lmao*. The inherent

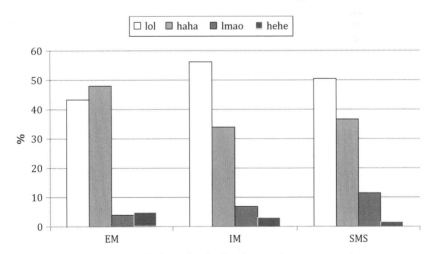

Figure 12.8 Distribution of major laughter variants across registers

characteristic of these registers comes to the fore. If *lol* indicates interlocutor involvement (Tagliamonte and Denis, 2008a: 11), it can be expected that EM, which generally has longer turns and fewer turns per conversation than IM and SMS would have fewer indicators of involvement and therefore fewer instances of either *haha* or *lol*. In IM and SMS the turns are shorter and more rapid and individuals need to show engagement, which results in more *lol* rather than the iconic *haha* for laughter.

To assess the potential functional differences among the variants of laughter, let's consider the effect of discourse position. Laughter variants occur at different points in the discourse, at the beginning of a turn as in (235b), (235i), (236b). They also occur at the end of a turn as in (237a–b) and in some cases all by themselves in a turn, as in (236b). Although I also originally tabulated middle positions as well, as in (239a), these were rare in every register (5.8 percent overall) and so were excluded from the statistical model. While true laughter might be expected to occur virtually anywhere, a form used to acknowledge an interlocutor's utterance can be expected at juncture points in the conversation.

235.   a. [d] a cinema course
        b. [friend] *lol* seriously?
        c. [friend] wat do u in dat course?
        d. [d] 1 lecture 1 movie screening and 1 tutorial a week
        e. [friend] wat do u do in lecture and tutorial
        f. [d] assess and learn the history and changes of horror movies
        g. [d] *hahaha*
        h. [d] watch movies
        i. [friend] *lol* d u need to take dat course?
        j. [d] nah electives (d, IM)

236.   a. [w] coz i came down to libarary.
        b. [w] *lol*.
        c. [friend] Studying for finals already? (w, IM)

237.   a. [friend] It's basically an excuse to drink beer *haha* (f, SMS)
        b. [friend] okay im gonna be gone for now *haha* [friend] ttyl! [j] k bb (j, IM)

238.   a. [friend] *lol* sickk now we both have one *hahah*
        b. [friend] oh yeah i might go to svp this weekend you want to come? (u, IM)

239.   a. i didn't get scared that much. just jumpy *lol* n i didnt c u today! (r, IM, 2009)
        b. ill come visit *haha* sound good? (M, IM, 2009)

Table 12.4 shows the distribution of *lol* according to register, discourse position, and sex.

The results in Table 12.4 show that *lol* patterns by register but not by sex. The fact that it occurs most often in closing and stand-alone contexts suggests

Table 12.4 *Distribution of* lol *register, discourse position, and sex*

	%	N
REGISTER		
Instant Messaging [IM]	60	1,017
Texting on phones [SMS]	50	241
Email [EM]	49	227
DISCOURSE POSITION		
Closing	65	322
Stand-alone	60	566
Initial	49	497
SEX		
Male	57	367
Female	51	588

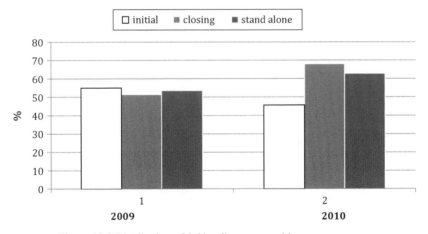

Figure 12.9 Distribution of *lol* by discourse position

that it is not simply laughter, but may be developing another function. This becomes evident in Figure 12.9 which shows a cross-tabulation of discourse position and year of data collection.

Figure 12.9 exposes a change from 2009 to 2010. In 2009 *lol* was used equally across all positions, which would be expected for an unpatterned insertion of laughter. However, by 2010 *lol* has shifted to a higher level of frequency in closing position and where it represents the only item in a turn. This result offers evidence of the development of *lol* from actual laughter into a marker that signals the end of a turn.

Orthographic variation

Another prominent feature of CMC language is the orthographic variation that occurs with the second-person pronoun *you/u* and the second-person singular form of "to be," *are/r*, as in (240). Note that in (240c) the writer alternates between forms.

240.   a. but hee loves *u* too, and i think *u* loook cute together (m, EM)
        b. no wonder people think *you* are a discombobulated idiot (g, SMS)
        c. It'll be like one of those blogs "pocky all around the world" where *u* take pics of *you* and the pocky all around the world! XD (z, EM)
        d. wat games are *u* playing? (d, IM)
        e. Was wondeirng if *u r* still in the pet therapy program. If *u r*, wud *u* like to continue being my partner for every other tuesday? (j, SMS)

The distribution of these two variables in the TIC is shown in Table 12.5, which reveals that standard full forms are dominant and that the CMC variants *u* and *r* are relatively infrequent. Examination of how the CMC variants pattern by register is shown in Figures 12.10 and 12.11.

The standard forms are by far the preferred choice in each register. Only *u* shows an incremental pattern of increasing use from EM → IM → SMS. While the shortening of forms can be explained by the character limit in SMS, these results show that it is not definitive. Writers clearly don't use "r" for "are" even when it seems likely that they would do so. Notice however that "you/u" occurs far more frequently than "are/r." It is unclear why writers do this. Further study of these alternations might reveal the underlying reason.

Figures 12.12 and 12.13 show each individual's use of *you/u* in 2009 and 2010 respectively. Each figure is arranged such that the black bars represent the standard forms and the white bars represent the short forms.

It is easy to see that the majority of individuals use the standard *you* categorically, though two speakers in 2009 are categorical *u*-users. Certain individuals use the non-standard form occasionally. This intermittent usage is likely a matter of style, as suggested by (240e). Next time someone sends you a text message, notice where *u* or *r* turn up. Is the person trying to be funky

Table 12.5 *Distribution of* you/u *and* are/r

Form	N	%
you	2,490	79.20
u	654	20.80
are	580	86.57
r	90	13.43

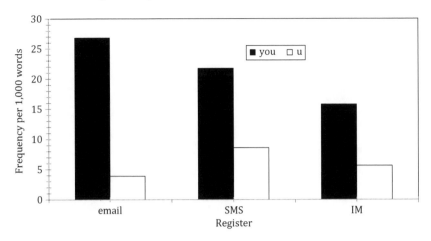

Figure 12.10 Distribution of *you* and *u* by register

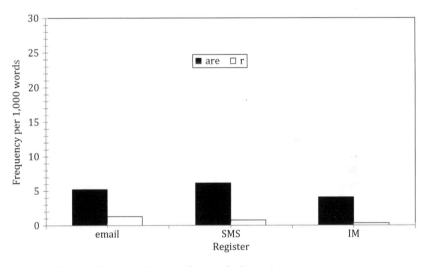

Figure 12.11 Distribution of *are* and *r* by register

and/or does the form turn up in certain linguistic contexts, such as questions, e.g. *r u curious*?

Intensifiers

The English intensifier system has been subject to considerable study (Stenström, 2000; Tagliamonte, 2008; Tagliamonte and Roberts, 2005; Van

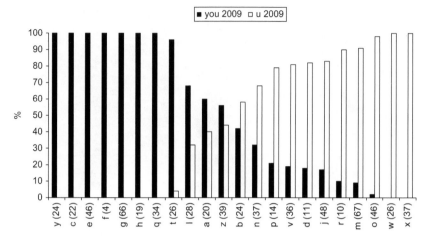

Figure 12.12 Distribution of *you* vs. *u* by individual in 2009

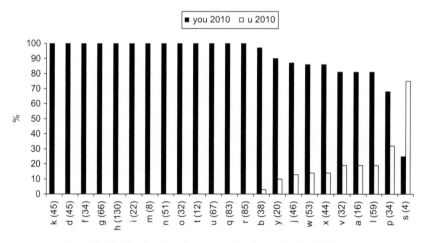

Figure 12.13 Distribution of *you* vs. *u* by individual in 2010

Herk, 2009). Rapid change, recycling, and forms jostling for position are the characteristics of this area of grammar. The Standard English form *very*, as in (241a), competes with *really* as in (241b) and *pretty* also makes up a sizable proportion of forms, as in (241c). This study capitalizes on the fact that the variant *so* in (241d) was increasing at the time among teenagers and especially girls (e.g. Tagliamonte, 2008).

241.   a. yehh we do have quiz tmr ... *very* easy one ... dun worry (l, SMS)
         b. That sucks im actually *really* bloated (m, IM)
         c. like i think im *pretty* lucky to be going to bg for uni stjll (v, EM)
         d. hazelnut is *soo* good! (q, IM)
         e. sooooo buttery (m, EM)

Different intensifiers are variably associated with non-standard and colloquial varieties of the language, which makes this an ideal linguistic site for the
investigation of variation in CMC. However, this study enables us to test for
which intensifiers are used in each CMC register.

Following the protocols in earlier research (Ito and Tagliamonte, 2003;
Tagliamonte, 2008; Tagliamonte and Roberts, 2005) all adjectives in the
TIC capable of being intensified, whether they were modified by an
intensifier or not, were extracted for analysis. Contexts that did not permit
intensification, such as comparatives and superlatives were excluded as
were negatives. Adjectives modified by downtoners (e.g. *kind of*, *sort of*)
were grouped with non-intensified contexts. Each context was coded for
year of data collection, individual, register, adjective type, and semantic
classification.

Figure 12.14 shows the distribution of adjective types in the data. It is
immediately apparent that the written data stand apart from all the CMC
registers. While the written data have over 60 percent attributive adjectives,
these represented less than 25 percent in each of the CMC registers. Predicative adjectives represent the vast majority of intensifiable adjectives in CMC,
as in (242–243).

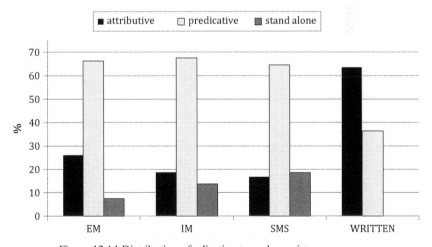

Figure 12.14 Distribution of adjective types by register

242.   a. But yea i sent u that txt cuz i was *sooo* bored . . . i took a nice nap that day
            (j, EM)
        b. hey im *so* cheesed i did bad on my article summary for astro! :((m, SMS)

243.   a. Visited one of the first catholic churches ever . . . *very* cool. (o, EM)
        b. yeah *so* amazing from be4 (m, IM)
        c. [m/09/IM] and i thought . . . ooo o *soo* sweet (m, IM)
        d. *very* good to hear from you (h, EM)

Table 12.6 shows the rate of intensification in the TIC overall and within
each register. Overall, the TIC corpus shows a rate of intensification of 24.9
percent when the written data are included. Notice, however, that this masks
the extreme difference between the written data and the CMC registers, all of
which hover around 30 percent intensification. Here again is strong evidence
for the divide between standard written language and CMC. How does the
frequency of rates compare to other studies of intensifiers across speech
and CMC?

Figure 12.15 compares the overall rate of intensification in the TIC (minus
the written materials) with those from five other studies: American English in
the television series *Friends* (Tagliamonte and Roberts, 2005), spoken British
English (Ito and Tagliamonte, 2003), the ambient community in Toronto
(Tagliamonte, 2008), and a study of Gay, Lesbian, Bisexual, and Queer
(GLBQ) individuals from Toronto (Tagliamonte and Uscher, 2009). These
corpora are shown along the *x*-axis.

Note that the TIC has rates of intensification comparable to studies of
face-to-face speech. This supports the idea that CMC patterns with spoken
language.

The four most common intensifiers reported for contemporary English at the
turn of the twenty-first century are *really*, *very*, *pretty*, and *so*. Table 12.7
shows the distributions of these forms along with all other intensifiers
occurring five or more times in the TIC.

Table 12.7 reveals that *so* is by far the most common intensifier (13.7
percent). The more standard variants – *really* and *pretty* and especially *very* –
occur at much lower frequencies.

Table 12.6 *Overall rate of intensification*

	% Intensification	Total N
TIC overall	24.9	2,003
Email	28.0	835
IM	29.0	920
SMS	31.0	248
WRITTEN	10.1	535

Table 12.7 *Distribution of intensifiers*

Intensifier	%	N
so	13.7	274
really	4.7	95
pretty	3.6	72
very	1.9	39
all	0.5	10
super	0.4	9
totally	0.4	8
just	0.3	7
too	0.3	6
quite	0.3	6
fucking	0.3	6
extremely	0.2	5
OTHER	2	41
Ø Intensification	71.1	1,425
TOTAL		2,003

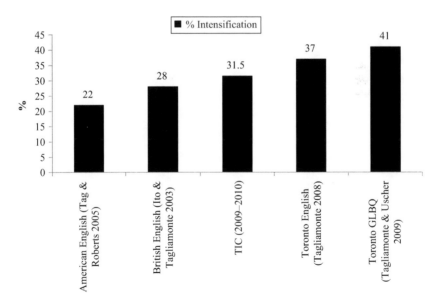

Figure 12.15 Comparison of overall rate of intensification across studies

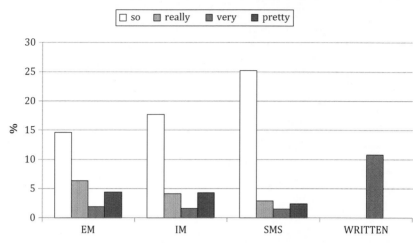

Figure 12.16 Distribution of major intensifiers by register

The key question however is how these intensifiers are distributed in the different registers. Figure 12.16 displays the proportion of *so*, *really*, *very*, and *pretty* by register in the TIC. The data are based on the frequency of intensifiers with 1,569 intensifiable adjectives.

Figure 12.16 exposes a powerful register difference between the written data and the CMC registers. The intensifier *very* is the only intensifier used in the written documents. In contrast, all the intensifiers are used in the CMC registers. Comparing their patterns across registers reveals a by now familiar trend. EM is conservative, followed by IM and SMS. The use of incoming intensifier *so* varies steadily by register. EM has the least *so*, IM more, and SMS the most. Two interpretations may be put forward. First, the shortness of *so* may favor its use in SMS where there is pressure on the writer for brevity. At the same time tokens of reduplicated "o's," e.g. *soooo*, are present. Second, it may be the case that SMS is the leading register for deploying new forms. These may be acting in tandem to produce the heightened rate of *so* in SMS.

The analyses that follow probe the variable grammar that underlies intensifier choice by testing the effects of two internal factors – semantic classification and adjective type. Different types of adjectives may be more or less amenable to innovating forms (Partington, 1993: 183). This continuum can be uncovered by systematically classifying the different adjectival heads by their semantic class (Dixon, 1977). The data offered sufficient numbers for two main classes of adjectives: those describing human propensities, e.g. *glad*, *sorry*, *crazy*, and those which express a value, e.g. *good, bad, cheap*. Figure 12.17 shows the distribution of predicative *so* by register according to

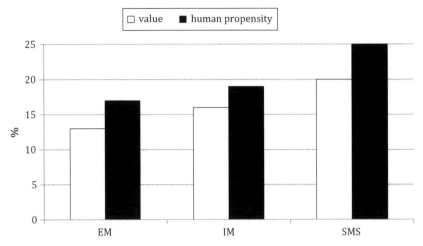

Figure 12.17 Distribution of *so* by semantic classification by register

this semantic classification of the adjective. Recall that *so* rarely occurs in attributive position.

Figure 12.17 reveals that while *so* occurs with both adjective classes, there is a variable pattern such that *so* tends to occur more often with adjectives of human propensity, as in (244), rather than adjectives of value, as in (245).

244.   a. I'm so sorry (f, IM)
         b. it made me *so* mad
         c. all the *really* hot people were left out (m, EM)

245.   a. its *reallllyyy* hard for me :((m, IM)
         b. loool but ya, *pretty* pointless (j, EM)
         c. u know he started laughing too? cause it was *so* akward (z, IM)

The critical evidence is that this pattern is parallel across registers. A grammatical constraint governs the use of *so*, and this is stable regardless of varying frequencies of the intensifiers or their forms.

Future temporal reference

The English future temporal reference system is a system that has been subject to a substantial range of research, both sociolinguistic and historical (e.g. Nesselhauf, 2007b; Poplack and Tagliamonte, 1999; Tagliamonte et al., 2014b; Torres-Cacoullos and Walker, 2009b). Unlike the intensifier system, this system has been involved in a long and gradual change. The use of *going to* arose in the late 1400s and is reported to be steadily displacing *shall* and *will*. At the time of this study, *going to* represented 53 percent of the spoken vernacular in Toronto English (Tagliamonte and D'Arcy, 2009). The TIC has all the variants reported in recent studies, including *shall*, *will*, *'ll*, *going to*, and many orthographic variants of these, as in (246).

246.   a. yo *shall* we go to see that on friday? (b, IM)
        b. wat *will* u be doing in the summer? (a, IM)
        c. okay *ill* get you a dog (y, IM)
        d. chem *is going to* own me (y, IM)
        e. *im gona* go brush my teeth (h, IM)
        f. *im* realy *guna* do it (p, IM)
        g. so is she *gonna* go bac tmr ? (w, IM)
        h. i swear man *imago* off (m, IM)

The form *going to* does not carry overt stigma in the spoken language; however, the orthographic forms of variably reduced pronunciations such as *gonna*, *gon* are judged colloquial and the form *ima* is decidedly non-standard. The form *will* is the standard variant while *shall* is reported to be formal and in decline across major varieties of English (e.g. Williams, 2015). Linguistic research documents distinct register differences among forms with *will* and its variants preferred in "speech-based" registers (Nesselhauf, 2007a: 291). The sheer number of different forms of varying degrees of formality and states of change will be useful for helping to discern the nature of the CMC registers in the TIC.

Following the protocols in earlier research (Poplack and Tagliamonte, 1999; Tagliamonte, 2002; Torres-Cacoullos and Walker, 2009a), all tokens of future temporal reference were extracted – excluding formulaic utterances, future present and progressive and future in the past, which overwhelmingly occur with *would*, e.g. *I thought she would come*. This enables us to focus on the robust variability between variants of *shall*, *will*, and especially the many orthographic variants of *going to*. Each context was coded for year of data collection, individual, register, grammatical person, animacy, type of clause, and type of sentence.

Figure 12.18 shows the distribution of future temporal reference variants by register in the TIC and reveals something unexpected: the form *will* dominates in all registers. The figure also adds further evidence for a linguistic divide between written data and CMC. Notably, writers employ *will* to the virtual exclusion of all other variants in the written essays. In addition, there is a split among the CMC registers. SMS stands apart due to the high rate of *'ll* whereas in EM and IM this form is a minor variant in the system. Why would this be the case? Nesselhauf (2007a) suggests that the use of *'ll* is emblematic of speech-based registers. However, these results show that it cannot simply be the speech-like nature of the register because SMS and IM are both speech-like. As with the heightened use of *so* in SMS, the use of *'ll* is likely due to the fact that it is short. Writers using SMS are said to

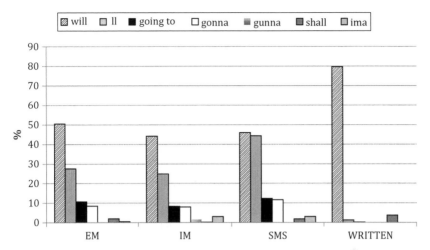

Figure 12.18 Distribution of future temporal reference variants by register

be under pressure to be brief and also responsive. It is notable that the overall frequency of "going to" variants in all the CMC registers is low and no register has more than a smattering of forms such as *gonna* and *ima*. In sum, although "going to" represents 53 percent of the future temporal reference system in the spoken vernacular in Toronto, these registers all evidence conservatism. Variants of the "go" future are never more than 30 percent. All the registers of CMC are lagging behind in the grammatical change towards the "go" future in English.

In order to further assess the state of the future temporal reference system in these CMC registers, it is possible to model the variable grammar that underlies the choice of *going to* over *will*. A composite of factors are known to constrain the use of *going to* including the nature of the subject, the type of clause, and type of sentence (e.g. Nesselhauf, 2006; Poplack and Tagliamonte, 1999; Szmrecsanyi, 2003; Tagliamonte et al., 2009; Torres-Cacoullos and Walker, 2009b). The configuration of these constraints is thought to differ in weight and constraint ranking (order) depending on the stage of development of *going to*, as in Table 12.8.

Table 12.9 shows the distribution of *going to* according to various contextual factors and the results confirm that the choice of *going to* is most frequent in IM followed by SMS and then EM. This accords with the building evidence that IM is the most progressive of the CMC registers. The effect of grammatical person demonstrates that the use of future variants in these data is linguistically structured. When *going to* occurs, it is frequent for second- and third-person human subjects, followed by first-person subjects: it occurs only

Table 12.8 *Predictions for stages of grammatical change of* going to *(adapted from Tagliamonte et al., 2014b: Table 4)*

	Early stage	Later stage
Sentence type	Negatives highly favor	Negatives favor
Clause type	Subordinate clauses favor	Expansion into main clauses
Grammatical person	Human second- and third-person subjects favor	Expansion into first-person and finally inanimates

Table 12.9 *Distributions of* going to *by register, grammatical person, and type of sentence*

	%	N
REGISTER		
Instant Messaging [IM]	27.6	482
Texting on phones [SMS]	23.9	163
Email [EM]	19.4	392
Range		
GRAMMATICAL PERSON		
2nd/3rd person	27.7	155
1st person	13.6	272
Inanimate	4.0	50
Range		
TYPE OF SENTENCE		
Affirmative	13.8	406
Negative	8.5	71

rarely with inanimates. The difference between negative and affirmative sentences is slight but shows that *going to* is barely used in negative contexts. Together with the comparatively low frequency of *going to* overall, these results corroborate the observation that CMC registers are well behind spoken English in the use of *going to* for future temporal reference. Since this is a well-documented change in progress it is worth questioning whether any of these patterns operates across each of the CMC registers. Given that written registers are claimed to lag behind spoken registers in linguistic change (Pintzuk, 2003: 525), it is starting to look like *going to* has not diffused equally into each one. Figure 12.19 assesses whether the CMC registers operate with a regular variable grammar.

Figure 12.19 reveals that human non-first-person subjects lead in the use of *going to* variants as in (247), while first-person subjects (248) and inanimates, as in (249), lag behind.

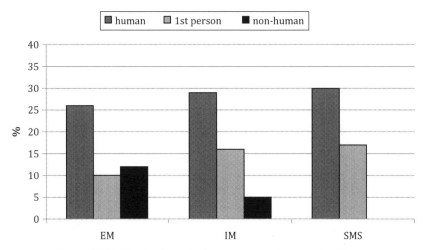

Figure 12.19 Distribution of *going to* variants by type of subject

247.　a.　well if ur *gonna* walk lemme no (m, IM)
　　　b.　Mom's *gonna* flip~ lol (m, EM)
　　　c.　the person is *gonna* be gassing me up and shit (j, IM)

248.　a.　They better be down or I *am going to* kick some ass (f, IM)
　　　b.　yah, *ill* go with you if you want ill talk to you tomorrow (f, IM)

249.　me too yo its *gonna* be so much fun (m, IM)

Moreover, this pattern is regular across all the CMC registers. Taken together, these results demonstrate that the forms used for future temporal reference in the TIC mirror the patterns found in contemporary studies of the future temporal reference system in spoken and written language – *will*, *'ll*, and *going*. Despite the varying orthographic variants in CMC for "going to" (*gunna*, *gonna*, *gunna*, etc.), the alternation between the major instantiations of the future (*will* vs. *going to*) adheres to a regular pattern that is the same across the board. This demonstrates that the CMC registers have the same systematic underlying grammar for the *go* future.

What does the cross-register comparison tell us about teen language?

The linguistic nature of CMC in cross-register perspective has been elucidated with reference to three phenomena: short forms of various types, intensifiers, and future temporal reference. The results from the analyses of each feature demonstrate tangible contrasts across writing, EM, IM, and

SMS. First, it must be emphasized that the standard language is intact in the written essays used by all these first-year university students. There is no breakdown of grammar; there is little to no infiltration of CMC forms and there are none of the decidedly vernacular features reported for CMC. This result is all the more striking when we compare the language behavior of *the same individuals* in EM, IM, and SMS. First, while many CMC forms occur in these registers, their frequency is modest at best. Second, the character of their use is systematically patterned and is the same across registers. EM is the most formal and the most like the written essays. It has the longest turns and the lowest frequency of CMC forms. EM also has the lowest frequency of intensifier *so* and future *going to*. The young people associate EM with parents, professors, and bosses and so it appears that they simply shun ill-regarded language in that register, even when communicating with their peers.

It is difficult to finely delineate linguistic differences between IM and SMS. The contrasts are a matter of degree and are likely dictated by extra-linguistic factors. IM and SMS are both used with equal vigor by youth to communicate with each other. At the time of the study, the difference between IM and SMS was delimited by device, SMS by type of phone restricted by character limits and type of keyboard; EM/computer. The technological restrictions imposed on SMS are reflected in the consistent finding that the shortest forms in each variable set, *so* and *'ll*, are favored in this register in comparison to EM and IM. SMS also has more spelling variants and more innovative forms at the extreme vernacular end of the spectrum (e.g. *ima*).

A key discovery comes from the comparative analyses of two sub-systems of grammar – intensifiers and future temporal reference. Although the forms and their frequency vary from one register to another, e.g. *so*, *SO*, *SOOO* or *going to*, *gon*, *gunna*, the grammar underlying the deployment of those forms remains stable. In other words, there is no breakdown of grammar.

Another important finding is that the nature of the linguistic feature under investigation – whether orthographic, lexical, or grammatical – is critical to delimiting register differences. Orthographic variants, e.g. *going to* vs. *gonna*, laughter, and incoming intensifiers conspicuously distinguish register. However, grammatical features such as future temporal reference do not. Indeed, a shocking result is that the CMC registers are united and pattern along with the written language in their conservative position on the trajectory of change towards the *go* future. This finding calls out for research on the impact of register in linguistic change and the necessity to include both written and spoken registers in the investigation.

A promising new territory awaits for exploring linguistic variables in CMC. Synthesizing across all the analyses and their results, one thing is certain: these young people are fluidly navigating a multifaceted range of new written registers and are using conventions that are particular to each one – from traditional written language to relatively formal EM to interactive, casual IM, to funky, flirty SMS.

Sociolinguist over the shoulder

When this research began, the biggest hurdle was finding a way for a middle-aged academic (Sali) to step into the world of teenagers on the Internet. The hiddenness of this community was, at the time, enshrined in its own acronym, *pos*, "parents over shoulder," based on the image of parents attempting to look over their teenagers' shoulders to see what they were typing on their computers or phones. With the collaboration of dozens of first-year students, an undergraduate assistant (Lawrence Kwok), and post-graduate students (Derek Denis and Dylan Uscher), I was able to successfully explore this alien terrain and uncover its authentic nature. In essence, I became "the sociolinguist over the shoulder." This rare perspective gives me the opportunity to share the following demonstration. In what follows imagine a day in the CMC world of individual "r" as he hands in an essay, emails one friend, chats with another in IM, and texts another on his phone. First, here is an excerpt from r's essay, in (250).

250.   [r] Therefore, the idea, that youth who play video games are responsible for violent crimes does not hold, since most of the games played by youth are not violent. Other factors, however, have contributed to the false notion that violence stems from video games.

Notice that the syntax is complex and there are a number of formal features, including the connectors "therefore" and "since" and the relative pronoun "who." Here is "r" in EM, in (251).

251.   [r] I hope all of your exams went well! We're FINALLY all done!! Since we're done our coaster, please bring 30$ on marks review day, as my mother is asking me for the money. (r, EM)

In (251), notice the use of upper case and exclamation marks. At the same time, there are formal features, including "since" and "as." The characterization of CMC as a hybrid is due to this type of mixture. Next, here is "r" in IM (252).

252.   [r] aww muffin ... ill keeps you companies till you sleep ... and me im just beefing up my music library seeing my commute has gotten boring of late .. .. ..if you want ill share some ... (r, IM)

In (252) notice the palpable psychological shift. The quality of the discourse is immediate, direct, interactional, beginning with *aww muffin*. The linguistic footprint of this register is patent: no capital letters or apostrophes, lexical colloquialisms are apparent, e.g. *beefing up*, the use of the *-s* suffix in non-standard environments, *keeps*, *companies*, and the use of the ellipsis to separate ideas. Still, the syntax remains relatively complex with clause markers *till*, *if*. Finally, here is "r" in SMS (253).

253.   [r] ahahah your crazy ... real talk ... and ill be on later and ill walk you through it ... the lab shit aint hard but the questions I feel for you soda (r, SMS)

In (253), note the same quality to this discourse as with the IM, interactional and personal. Here too there are no apostrophes and the ellipsis is used to demarcate sections of the discourse. What stands out here is the use of "your" rather than *you're* or *you are*, double negation, and a mild swear word, *shit* (one of the infrequent generics studied in Chapter 8). This heralds the quintessential nature of SMS – edgy.

Interactive CMC by youth writing to each other is a flagrant mix of reserved and trendy words and expressions. The differences across registers reflect fluid command of a continuum of different styles and practices and the students command them all.

Language puzzle

Among the many examples in Chapter 12 you will find a bounty of language features worthy of further study, many of which have been studied in the literature.

a. Find 5 variants of "okay."
b. What letters are sometimes doubled in a non-standard way?
c. How many ways do the writers spell "tomorrow"?
d. Find a colloquial term for pre-adolescents.
e. Find an unusual word for "angry/upset."
f. Study the exchange in example (202). How many spellings for "yes" are there?
g. Find an example of the CMC way to correct a previous typo using "*."
h. The students in the TIC often discuss classes and homework. Many of their courses have short forms, i.e. *math, econ, chem, bio, phy, tut "tutorial," soc.* How many shortened course names can you find?
i. Find a single example, where in the same context an apostrophe is used in one place but not another.
j. How many uncorrected typing errors can you find?

Answers
a. *k, kk, okay, 'kay, okie.*
b. *e, h, i, k, l, o, p, l, y.*
c. *tmr, 2morroe.*
d. *teeny bobbers. Although the term is usually "teenybopper."*

(*cont.*)

e. *"cheesed," e.g. hey im **so** cheesed i did bad on my article summary for astro! :(.*
f. *N=3, youp, yuppers, yup.*
g. *[3] I have a 30cm ne; [3] *one.*
h. *chimie, "chemistry"; astro, "astrology."*
i. *didn't* and *didnt* in (236a) used by a single speaker in the same transmission.
j. *Many!*

13   Are they always going to talk like that?

> I'm just thinking 'cause like when I think of stuff as far as like music
> and culture or like ah like trends and stuff like that, I always think of like
> I don't know the States and LA and New York and stuff like that.
>
> (Brent Kim, 21)

I have now investigated a host of words, phrases, and constructions that are typical of teen language at the turn of the twenty-first century. Given the findings and results and observations from each of the chapters, what does it all mean?

It should now be apparent that teenagers are not the ones to blame for variation and change in language. Language change is part of language itself. Every generation is different from the last and will be different from the next. Do teenagers use slang? Yes, but so does everyone else, at least some of the time. You have only to notice the many examples from the more elderly individuals in this book. It is even the case that a person will criticize teen language and then use that very same form him- or herself (see Gabrielle Prusskin's quote on page 34). What is slang anyway? It depends on what is included in the group of phenomena called slang at any given point in time. Such words and phrases are typically called "mistakes." However, language mistakes are not in teenagers; the mistake is in human nature. Who decides what is right and wrong? The only thing that makes a word "lazy," "sloppy," or "bad" is how society views it. The value judgment is social and historically time-stamped. What was once slang can as easily become the grammar of the next generation or it can fade into dated oblivion like *hwæt, whom, shall,* or *groovy*.

When I identified the funky features of teen language at the beginning of the book it may have seemed that they were all the same type of thing – the wacky things that kids say. In fact, they are actually a highly variegated group of linguistic phenomena. Most of them are developments that can be tracked back into much older populations; some have their roots hundreds of years in the past. Some of them are innovative extensions from what has come before. In rare cases words emerge and cover vast distances in time and space in a generation or two. In order to put all these jazzy, apparently teenage, features in context, I consistently compared their use among contemporary and recent teenagers (individuals born between the late 1970s and the early 1990s) with the language of the rest of the community. Where possible, I backed up those observations with evidence from the historical record (the OED) as well as corroboration with broad-scale databases, specifically Google Ngrams.

And I mean I always expect teenagers to have attitudes. (Julie Strand, 39)

Incrementation

Labov's model of language change in Figure 1.1 (Chapter 1) provided the prototype for understanding language change. Teenagers play a vital role in this process, which is intricately entwined with the human life span. When changes in language are viewed in terms of frequency and distribution according to the age of the individual, a complex stratum of stability and acceleration emerges out of the chaos. These patterns help us understand the change itself and how it is embedded in the community and in society more generally.

Among the 9–12-year-olds in these studies, the impact of caretakers is visible in their language use. Incoming forms tend to be at very low levels, mirroring the adults who the children are interacting with the most – typically their mother (see Kerswill, 1996: 194). In other cases, however, their use of forms is at levels beyond the adult model. I will return to this observation below.

Among senior citizens, we gain a glimpse of an earlier stage in the evolution of the language, c.1900–1940. In the studies in this book I have grouped the individuals born in the early decades of the twentieth century together. As the language of adults is predicted to remain relatively stable throughout their lifetime, these individuals mirror the state of the language at the time of their late adolescence. In every case, this cohort exposes an earlier stage.

The pre-adolescents – teenagers and young adults – have been the focus of most of my attention. During this phase in the life span, language brews up a hullabaloo and if there are changes afoot they progress via linguistic incrementation in adolescence. The use of incoming forms and phrases increases and in some cases these items extend their functions developing new patterns. This is also the phase from which new words emerge, often fading away quickly and forgotten. To the language scientist, however, this is the thrill – tracking which words come and go and which ones gradually evolve into the grammar.

The position of teenagers in linguistic change is a compelling one. Researchers once assumed that a language change "would continue in the same direction as the age group became younger and younger" (Labov, 2001: 454). However, when studies started including pre-adolescents and adolescents in their investigations, they discovered a repeating pattern – often a peak in apparent time rather than a regular upswing all the way to the youngest speakers (e.g. Cedergren, 1973; Labov, 2001; Tagliamonte and D'Arcy, 2009). Further, the heightened frequency of forms was found to be typical of females in late adolescence and early adulthood, suggesting that this was a principled part of the cycle. Labov (2001) argued for the model of incrementation enshrined in Figure 1.1. This model makes a number of predictions about linguistic change in progress and life stages, as I will review below.

When a change is beginning, it will be virtually imperceptible. At the other end of the cycle, a new form may never represent 100 percent of the variable. Frequency of use therefore becomes an important line of evidence critical to the interpretation of the trajectory of development. Nevalainen and Ramolin-Brunberg (2003: 55) propose the following frequency levels for linguistic change in progress (254).

254.   Incipient $\leq 15\%$
        New and vigorous   15–35%
        Mid-range   36–65%
        Nearing completion   65–85%
        Completed $\geq 85\%$

Taking the insights from the model of Incrementation and the Principles of Linguistic Change, let me now attempt to put the linguistic patterns I have laid out in this book into broad relief. In what follows, I will use the frequency distributions by speaker date of birth as foundational evidence. What do the data reveal and what explanations can be put forward? In earlier research, my colleague Alexandra D'Arcy and I argued that "to understand the location of the peaks or, conversely, to explain their absence, it appears essential to contextualize a language change in terms of its stage of development" (Tagliamonte and D'Arcy, 2009: 99). It is also necessary to interpret language in terms of the complexity of language acquisition through the human life cycle in the late twentieth and early twenty-first centuries.

Incrementation in adolescence (Labov, 2001; Tagliamonte and D'Arcy, 2009): When a change has taken hold and is accelerating, a peak in adolescence is predicted in apparent time data. In such a case, the change is moving quickly, with sufficient scope to increase in terms of frequency from pre-adolescence into early adulthood. According to the same model, once an innovation reaches approximately 50 percent of its system, the trajectory in apparent time smoothes out (see Figure 1.1). There is no longer a peak in apparent time. The corollary of this is that even though a change has not gone to completion, it may not evidence a heightened rate among teenagers in apparent time before stabilization. This is the key to understanding the advanced trajectories in apparent time with no peaks.

Predictions:

- When there is a peak in apparent time we can infer that this is the leading edge of linguistic change.
- When a change is new and vigorous up to mid-range, a peak will be visible.
- When a change is on the long tail towards its completion point, no peak is predicted.
- When a change is just beginning, watch for ripples in adolescence.

The position of pre-adolescence is a watershed. On one side is the language of the parental models; on the other side is the emerging next generation. How the pre-adolescents behave unavoidably depends on the stage of development of a change. The young people may pattern conservatively or be avant-garde. If a change is robustly variable they will acquire the variation at the level of the caretakers. The result in the community will be conservative frequency at both ends of the age spectrum. However, what if the change is at the saturation point? The change may be so advanced among the caretakers that it will be acquired at high levels by their children.

Life span change (Labov, 2001; Sankoff and Blondeau, 2007; Wagner and Sankoff, 2011; Wagner and Tagliamonte, submitted-a and submitted-b): This leads to another set of predictions:

- The usage patterns of the oldest members of the community will reflect older, conventional, forms.
- The usage patterns of young adults (late adolescence, early 20s) will reflect the leading edge of change, at least in rapidly advancing changes.
- Even in the case where there is retrograde shift across the life span – that is, where individuals readopt conventional forms – it is not enough to impede change in progress in the community.

Let's compare and contrast the results for some of the main words and innovating functions studied in the preceding chapters by plotting them together in Figure 13.1. In each case, the trajectory is shown for the relevant form and linguistic system found to be undergoing change: the use of quoting *like*, intensifier *really*, use of *like* in pre-sentential position, the GE *and stuff*, pre-verbal *just*, generic *stuff*, and adjective *weird*. This point is critical. Unless the analyst has thoroughly determined where and how the form is synchronizing within the grammar, its movement into a linguistic system may slip beneath the analytical radar.

Figure 13.1 exhibits considerable change in apparent time for the features investigated. Overall, comparing the individuals born in the early 1900s to those born in the last decade of the twentieth century exposes a multitude of palpable shifts. No wonder the elderly complain about teenagers! The oldest members of the community are traditional on all counts, but each of these

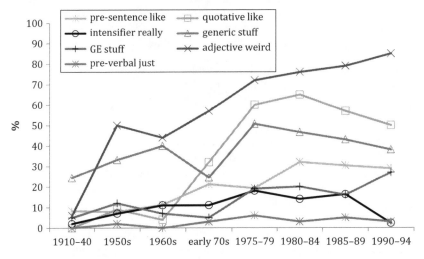

Figure 13.1 Composite portrait of major changes on the same scale by speaker date of birth

forms increase as the individuals get younger. Notice, however, that the whole community is shifting forward in tandem. Each age cohort is another step forward: English is changing and we are all in it together. At the same time, it is now apparent which individuals (which age group) are most implicated in one change or another.

Some changes erupt suddenly such as the shift to *weird* among people born in the 1950s or the shift to quotative *like* among the people born in the 1970s. Some changes exhibit a peak in apparent time. These are the accelerating changes of the late twentieth and early twenty-first centuries, which come to a pinnacle among individuals who passed through late adolescence during this period, leading the cutting edge of change in progress. Some of the changes have leveled out, e.g. the adjective *weird*. As change slows down the frequency of use does not accelerate so much across adolescence and therefore there is little to distinguish one generation from the next. Hence no peak in adolescence, just as predicted in Labov's (2001) model (see Figure 1.2).

Among the youngest age groups, some changes display the downturn in frequency that reflects the conservatism of young children, who are still patterning with their caretakers. This is evident with quoting *like*, generic *stuff*, pre-sentential *like*, and intensifier *really*. However, the curious finding was that in some cases – GE *and stuff* and adjective *weird* – the trajectory is a steady upswing across the board and there is no adolescent peak. I suggest that linguistic phenomena such as adjectival or general extender choice are unlikely to go to completion, i.e. they may never reach categorical dispersion in the variable system. These choices are inherently stylistic and creative with variability as part of the expressive nature of human language. In this case the relative categoricity evident among the pre-adolescents is the result of the fact that these young people have not yet developed the nuances of the respective system and simply use the majority form used by their models.

The most notable example of a generation in flux during this period are the individuals born between 1980 and 1989. This is the generation that took on quotative *like* in full force, having inherited it from the generation born in the 1970s. They also show visible incrementation for discourse *like*, GE *stuff*, generic *stuff*, and intensifier *really*. Can you guess how old these speakers were when the data were collected? They were aged between 13 and 16 – the teenagers.

Let's turn to the broad view from Google Ngrams as a backdrop as in Figure 13.2. In this case, I have attempted to isolate the relevant functions by employing one of the most frequent collocations from my analyses, i.e. *like* + first-person singular, *you know what, weird, or whatever, really good, just go/just going, and stuff, 's like,* and *I dunno*. This helps to make the Ngrams tap the form and function undergoing change.

The perspective from Google Ngrams must, of course, be taken with a grain of salt, but it offers another vantage point from which to interpret the trends in Figure 13.1. The main observations to attend to from this view are: (1) the time spans of stability and points of acceleration, and (2) the relative frequency of the forms/phrases. For most of this compendium of forms/phrases there is a very long period of stability across the nineteenth and into the twentieth centuries. This does not mean that there were no changes going on during that period, only that *these particular variables* were not mutable then. This is another important fact about language variation and change. At the outset, I specifically cherry-picked these features as exponents of change in progress: the peculiar features of teen language at the turn of the twenty-first century. But in reality, most of the grammar of a language is stable at any point in time.

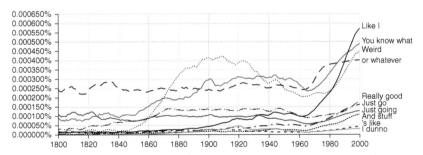

Figure 13.2 Google Ngrams search for frequent collocations of forms/functions

Consider the case of pre-sentential *like* in Figure 13.2. Before the 1960s nothing was happening. Then, there was a remarkable spurt upwards in the 1960s, signaling a shift. Yet in the vernacular community data (Figure 13.1) this change is step-wise in apparent time with a slight peak among the teenagers born between 1980 and 1984. This is a familiar pattern for a generational change in motion. I take these corroborating trends to vindicate my suggestion that the shift towards marking sentences with *like* is a grammatical change. It is potentially the development of a marker to signal topically linked sentences in discourse. Contrast this with the use of the adjective *weird*, which rises and falls and rises again over the same period in Google Ngrams yet shows steadfast increase right down to the pre-adolescents in Figure 13.2. This is a lexical change swaying with the trends of popular culture. The youth in this case learned *weird* from their caretakers at the get go and there is no peak in apparent time. It will be interesting to determine whether this is a typical pattern for incoming forms that have reached 50 percent or more of their system.

Similarly, compare the trajectories for generic and GE *stuff* to pre-verbal *just* in Figure 13.1. *Stuff* is at an advanced frequency, increasing incrementally to the young adults (born between 1975 and 1979), while *just* is at very low rates but shows a nascent peak among the individuals born in the late 1970s. These two changes precisely mirror the trajectory for changes for 1950 and 1925 in Figure 1.2. Now compare the community-based trajectories of these changes with the trajectories in Figure 13.2. Here we see *stuff* shoots up in the 1960s while *just* + finite verb (*just go*) shows a gradual incline from 1800 to the early 1960s. Then it too skyrockets, sweeping *just* + V-*ing* upwards along with it. The contrast between these two changes suggests that these are developments that are proceeding in distinct fashion, undoubtedly due to the nature of the change itself: one lexical, one grammatical. Research on these changes will need to pursue this issue further. It will also be of great interest to engage in more detailed comparisons of linguistic change across written and spoken language. They do not appear to be evolving in exactly the same way.

Over and above any of the differences from one change to the next, the comparison between the community-based analyses and Google Ngrams affirms the unquestionable impact of the 1960s as a pivotal time for this group of linguistic changes. There are notable break points in the 1960s and then again in the 1980s. The latter developments correspond with the teenage population in Figure 13.1. This is the cohort that is pushing these changes forward. Indeed, what we are looking at is linguistic incrementation *par excellence*.

[Sali to teenage daughter's boyfriend] Does Tara sound like you? [Boyfriend] No, she sounds like a girl. (9-30-2007)

The sex effect

Another important line of evidence is the difference between men and women, girls and boys. One of the most pervasive findings in variationist sociolinguistics is that women lead linguistic change – Labov's Principles 2, 3, and 4 (Labov, 2001). This reflects an overarching tendency that holds for by far the majority (90 percent) of recorded cases of linguistic change in progress. Gender asymmetry is said to develop early in language development, coming to the forefront in adolescence as boys retreat from and/or resist the use of words and phrases used by girls. A key indication of this is a peak in the apparent time trajectory for females, but not for males. Further, this split between the sexes is most exaggerated when the rate of change is most vigorous: in this situation men are often a generation behind. According to the Principles of Linguistic Change, the divide between male and female endures throughout the course of a change and is only gradually reduced as the change nears completion (Labov, 2001: 306–309). However, most of the evidence for these patterns in the literature has come from phonological changes. When other types of change have been investigated, including syntactic-semantic and discourse-pragmatic change, a gender-asymmetric view of language change has not obtained. Males have been found to participate in change similarly to women. They increment after pre-adolescence and stabilize sometime in late adolescence, only differing in their pace of change (see Tagliamonte and D'Arcy, 2009). Where do men and women contrast in their participation in linguistic changes and where do they align? The changes studied in this book offer new insights. Figures 13.3 and 13.4 now offer independent views of the population, by female and male, in order to elucidate this question.

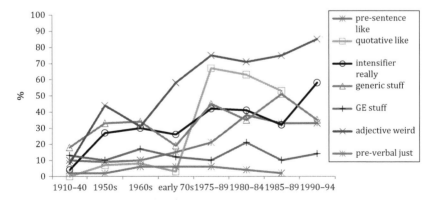

Figure 13.3 Composite display of major changes among females

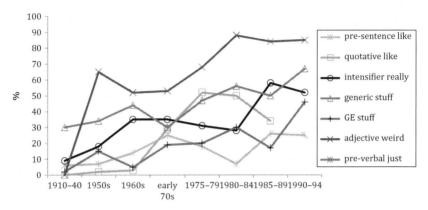

Figure 13.4 Composite display of major changes among males

Figures 13.3 and 13.4 expose a qualitative difference between female and male. Among the females, these changes present a relatively coherent set of peaks (5/7), as predicted by the incrementation model, each one located in adolescence. This peak is typically found at age 13–16 (1985–1989) or alternatively, at age 17–19 (1975–1979). This shows that teenage girls drive these popular features forward. The male trajectories have a somewhat different quality. There are some peaks, but they are found less consistently (3/7) and the men exhibit a broader life span period of incrementation. In some cases – quoting *like* – the guys have a peak in usage just as the girls do and at the same juncture. In the others it is earlier (*weird* and *really*). An intriguing result is that it is the males, not the females, who have the highest frequencies in pre-adolescence of generic *stuff* and GE *stuff.*

Taken together these findings suggest that linguistic changes in progress may evidence incrementation in the early life span in varied ways, depending on the change, the stage of the change, and the sex of the speakers. These differences notwithstanding, it is evident that a strict dichotomy between men and women in the incrementation process cannot be sustained. Among the changes documented in this book, some are progressing in tandem across the sexes (adjective *weird*), some are led by women (pre-sentence *like*), but at least one is distinctly led by men (generic *stuff*, whether in a GE or otherwise). This raises the question of which types of change may be more amenable to a male lead. It could be that males are more amenable to changes that involve generalization (*stuff, I dunno*). However, this suggestion requires verification from a greater range of linguistic phenomena.

It is time to turn to a deeper consideration of what all these changes mean, both for English in particular and linguistic variation and change more generally. The study of language variation and change (variationist sociolinguistics)

(Tagliamonte, 2012) is a relatively young field, originating in the 1960s. The study of discourse-pragmatic variation did not develop until the 1970s (see Figure 2.1). Why did it begin then? I suggest that it was likely because language scientists started noticing these changes going on in English and began to study them. Which brings me to the more comprehensive question – why is English undergoing precisely *these* types of changes at this particular point in time? When researchers first started studying discourse-pragmatic features, they thought of them as mysterious, almost as if such changes were exceptional and/or had never happened before. However, it soon became evident that many of the same features existed a thousand years ago, for example in Old English epics (*Beowulf*), albeit in different form. This confirms that despite the newness of studying discourse-pragmatic variation, the phenomenon itself is intrinsic to language. Moreover, discourse-pragmatic phenomena appear to be features from which grammatical devices evolve over the long term (e.g. Sankoff, 1990; Sankoff and Brown, 1976). Once we consider these two aspects – historical time-depth and the origins of grammar in discourse – it may well be the case that the changes I have discussed in this book are simply language reformations typical of this era in the history of the English language. If I am right, then other languages have undergone the same kind of discourse-pragmatic developments at some stages in their own history.

Moreover, as I have demonstrated, these words and phrases are not a monolithic collection. They cannot be judged as teenagers using a bunch of slang words or sloppy language. Instead, they represent diverse types of change in a wide range of grammatical sub-systems. The analyses in Chapters 4–12 have exposed lexical changes and grammatical changes, quick changes and slow changes, changes that have just begun, and changes that have been going on for a long time. The phenomena represent reorganization of the following systems: storytelling, the tense system, adverbial inventory, and sentence structure.

Yet the frequency and nature of these changes are independent of the acceleration in frequency of the words, features and expressions that can be observed across the 1970s and 1980s in the vernacular speech data. I suggest this is the result of the fact that the individuals born in 1970s and 1980s were teenagers and young adults when the data in the present study were collected. Of course they are the ones who are pushing the changes of our time up the slope of incrementation. The curiosity is that Google Ngrams plainly show a breakpoint in the early 1960s, *not* the 1970s and 1980s. This discrepancy between the two data sources is provocative. On the one hand, it may be that a revitalization in literary works presages later developments in the vernacular, but this would go against ideas about written/spoken register differences (see Pintzuk, 2003: 525). On the other hand, it may be that the ebb and flow of linguistic phenomena in the written language is actually a poor reflection of the regular evolving changes of the living spoken word. In fact, as the analyses in Chapter 12 highlighted, spoken and written registers are distinct on many levels with regard to the progression of linguistic change. Written language, even CMC registers, is far more conformist than speech with regard to grammatical change than expected. While it is beyond the scope of this book to address these issues in great detail, it will certainly be advantageous to explore them in greater detail in years to come.

I must now address the burning question that is often asked of me given my expertise as a language scientist who studies linguistic variation and change. What will happen to these teenagers as they get older? Given the trajectories of linguistic change patently visible in the many figures in this book, my prediction is that they will keep on using the same forms at near to the same frequency as they do now, conforming to the prediction of stability across the adult life span. As they grow older and into their senior years their language behavior will, from the perspective of society, be interpreted as the way "old people" talk. The younger generations will have moved on to new words and grammatical trends in the repeating cycle of language change across the human life span. It will always be true that teenagers use different words and expressions than older people. They are in the phase of life to play, be creative, make social contacts, and engage in the practices of youth, including the incrementation of linguistic change. In partaking in this process, their talk advances language along the pathway of development and diversification that is the nature of all complex systems.

In the twenty-first century adults will talk with *like*, *just*, *so*, and all that stuff. To the youth of tomorrow it will sound stuffy and old-fashioned. The teenagers who were at my kitchen table in the early 2000s will be complaining about their kids. As for me, I will be happily eavesdropping on my grandchildren and finding out how the current changes are evolving into the future.

Notes

1 WHAT'S ALL THE FUSS ABOUT TEEN LANGUAGE?

1. All examples and many quotes come from the corpora upon which this book is based. The names of all individuals are pseudonyms. Their age at the time of interview is indicated. The language in the examples and quotes has been lightly edited for readability. In this excerpt, note the use of discourse marker *like*, discourse marker *so*, and the reformulation of analytic to synthetic negation. Notes on linguistic features in the data are not meant to be exhaustive. Watch for novelties!
2. www.bbc.co.uk/birmingham/teens/2005/english_language.shtml, accessed September 21, 2007, 14:58.
3. Using the term "generation" is an idealized way of referring to successive cohorts of individuals as they move through the life span (Joseph and Janda, 2003: 77).

2 TEENS TALKING

1. www.ahdictionary.com/, accessed March 17, 2015, 14:07.
2. In some cases false starts, repetitions, and hesitations were removed from the cited examples in order to facilitate comprehension.
3. Special thanks are due to student participants in the six Research Opportunities courses I taught at the University of Toronto between 2002 and 2006: ROP2 *Jonille Clemente, Marion Hau, Madeleine Macdonald, Muhammad Velji,* and *Jessica Wertman*; ROP3 *Stephanie Cali, Louis Filipe, Karina von Stedingk, Seo-Lin Yang,* and *Stacy Yeh*; ROP 4 *Sidonia Couto, Derek Denis, Glenna Fraumeni,* and *Eric Woo*; ROP 5 *Jada Fung* and *Carol Tse*; ROP 6 *Dylan Uscher* – all students of the University of Toronto Faculty of Arts and Science. These students interviewed teenagers and extracted and coded some of the preliminary data on various features of interest.
4. The WORDLIST for the TTC is provided on the CUP website. Use it to solve some of the Linguistic Puzzles that appear at the end of each chapter and for other data exploration fun. The WORDLIST comprises only the words of the interviewee.
5. http://clu.uni.no/icame/colt/, accessed March 17, 2015, 14:27.
6. I would like to thank the students who made this corpus possible: the mentees: *Helen Tsang, Macy Siu, Vivian Li, Anita Li, Mile Foto, Tamar Friedman,* and *Catherine Kierans*; others who participated in the project: *Maria Abdoulavia, Patrick Dennis, David Hodgkiss, Chris Latendresse, Amy Levy, Holly Lloyd, Doug Marks, Stuart Marks, Katie Mayerson, Jesse McLean, Matt Scarlino, Michelle Sperling, Jessica Spindler,* and especially *Derek Denis*.

7. Note that the MSN software allows users the option of saving the text record of their conversations. It was our luck that the mentees in our study had previously saved documents of this type on their computers when our project began. Many of them simply opted to donate these files to the project with the permission of their interlocutors.

8. Both mentees and their conversational partners are included in these counts since the mentees were both fieldworkers and participants in the interactions.

9. Thanks to all the students for their contributions to this study. From HUM 199Y 2009, *Long Bai, Chui Chan, Hyea Cho, Matthew Chung, Hayyah Clairman, Minh Dang, Sarah Fisher, Vassil Halatchev, Sze Heong, Mina Hosseinian Arefi, Nusrat Ireen, Hyun-Woo Kim, Lawrence Kwok, Nathan Legiehn, Julieta Lischinsky, De Mao, Kody McWilliams, Evan O'Donnell, Wen Rao, Alexander Sadowski, Xin Tong, Jurgena Tusha,* and *Yang Zhao*. From HUM 199Y 2010, *Luke Albert, Julie Ardron, Kabe Chan, Erdal Cicek, Victoria Davis, Robin Farquharson, Tija Freimuta, Hilary Goodrow, Xiaojie Han, Annie Huang, Sung Jeon, Chen Ju, Young Jung, Nim Li, Osman Mahamud, Nader Mohamed, Justyna Ossowski, Mansurkhan Pathan, Samantha Pritchard, Felicia Romano, Rhian Thomas, Joseph Vasquez,* and *Rebecca Zagdanski*.

10. All examples are replicated verbatim from the corpora under investigation. The code in front of each line represents the individual who composed that line. Each line break with a code in front of it represents a single transmission or turn. A single letter code, e.g. "s," indicates that this writer is one of the 45 students. The students' interlocutors (all friends their own age) are simply indicated as <friend>, or female (F) or male (M).

11. My debt to the Social Sciences and Humanities Research Council of Canada [SSHRC] for funding my research on Canadian English is boundless. I am also deeply grateful to the Killam Trust for a Research Fellowship in 2013–2015, which enabled me to bring to synthesis much of my research, including the time to write this book.

12. The WORDLIST for the TEC is provided on the CUP website. Use it to solve some of the Linguistic Puzzles that appear at the end of each chapter and for other data exploration fun. The WORDLIST comprises only the words of the interviewee.

13. A big "thank you" to *Jonille De Los Santos* and *Larissa Teng* for their yearly get-together with my audio recorder on "play."

14. https://books.google.com/ngrams, accessed February 16, 2015.

15. I have omitted the word "unclear" (N=13,111) and the word "laugh" (N=3,876) both of which I assume were not words uttered by the teenagers, but indicators in the transcribed data that a bit of the discourse was not understood or that the individual laughed. I have also omitted another entry, "nv" (N=10,456), a tag for non-verbal events, e.g. coughs (Gisle Andersen pers. comm., April 7, 2015).

16. The MLE Corpus comes from a study of London adolescents. www.lancaster.ac .uk/fss/projects/linguistics/multicultural/overview.htm, accessed March 17, 2015, 16:18. Thanks to Paul Kerswill for access to the text files so that I could create these wordlists for comparison.

17. The word "Sue" refers to the main interviewer on the project Sue Fox. The word "unclear" is a transcription notation.

3 METHODS: *HOW TO TAP TEEN LANGUAGE?*

1. www.oed.com/, accessed March 7, 2015.

2. https://books.google.com/ngrams, accessed March 11, 2015, 07:11.

4 QUOTATIVES: *I'M LIKE, "OH MY GOD!"*

1. The examples labeled YRK and OTT come from the York English Storytelling Corpus described in Tagliamonte and Hudson (Tagliamonte and Hudson, 1999).
2. www.explainxkcd.com/wiki/index.php/1483:_Quotative_Like, accessed March 18, 2015, 08:18.

5 INTENSIFIERS: *UPPING THE ANTE* – SUPER *COOL!*

1. *Barney and Friends* was an American children's television series that aired from 1992–2009 featuring a character called Barney, a purple anthropomorphic Tyrannsaurus rex.

6 HOW DO YOU START A SENTENCE?

1. For straightforwardness, I will use the term "sentence" since it will be readily recognized by most people; however Schiffrin (1987) argues that "unit of talk" is more appropriate.
2. www.humanities.mcmaster.ca/~beowulf/, accessed March 2, 2015, 17:20; https:// docs.google.com/document/d/1E_kdJ4Qd0lkCh5p7U0lCJ05-7oFf8R1HfasQX7 T0ofI/edit?pli=1, accessed March 2, 2015, 17:20.
3. I distinguish here between a full elongated vowel in "ah," and various renditions of "uh" and "um," which occur as hesitation markers. I abstract away from the use of "uh" and "um" and their differences here although this would be an interesting study in its own right.
4. It might be objected that this is the result of reduplication; however, the sound quality of each "yeah" is different. Again, a more in-depth phonetic analysis of these forms would be very informative.
5. COCA is the only large and balanced corpus of American English. The corpus was created by Mark Davies of Brigham Young University, and it is used by tens of thousands of users every month (linguists, teachers, translators, and other research-ers). It is available at: http://corpus.byu.edu/coca/, accessed February 28 2015, 08:21.

8 GENERICS: *STUFFOLOGY*

1. The downturn in frequency of *stuff* among the early 1970s group is likely due to small N's in this cell, N=53, compared to the robust numbers in the other groups, N=193+ in each case.

9 JUST: JUST *WHAT?*

1. Similar high frequencies of *just* in corpora have been reported. Grant (2013: 176) reports high frequencies in New Zealand English and British English. Lindemann and Mauranen (2001: 463) document 5,254 examples in the MICASE corpus, a collection of spoken academic English: http://quod.lib.umich.edu/m/micase/, accessed February 26, 2015, 14:36.
2. http://quod.lib.umich.edu/cgi/c/corpus/corpus?page=home;c=micase;cc=micase, accessed March 7, 2015, 07:20.

3. https://books.google.com/ngrams/graph?content=just&year_start=1800&year_end=2000&corpus=1&smoothing=3&share=&direct_url=t1%3B%2Cjust%3B%2Cc0, accessed February 20, 2015, 17:42.
4. Special thanks to Alexandra D'Arcy who provided the data files for her analysis of *like* within the verb phrase. Much more exciting information about *like* can be found in her book (D'Arcy, forthcoming).
5. The example is the use of both "that" and "which" to mark relative clauses. Here is another example from 1889 in which "strange" and "funny" appear together: "To keap fun'rals waaitin' time efter time is a *straange funny* waay for a parson to go on" (E. Peacock Gloss, *Words*, Manley & Corringham, Lincs.).
6. The paucity of tokens in each of the verbal contexts makes it impossible to adequately assess their distribution by age group.
7. Notice how many linguistic features discussed in this book are present in this little quip from Hilda Tseng: pre-sentential "like," quoting "like," intensifier "really," pre-V-ing "just," downtoner "kind of," GE "or anything,"

10 ADJECTIVES: *THE GOOD, BAD, AND LOVELY*

1. "The Adjective Check List," www.mindgarden.com/products/acl.htm, accessed 16 July, 2012, 16:41.
2. Thanks to all the students for their contributions to this study: *Jon Bakos, Julia Cheng, Jessica Delisi, Amelia Dietrich, Devin Grammon, Ashley Hesson, Linda Konnerth, Hank Lester, Justin McBride, Jane Mitsch, Meredith Moss, Jenna Nichols, Colin Pitet, Rachelle Price, Gabe Radovsky, Wil Rankinen, Na-Young Ryu, Hayley Smith, Nick Toler,* and *Jack Toner.*
3. Other adjectives of strangeness were present, including *selcouth* (*c.*888), *selly* (OE), *ferly* (*c.*1225), etc.; however, all of these are moribund in contemporary varieties.
4. Another potential adjective of strangeness in the Toronto community, *random*, as in (i), was too infrequent for inclusion in the present study. (i) "I always have some sort of like *weird* experience that happens – like some *random* Pride thing" (TOR, DU, 20s).
5. Another potential adjective of strangeness is *queer* (*c.*1513); however, its contemporary connotations make it untenable as a member of the "strangeness" set. There were no instances of *queer* meaning "strange" in the data.
6. The somewhat generalized meaning of *funny* may be part of the reason it is so frequent in the data, occurring 1,108 times in the TEC. Further study of this form in order to disentangle its function is warranted.
7. Interestingly, the collocations *that's weird* and *that's strange* occur frequently among the interviewers in the TEC whereas the collocation *that's unusual* is found frequently in the British Corpora. Note the correspondence to the figures in Table 10.1.
8. Given the scarcity of tokens of the other adjectives I do not consider them further here.
9. The word "queer" for strange is also found in some of the British corpora, e.g. Roots N=23, e.g. *And you know rather queer it was, the first bus.* I have only included it in the set of comparison adjectives of strangeness found in the target data for simplicity's sake.

10. Due to the abundance of different historical spellings in the Helsinki Corpus I included all the orthographic forms listed in the OED, e.g. "weird" as *wyrde, werd, veird, weyard, weyward, weer'd, weïrd, weerd*; "strange" as *strange, straunge* 23, *strang* 46, *strawnge* 3, *strenge* 9; "odd" as *odd* 13, *odde* 4, *ode* 1, etc. An exhaustive search of adjectives of strangeness in these corpora is beyond the scope of this chapter. The historical trajectory of these adjectives warrants further investigation.

11. The corpora represented are as follows: Toronto = The Toronto English Corpus. Clara is a subset of these materials from a single individual interviewed every year from 2002–2011 (Tagliamonte, 2012). *Friends* refers to the television series *Friends* and comes from the dialogue of Seasons 1–8. These data were the basis of the analysis in Tagliamonte and Roberts (2005). DoC refers to a corpus of Southeastern Ontario English, a variety spoken in several small towns relatively distant from Toronto (i.e. 2–4 hours) (Tagliamonte, 2007–2010). York refers to the York English Corpus (Tagliamonte, 1996–1998), a variety of northern British English. Roots refers to the Roots Corpus and "South" to three communities in the south of England in each of Devon, Somerset, and Sussex (Tagliamonte, 2013). These data all come from small British and Northern Irish community-based samples of English. "Helsinki" refers to the Helsinki Corpus (1991), data from English in *c*.730–1710. The Google results were accessed on July 10, 2011.

12. According to Google, "American English" represents "Books predominantly in the English language that were published in the United States" and "British English" represents "Books predominantly in the English language that were published in Great Britain": http://books.google.com/ngrams/info, accessed August 12, 2013, 14:56.

13. The adverbs are ordered in the figures as follows: *peculiar* begins at the top of the left side of the graph, just underneath is *strange*; *weird* is the light line just underneath and the others are ordered thereafter. Note that these are gross patterns since other meanings associated with the forms would be included, e.g. "idiosyn-cratic" for *peculiar* and "non-even" for *odd*.

14. The adjective *odd* presents a curious case. It appears frequently in the British data; however, Google Ngrams show that it is never really ascendant. Note, however, that it increases over the 1900s, at least in British English, which corroborates the corpus trends. One wonders why it is not more frequent in the Helsinki corpus. This is likely due to the register/genre difference between the spoken and written (Helsinki) data. In addition, there is also the general trend towards more colloquial language over the twentieth century that may account for these discrepancies (e.g. Hundt and Mair, 1999).

15. Another obvious way to extend this research would be to analyze the linguistic contents of the comic books themselves.

16. www.ling.upenn.edu/~wlabov/Papers/DFLC.htm

12 INTERNET LANGUAGE: *EVERYONE'S ONLINE*

1. http://kelseystark.weebly.com/text-speak-in-the-classroom.html
2. http://news.bbc.co.uk/2/hi/uk/4471607.stm
3. www.npr.org/templates/story/story.php?storyId=126117811
4. www.winstonchurchill.org/support/the-churchill-centre/publications/chartwell-bul letin/2012/50-aug/1526-admiral-lord-fisher-to-churchill-omg, accessed January 19, 2015, 11:11.

5. www.silicon.com/tags/im.htm, accessed September 12, 2007, 14:10.

6. www.newhorizons.org/strategies/literacy/oconnor.htm, accessed September 23, 2005, 11:40.

7. Emoticons are among the most innovative features of IM. They are "abbreviations of expressions of mood, tone of voice, or instruction to the reader" (Randall, 2002: 27) made using typographical symbols. I did not consider emoticons in this study. The versions of the program at the time of our study automatically converted the keystrokes that make up emoticons into a graphical representation. These graphics, however, do not translate across platforms straightforwardly, making it difficult to study them systematically using the methods I have employed here.

8. The data contain many more IM forms than listed in Table 12.1; however, those listed are the most frequent.

9. This tabulation comprises all variants of *haha*, including *hahaha*, *hah*, *ahahaha*, etc.

10. The original meaning of *lol* as an acronym for "laugh out loud" is often lost in its uses by our teenage participants. It tends to be used in conversation as a signal of interlocutor involvement, just as one might say "mm-hm" in the course of speech. This is consistent with Baron's (2004: 416) comment that *lol* functions as a "phatic filler comparable to *okay, really,* or *yeah* in spoken discourse."

11. This tabulation comprised all variants of *hehe*, including *hehehe*, *heh*, *eheheh*, etc.

12. A widely accepted view is that language change originates in spoken language and then diffuses to written language with the assumption that "the written language reflects the spoken language of some earlier time" (Pintzuk, 2003: 525).

13. Find the video here: www.youtube.com/watch?v=up-RX_YN7yA, accessed January 22, 2015, 09:00.

References

Adamson, Sylvia (2000). A lovely little example: word order options and category shift in the premodfying string. In O. Fischer, A. Rosenbach, and D. Stein (eds.), *Pathways of Change: Grammaticalization in English*. Amsterdam and Phildadelphia: John Benjamins, 39–66.

Aijmer, Karin (1985a). Just. In S. Bäckman and G. Kjellmer (eds.), *Papers on Language and Literature Presented to Alvar Ellegård and Erik Frykman*. Göteborg: Acta Universitatis Gothoburgensis, 1–10.

(1985b). What happens at the end of our utterances? The use of utterance final tags introduced by "and" and "or." In O. Togeby (ed.), *Papers from the Eighth Scandinavian Conference of Linguistics*. Copenhagen: Institut for Philologie, 366–389.

(1997). I think – an English modal particle. In T. Swan and O. J. Westvick (eds.), *Modality in Germanic Languages: Historical and Comparative Perspectives*. Berlin: Mouton de Gruyter, 1–47.

(2002). *English Discourse Particles: Evidence from a Corpus*. Amsterdam and Philadelphia: John Benjamins.

Altenberg, Bengt (1990). Spoken English and the dictionary. In J. Svartvik (ed), *The London–Lund Corpus of Spoken English: Description and Research*. Lund University Press, 193–211.

Andersen, Gisle (1996). The pragmatic marker *like* from a relevance-theoretic perspective. In A. Jucker and Y. Ziv (eds.), *Discourse Markers: Selected Papers from the 5th International Pragmatics Conference*. Amsterdam and Philadelphia: John Benjamins.

(1997a). They gave us these yeah, and they like wanna see like how we talk and all that: the use of like and other discourse markers in London teenage speech. In U.-B. Kostsinas, A.-B. Stenström, and A.-M. Karlsson (eds.), *Ungdomsspråk i Norden*. Stockholm: Institutionen för nordiska språk, Stockholm University, 82–95.

(1997b). They like wanna see like how we talk and all that: the use of like as a discourse marker in London teenage speech. In M. Ljung (ed.), *Corpus-Based Studies in English: Papers from the 17th International Conference on English Language Research on Computerized Corpora*. Amsterdam: Rodopi, 37–48.

(1998). The pragmatic marker *like* from a relevance-theoretic perspective. In A. Jucker and Y. Ziv (eds.), *Discourse Markers: Descriptions and Theory*. Amsterdam and Philadelphia: John Benjamins, 147–170.

(2001). *Pragmatic Markers and Sociolinguistic Variation*. Amsterdam and Philadelphia: John Benjamins.

Androutsopolous, Jannis (ed.) (2014). *Mediatization and Sociolinguistic Change*. Berlin and Boston: Mouton de Gruyter.

Axtman, Kris (2002). "r u online?": the evolving lexicon of wired teens. *Christian Science Monitor*, December 12: www.csmonitor.com/2005/0311/p2001s2002-ussc.html.

Bäcklund, Ulf (ed.) (1973). *The Collocation of Adverbs of Degree in English*. Uppsala: Almqvist & Wiksell.

Bailey, Guy (2002). Real and apparent time. In J. K. Chambers, P. Trudgill, and N. Schilling-Estes (eds.), *The Handbook of Language Variation and Change*. Malden, MA: Wiley-Blackwell, 312–332.

Bailey, Guy, Wikle, Tom, Tillery, Jan, and Sand, Lori (1991). The apparent time construct. *Language Variation and Change* 3: 241–264.

Baron, Naomi S. (1998). Letters by phone or speech by other means: the linguistics of email. *Language and Communication* 18: 133–179.

(2003a). Language of the internet. In A. Farghali (ed.), *The Stanford Handbook for Language Engineers*. Stanford: CSLI Publications, 1–63.

(2003b). Why email looks like speech: proof-reading pedagogy and public face. In J. Atichison and D. M. Lewis (eds.), *New Media Language*. London and New York: Routledge, 85–94.

(2004). See you online: gender issues in college student use of instant messaging. *Journal of Language and Social Psychology* 23: 397–423.

(2008). *Always On: Language in an Online and Mobile World*. Oxford University Press.

Baron, Naomi S. and Ling, Rich (2003). IM and SMS: a linguistic comparison. Presented at the *Fourth International Conference of the Association of Internet Researchers*. Toronto, October 16–19.

Bayley, Robert (1994). Consonant cluster reduction in Tejana English. *Language Variation and Change* 6: 303–326.

Biber, Douglas (1988). *Variation across Speech and Writing*. Cambridge University Press.

Biber, Douglas and Finegan, Edward (1994). *Sociolinguistic Perspectives on Register*. Oxford University Press.

Biber, Douglas, Johansson, Stig, Leech, Geoffrey, Conrad, Susan, and Finegan, Edward (1999). *Longman Grammar of Spoken and Written English*. Harlow: Longman.

Blyth, Carl, Jr., Recktenwald, Sigrid, and Wang, Jenny (1990). I'm like, "say what?!": a new quotative in American oral narrative. *American Speech* 65: 215–227.

Bolinger, Dwight (1972). *Degree Words*. The Hague: Mouton de Gruyter.

Breban, Tine (2008). Grammaticalization, subjectification and leftward movement of English adjectives of difference in the noun phrase. *Folia Linguistica* 42: 259–306.

Brebieri, Federica (2009). Quotative "be like" in American English: ephemeral or here to stay? *English World-Wide* 30: 68–90.

Brinton, Laurel J. (1996). *Pragmatic Markers in English*. Berlin: Mouton de Gruyter.

Brinton, Laurel and Traugott, Elizabeth Closs (2005). *Lexicalization and Language Change*. Cambridge: Cambridge University Press.

Brooke, Julian and Tagliamonte, Sali A. (2012). Hunting the linguistic variable: using computational techniques for data exploration and analysis. *Presented at the*

Georgetown University Round Table 12 [GURT], Measured Language: Quantitative Approaches to Acquisition, Assessment, Processing and Variation. Georgetown University, Washington, DC, March 9–11.

Bucholtz, Mary (1999). "Why be normal?" Language and identity practices in a community of nerd girls. *Language in Society* 28: 203–223.

(2011). *White Kids: Language, Race and Styles of Youth Identity.* Cambridge University Press.

Buchstaller, Isabelle (2013). *Quotatives: New Trends and Sociolinguistic Implications.* Malden, MA: Wiley-Blackwell.

Buchstaller, Isabelle and D'Arcy, Alexandra (2009). Localized globalization: a multi-local, multivariate investigation of quotative *be like*. *Journal of Sociolinguistics* 13: 291–331.

Buchstaller, Isabelle, Rickford, John R., Traugott, Elizabeth Closs, Wasow, Thomas, and Zwicky, Arnold (2010). The sociolinguistics of a short-lived innovation: tracing the development of quotative *all* across spoken and internet newsgroup data. *Language Variation and Change* 22: 191–219.

Butters, Ronald R. (1982). Editor's note [on "be+like"]. *American Speech* 57: 149.

Bybee, Joan and Scheibman, Joanne (1999). The effect of usage on degrees of constituency: the reduction of don't in *English. Linguistics* 37: 575–596.

Cedergren, Henrietta J. (1973). *The interplay of social and linguistic factors in Panama.* PhD dissertation, Cornell University.

(1984). *Panama revisited: sound change in real time.* Presented at New Ways of Analyzing Variation in English 13. University of Pennsylvania.

(1988). The spread of language change: verifying inferences of linguistic diffusion. In P. Lowenberg (ed.), *Language Spread and Language Policy: Issues, Implications, and Case Studies.* Washington, DC: Georgetown University Press, 45–60.

Cedergren, Henrietta J. and Sankoff, David (1974). Variable rules: performance as a statistical reflection of competence. *Language* 50: 333–355.

Chafe, Wallace (1984). Integration and involvement in speaking, writing and oral literature. In D. Tannen (ed.), *Spoken and Written Language: Exploring Orality and Literacy.* Norwood, NJ: Ablex, 35–53.

Chambers, J. K. (2003a). *Sociolinguistic Theory: Linguistic Variation and its Social Significance.* Oxford: Blackwell.

(2003b). Sociolinguistics of immigration. In D. Britain and J. Cheshire (eds.), *Social Dialectology.* Amsterdam and Philadelphia: John Benjamins, 97–113.

Channell, Joanna (1994). *Vague Language.* Oxford University Press.

Cheshire, Jenny (1987). Syntactic variation, the linguistic variable, and sociolinguistic theory. *Linguistics* 25: 257–282.

(1998). English negation from an interactional perspective. In I. Tieken-Boon van Ostade, G. Tottie, and W. van der Wurff (eds.), *Negation in the History of English.* Berlin: Mouton de Gruyter, 29–54.

(2003). Social dimensions of syntactic variation. In D. Britain and J. Cheshire (eds.), *Social Dialectology.* Amsterdam and Philadelphia: John Benjamins, 245–261.

(2007). Discourse variation, grammaticalisation and stuff like that. *Journal of Sociolinguistics* 11: 155–193.

Cheshire, Jenny and Fox, Sue (2007). "This is me": an innovation in waiting and other quotative use among adolescents in London. Presented at the International Conference on Language Variation in Europe (ICLaVE) 4. Cyprus.

(2009). *Multiracial vernacular in London: age-grading or language change?* Paper presented at UK-LVC 7. University of Newcastle.

Cheshire, Jenny, Fox, Sue, Kerswill, Paul, Khan, Arfaan, and Torgersen, Eivind (2007–2010). Multicultural London English: the emergence, acquisition and diffusion of a new variety. Economic and Social Science Research Council (ESRC) Grant.

Crystal, David (1995). *The Cambridge Encyclopedia of the English Language.* Cambridge University Press.

(2001). *Language and the Internet.* Cambridge University Press.

(2003). *English as a Global Language.* Cambridge University Press.

(2006). *Language and the Internet,* 2nd edition. Cambridge University Press.

Cukor-Avila, Patricia (2002). She say, she go, she be like: verbs of quotation over time in African American vernacular English. *American Speech* 77: 3–31.

Culpepper, Jonathon and Kytö, Merja (2000). The conjunction *and* in early Modern English: frequencies and uses in speech-related writing and other texts. In R. Bermúdez-Otero, D. Denison, R. M. Hogg, and C. B. McCully (eds.), *Generative Theory and Corpus Studies.* Berlin and New York: Mouton de Gruyter, 299–326.

D'Arcy, Alexandra (2005). *Like: syntax and development.* PhD dissertation, University of Toronto.

(2006). Lexical replacement and the like(s). *American Speech* 81: 339–357.

(2007). *Like* and language ideology: disentangling fact from fiction. *American Speech* 82: 386–419.

(2008). Canadian English as a window to the rise of like in discourse. In M. Meyer (ed.), *Focus on Canadian English. Special issue of Anglistik: International Journal of English Studies.* Heidelberg: Winter, 125–140.

(2014). Evolving intensifiers: stability, stasis, and change. Presented at *Discourse-Pragmatic Variation and Change (DiPVaC) 2.* Newcastle University, April.

(forthcoming). *Discourse-Pragmatic Variation in Context.* Amsterdam and New York: John Benjamins.

Davies, Diane (2005). *Varieties of Modern English: An Introduction.* Harlow: Pearson Longman.

Denis, Derek (2011). Innovators and innovation: tracking the innovators of and stuff in York English. *UPenn Working Papers in Linguistics* 17: Article 8.

(2015). *The development of pragmatic markers in Canadian English.* PhD dissertation, University of Toronto.

Dines, Elisabeth R. (1980). Variation in discourse and stuff like that. *Language in Society* 9: 13–33.

Dixon, R. M. W. (1977). Where have all the adjectives gone? *Studies in Language* 1: 19–80.

Dobson, Roger (2003). Text messaging is spoiling teenagers' sleep. *British Medican Journal* 327: 582.

Dubois, Sylvie (1992). Extension particles, etc. *Language Variation and Change* 4: 163–203.

Durham, Mercedes, Haddican, Bill, Zweig, Eytan, Johnson, Daniel Ezra, Baker, Zipporah, Cockeram, David, Danks, Esther, and Tyler, Louise (2012). Constant linguistic effects in the diffusion of be like. *English Language and Linguistics* 40: 316–337.

Eckert, Penelope (1988). Adolescent social structure and the spread of linguistic change. *Language in Society* 17: 183–207.

(1989). *Jocks and Burnouts*. New York: Teachers College Press.

(1997). Age as a sociolinguistic variable. In F. Coulmas (ed.), *The Handbook of Sociolinguistics*. Oxford: Blackwell, 151–167.

(2000). *Language Variation as Social Practice*. Oxford: Blackwell.

(2003). Language and gender in adolescence. In J. Holmes and M. Meyerhoff (eds.), *The Handbook of Language and Gender*. Malden, MA: Wiley-Blackwell, 381–400.

(2005). Stylistic practice and social order. In A. Williams and C. Thurlow (eds.), *Talking Adolescence: Perspectives in the Teenage Years*. New York: Peter Lang, 93–110.

(2011). Language and power in the preadolescent heterosexual market. *American Speech* 86: 85–97.

Enkvist, Nils Erik (1972). Old English adverbial þa – an action marker? *Neuphilologische Mitteilungen* 73: 90–96.

Entwhistle, Doris R. and Garvey, Catherine (1969). *Adjective Usage*. Baltimore, MD: Johns Hopkins University, Center for the Study of Social Organization of Schools.

Erman, Britt (1995). Grammaticalization in progress: the *case of or something*. In I. Moen, H. Gram Simonsen, and H. Lødrup (eds.), *Papers from the XVth Scandinavian Conference of Linguistics, Oslo, January 13–15, 1995*. Oslo: Department of Linguistics, University of Oslo, 136–147.

(1997). "Guy's *just* such a dickhead": the context and function of *just* in teenage talk. *Proceedings from the Conference on Teenage Language, 14–16 June 1996, Stockholm, Sweden*.

(2001). Pragmatic markers revisited with a focus on *you know* in adult and adolescent talk. *Journal of Pragmatics* 33: 1337–1359.

Fasold, Ralph (1972). *Tense Marking in Black English: A Linguistic and Social Analysis*. Washington, DC: Center for Applied Linguistics.

Ferguson, Charles A. (1994). Dialect, register, and genre: working assumptions about conventionalization. In D Biber and E. Finegan (eds.), *Sociolinguistic Perspectives on Register*. Oxford University Press, 15–30.

Ferrara, Kathleen and Bell, Barbara (1995). Sociolinguistic variation and discourse function of constructed dialogue introducers: the case of be+like. *American Speech* 70: 265–289.

Ferrara, Kathleen, Brunner, Hans, and Whittemore, Greg (1991). Interactive written discourse as an emergent grammar. *Written Communication* 8: 8–34.

Fischer, Olga and Rosenbach, Anette (2000). Introduction. In O. Fischer, A. Rosenbach, and D. Stein (eds.), *Pathways of Change: Grammaticalization in English*. Amsterdam and Philadelphia: John Benjamins, 1–38.

FormyDuval, Deborah L., Williams, John E., Patterson, Donna J., and Fogle, Ellen E. (1995). A "big five" scoring system for the item pool of the Adjective Check List. *Journal of Personality Assessment* 65: 59–76.

Forston, Benjamin (2003). An approach to semantic change. In B. D. Joseph and R. D. Janda (eds.), *The Handbook of Historical Linguistics*. Oxford: Blackwell, 648–666.

Fortman, Jennifer (2003). Adolescent language and communication from an intergroup perspective. *Journal of Language and Social Psychology* 22: 104–111.

Fowler, Henry W. (1927). *A Dictionary of Modern English Usage.* Oxford: Clarendon Press.

Fraser, Bruce (1988). Types of English discourse markers. *Acta Linguistica Hungarica* 38: 19–33.

Fries, Charles Carpenter (1940). *American English Grammar.* New York: Appleton, Century, Crofts.

Gauchat, Louis (1905). L'unité phonétique dans le patois d'une commune. In *Aus romanischen sprachen und literaturen: Festschrift Heinrich Mort.* Halle: Niemeyer, 175–232.

Ghenu, Mike (2005). Ill communication: how email, text and instant messaging affect language. *The Varsity.*

Gough, Harrison G. and Heilbrun, Alfred B. Jr. (1965). *The Adjective Check List Manual.* Palo Alto, CA: Consulting Psychologists Press.

(1983). *The Adjective Check List: 1980 Edition.* Palo Alto, CA: Consulting Psychologists Press.

Grant, Lynn (2013). The frequency and function of just in British and New Zealand engineering lectures. *IEEE Transactions on Professional Communication* 56: 176–190.

Grinter, Rebecca E. and Palen, Leysia (2002). Instant messaging in teen life. In *Proceedings of the 2002 ACM Conference on Computer Supported Cooperative Work.* New York: ACM, 21–30.

Guy, Gregory R. (1980). Variation in the group and the individual: the case of final stop deletion. In W. Labov, (ed.), *Locating Language in Time and Space.* New York: Academic Press, 1–36.

(1991). Explanation in variable phonology: an exponential model of morphological constraints. *Language Variation and Change* 3: 1–22.

Harvey, Mark (2011). Lexical change in pre-colonial Australia. *Diachronica* 28: 345–381.

Heine, Bernd, Claudi, Ulrike, and Hünnemeyer, Friederike (1991). *Grammaticalization: A Conceptual Framework.* University of Chicago Press.

Heine, Bernd and Kuteva, Tania (2005). *Language Contact and Grammatical Change.* Cambridge University Press.

Hermann, M. E. (1929). Lautverändergungen in der individualsprache einer Mundart. *Nachrichten der gesellschaft der wissenschaften zu Göttingen, Philosophisch-historische Klasse* 11: 195–214.

Herring, Susan C. (ed.) (1996). *Computer-Mediated Communication.* Amsterdam and Philadelphia: John Benjamins.

(2003). Gender and power in on-line communication. In J. Holmes and M. Meyerhoff (eds.), *The Handbook of Language and Gender.* Malden, MA: Wiley-Blackwell, 202–228.

(2004). Slouching toward the ordinary: current trends in computer-mediated communication. *New Media & Society* 6: 26–36.

(2007). A faceted classification scheme for computer-mediated discourse. *Language@Internet* 4.

Herring, Susan C. and Paolillo, John C. (2006). Gender and genre variation in weblogs. *Journal of Sociolinguistics* 10: 439–459.

Hinrichs, Lars (2010). How to spell the vernacular: a multivariate study of Jamaican e-mails and blogs. In A. Jaffe, J. Androutsopoulos, M. Sebba, and S. Johnson (eds.), *Orthography as Social Action: Scripts, Spelling, Identity, and Power.* Berlin: Mouton de Gruyter, 325–58.

Hook, Peter Edwin (1991). The emergence of perfective aspect in Indo-Aryan languages. In E. Closs Traugott and B. Heine (eds.), *Approaches to Grammaticalization, Volume 2.* Amsterdam and Philadelphia: John Benjamins, 59–89.

Hopper, Paul J. (1991). On some principles of grammaticization. In E. Closs Traugott and B. Heine (eds.), *Approaches to Grammaticalization, Volume 1: Focus on Theoretical and Methodological Issues.* Amsterdam and Philadelphia: John Benjamins, 17–35.

Hopper, Paul J. and Traugott, Elizabeth Closs (1993). *Grammaticalization.* Cambridge University Press.

Huddleston, Rodney and Pullum, Geoffrey, K. (2002). *The Cambridge Grammar of the English Language.* Cambridge University Press.

Hundt, Marianne and Mair, Christian (1999). "Agile" and "uptight" genres: the corpus-based approach to language change in progress. *International Journal of Corpus Linguistics* 4: 221–242.

Ito, Rika and Tagliamonte, Sali A. (2003). *Well* weird, *right* dodgy, *very* strange, *really* cool: layering and recycling in English intensifiers. *Language in Society* 32: 257–279.

Itzhar-Nabarro, Sohar, Silberschatz, George, and Curtis, John (2009). The Adjective Check List as an outcome measure: assessment of personality change in psychotherapy. *Psychotherapy Research* 19: 707–717.

Jespersen, Otto H. (1922). *Language: Its Nature, Development, and Origin.* London: Allen & Unwin.

(1933). *A Modern English Grammar on Historical Principles: Part VI. Syntax.* London: Allen & Unwin.

Jones, Graham M. and Schieffelin, Bambi B. (2009). Enquoting voices, accomplishing talk: uses of be + like in instant messaging. *Language and Communication* 29: 77–113.

Joseph, Brian D. and Janda, Richard D. (2003). On language, change, and language change: or, of history, linguistics, and historical linguistics. In B. D. Joseph and R. D. Janda (eds.), *The Handbook of Historical Linguistics.* Oxford: Blackwell, 3–180.

Joshi, S. T. (1990). *The Weird Tale.* Austin: University of Texas Press.

Jucker, Andreas H. and Ziv, Yael (eds.) (1998). *Discourse Markers.* Amsterdam and Philadelphia: John Benjamins.

Kerswill, Paul (1996). Children, adolescents, and language change. *Language Variation and Change* 8: 177–202.

Kerswill, Paul and Cheshire, Jenny (2004–2007). Linguistic innovators: the English of adolescents in London. ESRC Research Grant (RES-000-23-0680).

Kiesler, Sara, Siegel, Jane, and McGuire, Timothy W. (1984). Social psychological aspects of computer-mediated communication. *American Psychologist* 39: 1123–1134.

Kiesling, Scott F. (2001). Stances of whiteness and hegemony in fraternity men's discourse. *Journal of Linguistic Anthropology* 11: 101–115.

Kishner, Jeffrey M. and Gibbs, Raymond W. (1996). How "just" gets its meanings: polysemy and context in psychological semantics. *Language and speech* 39: 19–36.

Kleiner, Brian (1998). Whatever: its use in "pseudo-argument." *Journal of Pragmatics* 30: 589–613.

Kroch, Anthony S. (1989). Reflexes of grammar in patterns of language change. *Language Variation and Change* 1: 199–244.

Labov, William (1963). The social motivation of a sound change. *Word* 19: 273–309.

(1966). *The Social Stratification of English in New York City*. Washington, DC: Center for Applied Linguistics.

(1969). Contraction, deletion, and inherent variability of the English copula. *Language* 45: 715–762.

(1970). The study of language in its social context. *Studium Generale* 23: 30–87.

(1972a). *Sociolinguistic Patterns*. Philadelphia: University of Pennsylvania Press.

(1972b). The transformation of experience in narrative syntax. In William Labov, *Language in the Inner City*. Philadelphia: University of Pennsylvania Press, 354–396.

(1981). What can be learned about change in progress from synchronic descriptions? In D. Sankoff and H. J. Cedergren (eds.), *Variation Omnibus* [NWAV VIII]. Edmonton: Linguistic Research Inc., 177–200.

(1982). Building on empirical foundations. In W. P. Lehmann and Y. Malkiel (eds.), *Perspectives on Historical Linguistics*. Amsterdam and Philadelphia: John Benjamins, 17–92.

(1984). The interpretation of zeroes. In W. U. Dressler (ed.), *Phonologica 1984: Proceedings of the Fifth International Phonology Meeting, Eisenstadt*. Cambridge University Press, 135–156.

(1990). The intersection of sex and social class in the course of linguistic change. *Language Variation and Change* 2: 205–254.

(1994). *Principles of Linguistic Change, Volume 1: Internal Factors*. Oxford: Blackwell.

(2001). *Principles of Linguistic Change, Volume 2: Social Factors*. Oxford: Blackwell.

(2002). Driving forces in linguistic change. Presented at the *International Conference on Korean Linguistics*. Seoul National University, South Korea, August 2. http://www.ling.upenn.edu/~wlabov/Papers/DFLC.htm.

Labov, William, Cohen, Paul, Robins, Clarence, and Lewis, John (1968). *A Study of the Non-Standard English of Negro and Puerto Rican Speakers in New York City*. Philadelphia: U.S. Regional Survey.

Labov, William and Waletzky, Joshua (1967). Narrative analysis: oral versions of personal experience. In J. Helm (ed.), *Essays on the Verbal and Visual Arts*. Seattle: University of Washington Press, 12–44.

Lavandera, Beatriz R. (1978). Where does the sociolinguistic variable stop? *Language in Society* 7: 171–183.

Lenhart, Amanda, Rainie, Lee, and Lewis, Oliver (2001). Teenage life online: the rise of the instant-message generation and the internet's impact on friendships and family relationships. Washington, DC: Pew Internet & American Life Project.

Levey, Stephen (2012). General extenders and grammaticalization: insights from London pre-adolescents. *Applied Linguistics* 33: 257–281.

Liebersen, Stanley (2001). *A Matter of Taste*. Cambridge, MA: Harvard University Press.

Lindemann, Stephanie and Mauranen, Anna (2001). "It's just real messy": the occurrence and function of *just* in a corpus of academic speech. *English for Specific Purposes* 20: 459–475.

Ling, Rich (2005). The sociolinguistics of SMS: an analysis of SMS use by a random sample of Norwegians. In R. Ling and P. E. Pedersen (eds.), *Mobile Communications: Re-negotiation of the Social Sphere.* London: Springer-Verlag, 335–349.

Longacre, Robert E. (1976). Mystery particles and affixes. In S. S. Mufwene, C. A. Walker, and S. B. Steever (eds.), *Papers from the 12th Regional Meeting of the Chicago Linguistic Society.* Chicago Linguistic Society, 468–475.

Macaulay, Ronald (2001). You're like "why not?" The quotative expression of Glasgow adolescents. *Journal of Sociolinguistics* 5: 3–21.

(2007). Pure grammaticalization: the development of a teenage intensifier. *Language Variation and Change* 18: 267–283.

Mayer, John D. (2004). How does psychotherapy influence personality? A theoretical integration. *Journal of Clinical Psychology* 60: 1291–1315.

Media and Language Change (2014). Special Issue of *Journal of Sociolinguistics* 18.

Meehan, Teresa (1991). It's like, "What's happening in the evolution of like?" A theory of grammaticalization. *Kansas Working Papers in Linguistics* 16: 37–51.

Meillet, Antoine (1912). *Linguistique historique et linguistique générale.* Paris: Champion.

Mencken, Henry Louis (1971). *The American Language.* New York: Alfred A. Knopf.

Méndez-Naya, Belén (2003). Intensifiers and grammaticalization: the case of swipe. *English Studies* 84: 372–391.

Meyerhoff, Miriam and Niedzielski, Nancy (2003). The globalization of vernacular variation. *Journal of Sociolinguistics* 7: 534–555.

Miller, Jim and Weinert, Regina (1995). The function of LIKE in dialogue. *Journal of Pragmatics* 23: 365–393.

Miller, Kristie (2009). Stuff. *American Philosophical Quarterly* 46: 1–18.

Milroy, James and Milroy, Lesley (1985). *Authority in Language: Investigating Language Prescription and Standardisation.* London and New York: Routledge & Kegan Paul.

Milroy, Lesley (1980). *Language and Social Networks.* Baltimore, MD: University Park Press.

(1987). *Observing and Analysing Natural Language.* Oxford: Blackwell.

(2007). Off the shelf or under the counter? On the social dynamics of sound changes. In C. M. Cain and G. Russom (eds.), *Studies in the History of the English Language III. Managing Chaos: Strategies for Identifying Change in English.* Berlin: Walter de Gruyter, 149–172.

Nesselhauf, Nadja (2006). The decline of *be to* and the rise of *be going to* in late Modern English: connection or coincidence? In C. Houswitschka, G. Knappe, and A. Müller (eds.), *Anglistentag 2005 Bamberg Proceedings.* Trier: WVT, 515–529.

(2007a). Diachronic analysis with the internet? *Will* and *shall* in ARCHER and in a corpus of e-texts from the web. In M. Hundt, N. Nesselhauf, and C. Biewer (eds.), *Corpus Linguistics and the Web.* Amsterdam and New York: Rodopi, 287–305.

(2007b). The spread of the progressive and its "future" use. *English Language and Linguistics* 11: 193–209.

Nevalainen, Terttu (1991). *But, Only, Just: Focusing Adverbial Change in Modern English 1500–1900.* Helsinki: Société Néophilologique.

Nevalainen, Terttu and Raumolin-Brunberg, Helena (2003). *Historical Sociolinguistics: Language Change in Tudor and Stuart England*. Harlow: Pearson Education.

Nevalainen, Terttu, Raumolin-Brunberg, Helena, and Mannila, Heikki (2011). The diffusion of language change in real time: progressive and conservative individuals and the time depth of change. *Language Variation and Change* 23: 1–43.

Orwell, George (1946). *Politics and the English Language*. London: Horizon.

Östman, Jan-Ola (1995). Pragmatic particles twenty years after. In B. Wårvik, S.-K. Tanskanen, and R. Hiltunen (eds.), *Organization in Discourse*. University of Turku, Department of English, 95–108.

Overstreet, Maryann (1999). *Whales, Candlelight, and Stuff Like That: General Extenders in English Discourse*. Oxford University Press.

Overstreet, Maryann and Yule, George (1997). On being inexplicit and stuff in contemporary American English. *Journal of English Linguistics* 25: 250–258.

Overstreet, Robert M. and Carter, Gary M. (2000). *The Overstreet Comic Book Grading Guide*. New York: HarperCollins.

Oxford English Dictionary (1989). Oxford University Press.

Paolillo, John C. (2001). Language variation on Internet Relay Chat: a social network approach. *Journal of Sociolinguistics* 5: 180–213.

Partington, Alan (1993). Corpus evidence of language change: the case of intensifiers. In M. Baker, G. Francis, and E. Tognini-Bonelli (eds.), *Text and Technology: In Honour of John Sinclair*. Amsterdam and Philadelphia: John Benjamins, 177–192.

Pelletier, Francis Jeffry (ed.) (2010). *Kinds, Things, and Stuff: Mass Terms and Generics*. Oxford University Press.

Peters, Hans (1994). Degree adverbs in early modern English. In D. Kastovsky (ed.), *Studies in Early Modern English*. Berlin and New York: Walter de Gruyter, 269–288.

Pichler, Heike (2007). Form–function relations in discourse: the case of I DON'T KNOW. *Newcastle Working Papers in Linguistics* 13: 174–187.

(2009). The functional and social reality of discourse variants in a northern English dialect: I DON'T KNOW and I DON'T THINK compared. *Intercultural Pragmatics* 6: 561–596.

(2010). Methods in discourse variation analysis: reflections on the way forward. *Journal of Sociolinguistics* 14: 581–608.

(2013). *The Structure of Discourse-Pragmatic Variation*. Philadelphia and Amsterdam: John Benjamins.

Pichler, Heike and Levey, Stephen (2010). Variability in the co-occurrence of discourse features. In L. J. O'Brien and D. S. Giannoni (eds.), *University of Reading: Language Studies Working Papers*. University of Reading, 17–27.

(2011). In search of grammaticalization in synchronic dialect data: general extenders in north-east England. *English Language and Linguistics* 15: 441–471.

Pintzuk, Susan (1995). Variation and change in Old English clause structure. *Language Variation and Change* 7: 229–260.

(2003). Variationist approaches to syntactic change. In B. D. Joseph and R. D. Janda (eds.), *The Handbook of Historical Linguistics*. Oxford: Blackwell, 509–528.

Pintzuk, Susan and Kroch, Anthony S. (1989). The rightward movement of complements and adjuncts in the Old English of Beowulf. *Language Variation and Change* 1: 115–143.

Poplack, Shana and Tagliamonte, Sali A. (1999). The grammaticalization of going to in (African American) English. *Language Variation and Change* 11: 315–342.

(2001). *African American English in the Diaspora: Tense and Aspect.* Oxford: Blackwell.

Quirk, Randolph, Greenbaum, Sidney, Leech, Geoffrey, and Svartvik, Jan (1972). *A Grammar of Contemporary English.* New York: Harcourt Brace Jovanovich.

(1985). *A Comprehensive Grammar of the English Language.* New York: Longman.

Randall, Neil (2002). *Lingo Online: A Report of the Language of the Keyboard Generation.* University of Waterloo.

Richard, E. Grandy (1975). Stuff and things. *Synthese* 31: 479–485.

Rickford, John R. (1975). Carrying the new wave into syntax: the case of Black English BIN. In R. Fasold and R. Shuy (eds.), *Analyzing Variation in Language.* Washington, DC: Georgetown University Press, 162–183.

Rickford, John R., Wasow, Thomas, Zwicky, Arnold, and Buschtaller, Isabelle (2007). Intensive and quotative all: something old; something new. *American Speech* 82: 3–31.

Roberts, Julie (2002). Child language variation. In J. K. Chambers, P. Trudgill, and N. Schilling-Estes (eds.), *The Handbook of Language Variation and Change.* Malden, MA: Wiley-Blackwell, 349–372.

Romaine, Suzanne (1994). On the creation and expansion of registers: sports reporting in Tok Pisin. In D. Biber (ed.), *Sociolinguistic Perspectives on Register.* Cambridge University Press, 59–81.

Romaine, Suzanne and Lange, Deborah (1991). The use of *like* as a marker of reported speech and thought: a case of grammaticalization in progress. *American Speech* 66: 227–279.

Sankoff, David (1973). Mathematical developments in lexicostatistical theory. In T. Sebeok, H. Hoenigswald, and R. Longacre (eds.), *Current Trends in Linguistics*, vol. 11. The Hague: Mouton, 93–112.

(1988a). Sociolinguistics and syntactic variation. In F. J. Newmeyer (ed.), *Linguistics: The Cambridge Survey.* Cambridge University Press, 140–161.

(1988b). Variable rules. In U. Ammon, N. Dittmar, and K. J. Mattheier (eds.), *Sociolinguistics: An International Handbook of the Science of Language and Society*, Volume 2. Berlin: Walter de Gruyter, 984–997.

Sankoff, David and Sankoff, Gillian (1973). Sample survey methods and computer-assisted analysis in the study of grammatical variation. In R. Darnell (ed.), *Canadian Languages in their Social Context.* Edmonton: Linguistic Research Inc., 7–63.

Sankoff, David and Thibault, Pierrette (1981). Weak complementarity: tense and aspect in Montreal French. In B. B. Johns and D. R. Strong (eds.), *Syntactic Change.* Ann Arbor, MI: University of Michigan Press, 205–216.

Sankoff, David, Thibault, Pierrette, and Bérubé, Hélène (1978). Semantic field variability. In D. Sankoff (ed.), *Linguistic Variation: Models and Methods.* New York: Academic Press, 23–43.

Sankoff, Gillian (1971). Language use in multilingual societies: some alternate approaches. In G. Sankoff (ed.), *The Social Life of Language.* Philadelphia: University of Pennsylvania Press, 29–46.

(1973). Above and beyond phonology in variable rules. In C.-J. N. Bailey and R. W. Shuy (eds.), *New Ways of Analyzing Variation in English.* Washington, DC: Georgetown University Press, 44–62.

284   References

(1974). A quantitative paradigm for the study of communicative competence. In R. Bauman and J. Sherzer (eds.), *Explorations in the Ethnography of Speaking*. Cambridge University Press, 18–49.

(1980). The origins of syntax in discourse: a case study of Tok Pisin relatives. In G. Sankoff (ed.), *The Social Life of Language*. Philadelphia: University of Pennsylvania Press, 211–255.

(1990). The grammaticalization of tense and aspect in Tok Pisin and Sranan. *Language Variation and Change* 2: 295–312.

Sankoff, Gillian and Blondeau, Hélène (2007). Language change across the lifespan: /r/ in Montreal French. *Language* 83: 560–588.

Sankoff, Gillian and Brown, Penelope (1976). The origins of syntax in discourse. *Language* 52: 631–666.

Sankoff, Gillian and Evans Wagner, Suzanne (2006). Age grading in retrograde movement: the inflected future in Montreal French. *U. Penn Working Papers in Linguistics* 12.

Sankoff, Gillian and Laberge, Suzanne (1980). On the acquisition of native speakers by a language. In G. Sankoff (ed.), *The Social Life of Language*. Philadelphia: University of Pennsylvania Press, 195–209.

Santa Ana, Otto A. (1996). Sonority and syllable structure in Chicano English. *Language Variation and Change* 8: 63–90.

Scheibman, Joanne (2000). *I dunno*: A usage-based account of the phonological reduction of *don't* in American English conversation. *Journal of Pragmatics* 32: 105–124.

Schiano, Diane J., Chen, Coreena P., Ginsberg, Jeremy, Gretarsdottir, Unnur, Huddleston, Megan, and Isaacs, Ellen (2002). Teen use of messaging media. *Proceedings of ACM Conference on Human Factors in Computing Systems*. Minneapolis, April 20–25, 594–595.

Schiffrin, Deborah (1982). *Discourse markers*. PhD dissertation, University of Pennsylvania.

(1987). *Discourse Markers*. Cambridge University Press.

Schilling-Estes, Natalie and Wolfram, Walt (1997). Symbolic identity and language change: a comparative analysis of post-insular /ay/ and /aw/. *U. Penn Working Papers in Linguistics 4.1*.

Schourup, L. C. (1985). *Common Discourse Particles in English Conversation*. New York: Garland Publishing.

Segerstad, Ylva af Hård (2005). Language in SMS: a socio-linguistic view. In R. Harper, L. Palen, and A. Taylor (eds.), *The Inside Text: Social, Cultural and Design Perspectives on SMS*. Dordrecht: Springer, 33–51.

Siegel, Muffy E. A. (2002). Like: the discourse particle and semantics. *Journal of Semantics* 19: 35–71.

Squires, Lauren (2007). Whats the use of apostrophes? Gender difference and linguistic variation in instant messaging. *American University TESOL Working Papers* 4: www.american.edu/tesol?CMCSquiresFinal.pdf.

Stenström, Anna-Brita (1999). He was really gormless – She's bloody crap: girls, boys and intensifiers. In H. Hasselgård and S. Okesfjell (eds.), *Out of Corpora: Studies in Honour of Stig Johansson*. Amsterdam and Atlanta: Rodopi, 69–78.

(2000). It's enough funny, man: intensifiers in teenage talk. In J. Kirk (ed.), *Corpora Galore: Analyses and Techniques in Describing English: Papers from the*

Nineteenth International Conference on English Language Research on Computerised Corpora (ICAME 1998). Amsterdam and Atlanta: Rodopi, 177–190.

Stenström, Anna-Brita and Andersen, Gisle (1996). More trends in teenage talk: a corpus-based investigation of the discourse items cos and innit. In C. E. Percy, C. F. Meyer, and I. Lancashire (eds.), *Synchronic Corpus Linguistics. Papers from the Sixteenth International Conference on English Language Research on Computerized Corpora, Toronto 1995*. Amsterdam: Rodopi. 189–203.

Stenström, Anna-Brita, Andersen, Gisle, and Hasund, Ingrid Kristine (2002). *Trends in Teenage Talk: Corpus Compilation, Analysis and Findings*. Amsterdam: John Benjamins.

Stoffel, Cornelis (1901). *Intensives and Down-Toners*. Heidelberg: Carl Winter.

Stuart-Smith, Jane (1999). Glottals past and present: a study of T-glottalling in Glaswegian. *Leeds Studies in English* 30: 181–204.

(2002–2005). Contributory factors in accent change in adolescents. Economic and Social Science Research Council of the United Kingdom. Grant #R000239757.

Stubbe, Maria and Holmes, Janet (1995). You know, eh and other "exasperating expressions": an analysis of social and stylistic variation in the use of pragmatic devices in a sample of New Zealand English. *Language & Communication* 15: 63–88.

Szmrecsanyi, Benedikt (2003). "Be going to" versus "will/shall": does syntax matter? *Journal of English Linguistics* 31: 295–323.

Tagliamonte, Sali A. (1996–1998). Roots of identity: variation and grammaticization in contemporary British English. Economic and Social Sciences Research Council (ESRC) of Great Britain. Reference #R000221842.

(1998). Was/were variation across the generations: view from the city of York. *Language Variation and Change* 10: 153–191.

(2002). Comparative sociolinguistics. In J. K. Chambers, P. Trudgill, and N. Schilling-Estes (eds.), *The Handbook of Language Variation and Change*. Malden, MA: Wiley-Blackwell, 729–763.

(2003–2006). Linguistic changes in Canada entering the 21st century. Research Grant. Social Sciences and Humanities Research Council of Canada (SSHRC). #410-2003-0005. http://individual.utoronto.ca/tagliamonte/.

(2005). So who? Like how? Just what? Discourse markers in the conversations of young Canadians. *Journal of Pragmatics, Special Issue, Guest Editors: Anna-Brita Stenström and Karin Aijmer* 37: 1896–1915.

(2006a). *Analysing Sociolinguistic Variation*. Cambridge University Press.

(2006b). "So cool, right?" Canadian English entering the 21st century. *Canadian English in a Global Context. Theme Issue of Canadian Journal of Linguistics* 51 (2/3): 309–331.

(2007). Representing real language: consistency, trade-offs and thinking ahead! In J. Beal, K. Corrigan, and H. Moisl (eds.), *Using Unconventional Digital Language Corpora. Volume 1: Synchronic Corpora*. Basingstoke: Palgrave Macmillan, 205–240.

(2007–2010). Directions of change in Canadian English. Research Grant. Social Sciences and Humanities Research Council of Canada (SSHRC). #410-070-048.

(2008). So different and pretty cool! Recycling intensifiers in Canadian English. *Special Issue of English Language and Linguistics: Intensifiers, Guest Editor: Belén Mendez-Naya* 12: 361–394.

(2010–2013). Transmission and diffusion in Canadian English. Standard Research Grant. Social Sciences and Humanities Research Council of Canada (SSHRCC). #410-101-129.

(2012). *Variationist Sociolinguistics: Change, Observation, Interpretation.* Malden, MA and Oxford: Wiley-Blackwell.

(2013). *Roots of English: Exploring the History of Dialects.* Cambridge University Press.

(2013–2018). *Social determinants of linguistic systems.* Insight Grant. Social Sciences and Humanities Research Council of Canada (SSHRCC).

Tagliamonte, Sali A. and Brooke, Julian (2014). A weird (language) tale: variation and change in the adjectives of strangeness. *American Speech* 89: 4–41.

Tagliamonte, Sali A. and D'Arcy, Alexandra (2007a). Frequency and variation in the community grammar: tracking a new change through the generations. *Language Variation and Change* 19: 1–19.

(2007b). The modals of obligation/necessity in Canadian perspective. *English World-Wide* 28: 47–87.

(2009). Peaks beyond phonology: adolescence, incrementation, and language change. *Language* 85: 58–108.

Tagliamonte, Sali A., D'Arcy, Alexandra, and Jankowski, Bridget (2010). Social work and linguistic systems: marking possession in Canadian English. *Language Variation and Change* 22: 1–25.

Tagliamonte, Sali A., D'Arcy, Alexandra, and Rodrigues-Louro, Celeste (2014a). *Outliers, Impact and Rationalization in Linguistic Change.* Minneapolis: Linguistic Society of America.

Tagliamonte, Sali A. and Denis, Derek (2008a). Linguistic ruin? LOL! Instant messaging, teen language and linguistic change. *American Speech* 83: 3–34.

(2008b). The stuff of change: general extenders in North American English. *American Dialect Society Annual Meeting*, Chicago, January 4.

(2010). The stuff of change: general extenders in Toronto, Canada. *Journal of English Linguistics* 38: 335–368.

(2014). Expanding the transmission/diffusion dichotomy: evidence from Canada. *Language* 90: 90–136.

Tagliamonte, Sali A., Durham, Mercedes, and Smith, Jennifer (2009). Grammaticalization in time and space: tracing the pathways of FUTURE *going to* across the British Isles. UK LVC 7 (Language Variation and Change) conference, Newcastle, UK, September 1–3.

(2014b). Grammaticalization at an early stage: future "be going to" in conservative British dialects. *English Language and Linguistics* 18: 75–108.

Tagliamonte, Sali A. and Hudson, Rachel (1999). Be like et al. beyond America: the quotative system in British and Canadian youth. *Journal of Sociolinguistics* 3: 147–172.

Tagliamonte, Sali A. and Roberts, Chris (2005). So cool, so weird, so innovative! The use of intensifiers in the television series *Friends. American Speech* 80: 280–300.

Tagliamonte, Sali A. and Uscher, Dylan (2009). Queer youth in the speech community: a comparative analysis of variation and change. *Presented at NWAV 38 (New Ways of Analyzing Variation) conference*, Ottawa, Canada, October 22–25.

Thibault, Pierette and Vincent, Diane (1990). *Un corpus de français parlé*. Québec: Bibliothèque nationale du Québec.

Thompson, Sandra A. (2002). "Object complements" and conversation: towards a realistic account. *Studies in Language* 26: 125–164.

Thompson, Sandra A. and Mulac, Anthony (1991). A quantitative perspective on the grammaticization of epistemic parentheticals in English. In E. C. Traugott and B. Heine (eds.), *Approaches to Grammaticalization*. Amsterdam and Philadelphia: John Benjamins, 313–329.

Thurlow, Crispin (2003). Generation Txt? Exposing the sociolinguistics of young people's text-messaging. *Discourse Analysis Online* 1.

(2006). From statistical panic to moral panic: the metadiscursive construction and popular exaggeration of new media language in the print media. *Journal of Computer Mediated Communication* 11: 667–701.

Torres-Cacoullos, Rena and Walker, James A. (2009a). On the persistence of grammar in discourse formulas: a variationist study of *that*. *Linguistics* 47: 1–43.

(2009b). The present of the English future: grammatical variation and collocations in discourse. *Language* 85: 321–354.

Tottie, Gunnel (2015). Uh and uhm in British and American English: are they words? In N. Dion, R. Torres-Cacoullos, and A. LaPierre (eds.), *Linguistic Variation: Confronting Fact and Theory*. New York: Routledge, 38–54.

Traugott, Elizabeth Closs (1997). Subjectification and the development of epistemic meaning: *the case of promise and threaten*. In T. Swan and O. Westvik (eds.), *Modality in Germanic Languages: Historical and Comparative Perspectives*. Berlin: Mouton de Guyter, 185–210.

(2013). I must wait on myself, must I? On the rise of pragmatic markers at the right periphery of the clause in English. Paper presented at Lund University, September 4.

Traugott, Elizabeth Closs and Heine, Bernd (1991a). *Approaches to Grammaticalization*, Vol. I. Amsterdam and Philadelphia: John Benjamins.

(1991b). *Approaches to Grammaticalization*, Vol. II. Amsterdam and Philadelphia: John Benjamins.

Trudgill, Peter J. (1972). Sex, covert prestige, and linguistic change in urban British English. *Language in Society* 1: 179–195.

(1974). *The Social Differentiation of English in Norwich*. Cambridge University Press.

(1986). *Dialects in Contact*. Oxford: Blackwell.

(2011). *Sociolinguistic Typology: Social Determinants of Linguistic Complexity*. Oxford University Press.

Tsui, Amy B. M. (1991). The pragmatic functions of *I don't know*. *Text* 11: 607–622.

Underhill, Robert (1988). Like is like, focus. *American Speech* 63: 234–246.

University of Helsinki (1991). *The Helsinki Corpus of English Texts*. Helsinki: Department of English, University of Helsinki.

Van Herk, Gerard (2009). *That's so tween: intensifier use in on-line subcultures*. Department of Linguistics, Memorial University, Newfoundland.

Vincent, Diane (1992). The sociolinguistics of exemplification in spoken French in Montréal. *Language Variation and Change* 4: 137–162.

Vincent, Diane and Sankoff, David (1992). Punctors: a pragmatic variable. *Language Variation and Change* 4: 205–216.

288   References

von Schneidemesser, Luanne (2000). Lexical change, language change. *American Speech* 75: 420–422.

Wagner, Suzanne Evans and Sankoff, Gillian (2011). Age grading in the Montréal French inflected future. *Language Variation and Change* 23: 275–313.

Wagner, Suzanne Evans and Tagliamonte, Sali A. (submitted-a). Incrementation in adolescence: tapping the force that drives linguistic change.

(submitted-b). What makes a panel study work? Researcher and participant in real time. In S. Evans Wagner and I. Buchstaller (eds.), *Panel Studies of Language Variation and Change*. New York: Routledge.

Weinreich, Uriel, Labov, William, and Herzog, Marvin (1968). Empirical foundations for a theory of language change. In W. P. Lehmann and Y. Malkiel (eds.), *Directions for Historical Linguistics*. Austin: University of Texas Press, 95–188.

Wierzbicka, Anna (1988). Oats and wheat: mass nouns, iconicity, and human categorization. In A. Wierzbicka, *The Semantics of Grammar*. Amsterdam: John Benjamins, 499–560.

Williams, Christopher (2015). Changes in the verb phrase in legislative language in English. In B. Aarts, J. Close, G. Leech, and S. A. Wallis (eds.), *The Verb Phrase in English: Investigating Recent Language Change with Corpora*. Cambridge University Press, 353–371.

Winter, Joanne and Norrby, Catrin (2000). Set marking tags "and stuff." In J. Henderson (ed.), *Proceedings of the 1999 Conference of the Australian Linguistic Society*. www.als.asn.au/proceedings/als1999/winter&norrby.pdf.

Witten, Ian H. and Eibe, Frank (2005). *Data Mining: Practical Machine Learning Tools and Techniques*. San Francisco, CA: Morgan Kaufmann.

Wolfram, Walt (1969). *A Sociolinguistic Description of Detroit Negro Speech*. Washington, DC: Center for Applied Linguistics.

Yates, Simeon J. (1996). Oral and written linguistic aspects of computer conferencing: a corpus-based study. In S. C. Herring (ed.), *Computer-Mediated Communication*. Amsterdam and Philadelphia: John Benjamins, 29–46.

Youssef, Valerie (1993). Marking solidarity across the Trinidad speech community: the use of an Ting in medical counseling to break down power differentials. *Discourse & Society* 4: 291–306.

Author index

Keyword index

Made in United States
Troutdale, OR
01/02/2024

16619559R00175